D1489158

Cognitive Strategies and

MATHEMATICS for the

LEARNING DISABLED

Contributors

Dan G. Bachor

Colleen S. Blankenship

Miriam Cherkes-Julkowski

Jeannette E. Fleischner

Anne M. Fitzmaurice Hayes

Michael O'Loughlin

Paulette J. Thomas

Cognitive Strategies and

MATHEMATICS for the

LEARNING DISABLED

Edited by

John F. Cawley, Ph.D.
University of New Orleans
Lakefront

AN ASPEN PUBLICATION®
Aspen Systems Corporation

1985

Rockville, Maryland
Royal Tunbridge Wells

Library of Congress Cataloging in Publication Data

Main entry under title:
Cognitive strategies and mathematics for the learning
disabled.

Includes bibliographies and index.
1. Mathematics—Study and teaching (Elementary)
2. Cognition in children. 3. Learning disabilities.
I. Cawley, John F.
QA135.5.C5723   1985   371.1'044   85-11131
ISBN: 0-87189-120-4

Editorial Services: Jane Coyle

Library of Congress Catalog Card Number: 85-11131
ISBN: 0-87189-120-4

Printed in the United States of America

1 2 3 4 5

Table of Contents

Preface

An examination of the literature and practices in mathematics for the learning disabled is highlighted by an emphasis on arithmetic computations. Within the computational emphasis, practice seems limited to rote learning via drill and practice. Little effort is directed toward meanings or to the use of arithmetic tasks to facilitate cognition, yet such an effort is needed. Accordingly, this book concentrates on selected facets of cognition and mathematics in the hope that related research and application will receive greater attention.

Cognition is an all-emcompassing term used as a concept heading for activities such as reasoning, problem solving and thinking, and the multitude of cognitive acts (e.g., discrimination, analogy, transitivity) that are employed when one acts cognitively.

Chapter 1 reviews cognition and the learning disabled. Mainly, the learning disabled seem to be less efficient in the performance of cognitive tasks than lacking the capabilities to perform them. They tend not to use the cognitive abilities they possess. When motivated or stimulated to use different tactics, the success of the motivational strategies seems dependent upon knowledge or skill. Further, there are numerous dimensions to each type of cognition. Verbal problem-solving performance, for example, can be influenced by any number of cognitive factors.

Chapter 2 is procedural. The thrust of this chapter is the development or explanation of procedures teachers can use to determine cognitive qualities of the learning disabled. This is an important chapter because so much depends on the teacher. A lack of tests and other instrumentation necessitates informal and teacher-made inventories. Chapter 2 is designed to guide the teacher in completing this process.

A behavioral perspective on mathematical learning problems is presented in Chapter 3. Behavioral research is popular in the field of special education, whereas there is only modest interest in mathematics.

Greater attention needs to be given to behavioral principles, particularly those stressing the high levels of percent correct and positive reinforcement. Given the fact that more students fail mathematics than any other subject, the implications are obvious.

Chapter 4 outlines a developmental model of mathematics instruction for the learning disabled. The model acknowledges variations in developmental levels among children and within individual youngsters. Discussion is directed to two types of development—an accelerated type, wherein the youngster moves from one stage to another, and a horizontal type, wherein the youngster learns more and more at the same level. Bringing about integration and the relationships among many components is a further element in the developmental perspective.

Do the learning disabled fail because they can't do or because they don't know how, when, or what to do when called upon? The individual may not respond correctly to $2 + 3 =$ because he or she did not rehearse it when first taught.

In this sense, as shown in Chapter 5, as much emphasis might have to be placed on teaching the individual to plan or to practice effectively as is placed on teaching the original task, $2 + 3 =$. Metacognitive alternatives have much to offer the learning disabled. Their applications in mathematics need to be pursued.

Processing information involves more than reception and expression. Information processing involves analysis, synthesis, decision making, and a host of other executive functions. Learning disabled children do not process information effectively. They omit information, include unnecessary information, forget steps, and include the wrong steps. Chapter 6 presents the issues and offers alternatives concerning information processing and mathematics.

Chapter 7 is devoted to thinking. Thinking is presented as a multivariate trait involving metacognitive understandings and specific cognitive acts. Thinking is interpreted to be more than "getting to it and getting your work done." Thinking is a process that takes time and, therefore, requires time. Learning disabled children can think. How complex their thinking can be is a topic in need of considerable inquiry. Without integrating carefully planned activities into the math program, we will never know how sophisticated these children may become.

For the National Council of Teachers of Mathematics, problem solving is the primary concern of the 1980s. The subject of Chapter 8, problem solving, needs to become a greater priority in special education. The chapter by Fleischner and O'Loughlin should stimulate a much needed redirection from computation to problem solving.

Chapter 9 focuses on questions. An inappropriate response may be the result of a poor question, a question that was not interpreted properly, or one that was too difficult. Or the question may not be answered because the learning disabled are not given the time to review the question and generate a response. These and other issues are attended to in Chapter 9.

Chapter 10 brings together classroom implications for cognition, mathematics, and the learning disabled. The presentation centers on postinstrumental methodology across a variety of topics. An emphasis is placed on computation because it is an important subject and because cognitive principles and practices are so intertwined with computation.

All in all an attempt has been made to make a case for a broadened perspective on mathematics for the learning disabled. This perspective stresses an optimism about learning disabilities, one that can be validated by long-term and comprehensive qualitative programming.

As authors we would like someday to look back upon this book as one of many directed toward various cognitive emphases in mathematics programming for the learning disabled.

Chapter 1

Cognition and the Learning Disabled

John F. Cawley

The general purpose of this book is to present the cautions, meanings, and educational implications of selected views of the broad topics of cognitive functioning, mathematics, and the learning disabled.

As used in this work, the term *cognitive functioning* includes thinking, reasoning, problem solving, information processing, conceptualization and some of the basic processes (e.g., short-term memory) that mediate the foregoing.

Although each of the components of cognitive functioning can be defined and differentiated rationally, this same degree of differentiation may not be possible from empirical or behavioral perspectives. It may be much easier to generate support for the existence of a general intellectual factor across the components of cognitive functioning than to demonstrate clear-cut independence among the factors. This may be true for a number of reasons, including:

- the multiple interaction of many parts of the human brain during cognitive activity and mathematics performance
- variations in the experiential background of children in terms of child-rearing practices, linguistic development, and the curricula and instructional experiences of school
- the complexity of the subject matter or content and the capability of the individual to activate the appropriate cognitive processes to manage that content

Within the realm of cognitive functioning, it is also necessary to consider the extent to which different authorities subordinate tasks under specific headings. Is *analogy,* for example, thinking, reasoning, or conceptualization? Is word fluency a measure of productive thinking (Torrance, 1965) or a primary mental ability (Thurstone & Thurstone, 1941)? Which and what combinations, if any, of these cognitive functions interact with which and what combinations of mathematics?

If shown the items in Figure 1-1 and instructed to mark all instances of a square, would the cognitive function involved be concept formation? Suppose an older individual is asked to examine the items in Figure 1-1 and prove that some are squares and others are not squares. Would this be reasoning? Problem solving? What is the role of prior knowledge? Put another way, can the individual demonstrate effective reasoning without the proper knowledge base? I think not, and for that reason, I believe that the learning disabled are in need of a comprehensive approach to mathematics. Programs cannot be limited to computation. Rather, they should include representation from fractions, geometry, measurement, problem solving, and applications (Cawley, 1984a; Sharma, 1984).

Figure 1-1 Squares or Not Squares

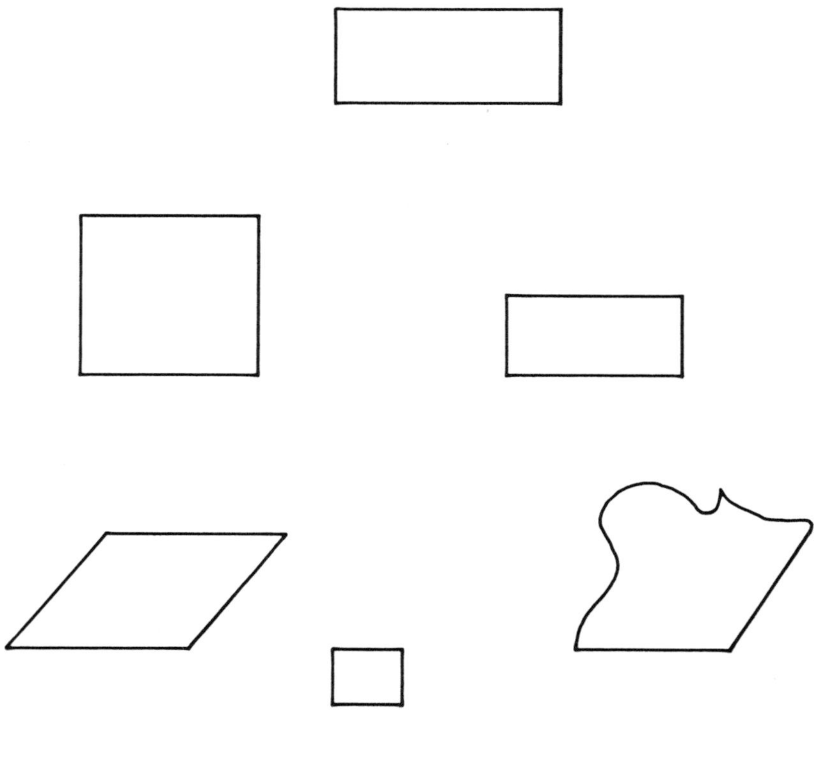

Halpern (1981), by contrast, indicates that 83 percent of the math that adults use deals with buying and selling and that 11 percent deals with money in other ways. Halpern suggests that learning disabled children should be taught only the computational and mathematical skills they will need as adults, a viewpoint with many implications.

Estimation, a process valued by Halpern (1981), requires experience and the opportunity to state hypotheses, evaluate them, restate them, and to function in a setting that is neither exact nor absolute. Four youngsters may be told to assume they do not know the answer but to estimate the answer to 8 × 4. To do so might require that all know that 8 × 4 is 32 and that each be aware that neither he nor she wants to give the exact answer. One might say, "I know that 8 times 4 is 32. I don't want to be exact. That's not estimating. I will say 30." Another might say, "I don't want to get too close. I'll say 28." A third may say, "Thirty and 28 have been used. I'll try 31." A fourth might say. "The others have all estimated lower, so I'll try one higher. My estimate is 33." In these illustrations, the individuals are learning about the process of estimation. They are not truly estimating, for they already know the exact answer. In effect, the information or knowledge they possess is integral to developing the process of estimation. A different situation occurs when they are asked to estimate the answer to 327 × 19. Here the answer is not known. Knowledge of place value and rounding would be required. A tolerance for individual variation and an understanding of the procedure each child uses are important. One child may respond with 6,000 and another, with 3,000. Would the latter be criticized if he or she used 3,000 only because 6,000 had already been used? Even though the estimate might not be close, is the cognition involved any more or less sophisticated?

McLeod and Armstrong (1982) surveyed 69 middle school and 35 high school teachers of the learning disabled. Two components of the survey have important implications.

The first factor is the content concerns of the teachers relative to the deficits of the children. The six most commonly reported deficit concerns were (1) division, (2) operations with fractions, (3) decimals, (4) percent, (5) fractions terminology, and (6) multiplication of whole numbers.

The second factor was the need to develop remedial approaches dominated by the ultimate need to relate to the mainstream text and by the development of teacher-made materials. The latter were judged necessary because of a lack of sufficient practice exercises in the regular text. One might consider that the child in need of excessive practice exercises is one who lacks the prerequisites for the task and, in effect, is not ready for it. They key question is whether the additional practice is used at the acquisition level or whether it is truly practice in the form of overlearning. Should the latter be the case, strategy training and self-monitoring techniques might possibly accentuate performance. Given that strategy orientations were not part of the McLeod and Armstrong survey, one can only speculate on how frequently they are used in the classroom. That is, had the teachers used one of these types of strategies, would the amount of practice have been reduced?

The influence of the regular class text suggests the need for using tactics that will reduce the need for extra practice and increase the speed at which the individual performs, since most regular class teachers proceed at the rate embedded in the text. Whether the special education teacher can influence the regular class teacher to consider qualitative mediational alternatives for the learning disabled remains to be seen.

Cognitive functioning consists of a rationally defined set of constructs; in addition, it is mediated by processes such as metacognition, attention, learning/cognitive styles, generalization and strategy tactics, and phenomena such as short-term and long-term memory.

A display of the content-by-mediation-by-cognitive-function framework is shown in Figure 1-2.

Two conditions need to be controlled in the study and application of cognitive functions in mathematics for the learning disabled. These conditions can be labeled task-by-age and task-alone.

Figure 1-2 Content by Mediation by Cognitive Function

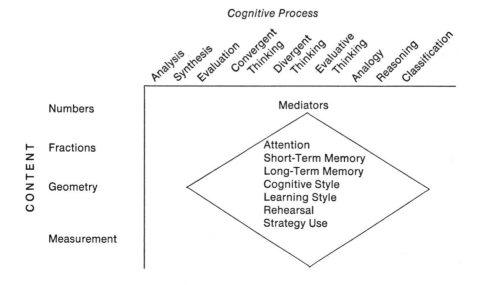

In the task-by-age condition, different tasks are introduced to people at varying ages or developmental levels. The Stanford-Binet and the Beginning Education Assessment (BEA) (J. Cawley, L. Cawley, Cherkes, & Fitzmaurice, 1980) are examples, respectively, of an intelligence test and an achievement test that are constructed on a task-by-age perspective (see Table 1-1). The Stanford-Binet and the BEA assign different tasks to different age levels. The assignments are based upon the satisfactory performance of large percentages of children (e.g., 75 percent) at each particular level.

In the task-alone condition, the same task is presented to all age groups, and the content of the task varies in complexity. The Peabody Picture Vocabulary Test-R and the Wechsler Intelligence Scale for Children-R are examples of the task-alone approach.

Given that mathematics is a task-by-age phenomenon (i.e., different topics are introduced at different age levels), it would seem that the task-by-age approach is ultimately a more logical research and theoretical perspective than the task-alone approach. Indeed, it is a more difficult perspective because it requires that both content and task be determined for each developmental level. Two procedures seem practical.

The first is to examine test responses in terms of raw scores. Any set of stable responses (e.g., eight of ten correct and then persistent difficulty) in a given cognitive activity would seem to indicate that the individual is task capable and that the ceiling was reached because the content became difficult. For example, Table 1-2, the Similarities subtest of the WISC-R and the Verbal Opposites subtest of the Detroit Tests of Learning Aptitude, are two rationally different cognitive activities.

In Table 1-2, the key terms could be *add* and *subtract*. Each could be defined as an operation in arithmetic, and either could reflect the opposite of the other. Entire systems of curriculum-based assessment could be developed to assess the cognitive functions of mathematics or to assess cognitive functions using mathematics content. In the former case, one could examine a topic such as subtraction and determine the sequence and variability of cognitive functions for subtraction (Carpenter, Moser, & Romberg, 1982; Resnick and Ford, 1981). In the latter case, one could assess functions such as analogies, reasoning, discrimination, and so forth using a single topic, such as division, or a combination of topics, such as numbers and geometry.

Another alternative consistent with the task-by-age condition is to determine the age at which most or all children respond efficiently to instruction for each topic, and to delay instruction until that time. Delaying the age at which topics are introduced would seem an efficient step since more children would master the topic more rapidly once it has been introduced

Table 1-1 Task-by-Age Illustrations

Beginning Education Assessment	*Stanford-Binet*
4-0 Visual Matching Auditory Picture Closure Auditory Picture Rhymes Auditory Attention Auditory Comprehension Silly Pictures Visual Oddities Generalization Combining Information Developmental Mathematics	4-0 Picture Vocabulary Naming Objects from Memory Opposite Analogies Pictorial Identifications Discrimination of Forms Comprehension Memory for Sentences I 4-6 Aesthetic Comparison Opposite Analogies Pictorial Similarities and Differences I Materials Three Commissions Comprehension III
5-0 Letter Recognition Picture-to-Picture Rhymes Sound–Picture Relations Auditory Classifications Visual Synthesis Sequencing Generalization Visual Oddities Negation Developmental Mathematics	5-0 Picture Completion: Man Paper Folding: Triangle Definitions Copying a Square Pictorial Similarities and Differences II Patience: Rectangles
6-0 Auditory Word Rhymes Sound–Letter Relations Adding Sounds Taking Sounds Away Letter Recognition Blending Words in Sentences Reading Comprehension Picture Opposites Visual Closure Finding Causes Developmental Mathematics Mathematics Achievement	6-0 Vocabulary Differences Mutilated Pictures Number Concepts Opposite Analogies II Maze Tracing

Table 1-2 Similarities and Word Opposites Comparison

	Similarities	*Verbal Opposites*
	"Listen, I am going to say two words. Tell me how they are similar."	"Listen, I am going to say a word. Tell me a word that shows the opposite."
Age 7–10	Add–Subtract	Add: _____
Age 10–0	Multiply–Divide	Divide: _____

and fewer children would develop inappropriate habits. This would be beneficial to learning disabled (LD) children, not necessarily in terms of increasing grade level performance, but in reducing the difficulties that stem from consistent failure.

The great majority of attention relative to cognitive functioning, mathematics, and the learning disabled has been focused on the role cognitive functions play in mathematics and the extent to which deficiencies in these functions impair performance in mathematics. A restructuring of the emphasis among these factors could possibly lead to long-term enhancement of the status of the learning disabled. This emphasis (Cawley, 1984b) would recognize that "mathematics must be capable of doing more for the learning disabled than meeting the needs of the individual in mathematics alone." (p. 2) This emphasis would capitalize on the stimulus properties of mathematics and use them in the conduct of cognitive activities as illustrated in Figure 1-3.

COGNITION AND MATH

In some respects, many special educators view the various comparisons between brain-injured and non-brain-injured children as a precursor to the development of the field of learning disabilities. Strauss and Lehtinen (1947), who are associated with these early developments, devoted an entire chapter, "Thinking Disorders in Brain-Injured Children," to this topic in their classic text. Their stress was on the aberrant or disordered aspects of thinking, and they described the cognitive disorders of thinking, reasoning, and concept formation of the brain-injured as being markedly different from those of the non-brain-injured.

Over the years there seems to have been a gradual transition from research that compared brain-injured and non-brain-injured mentally retarded children (e.g., Capobianco, 1957) to research that focused upon children of average or above-average intellectual ability.

Figure 1-3 Illustrations of Cognitive Functions Using Mathematics

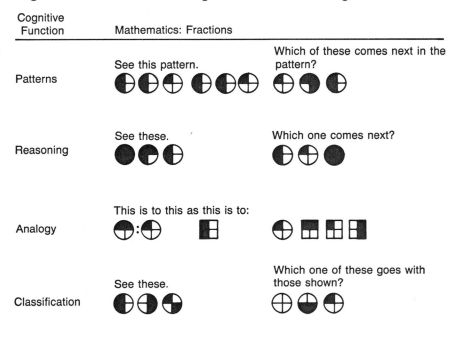

The definition of learning disability, as put forth in Public Law 94-142, stipulates that *"specific learning disability is a disorder in one or more of the basic psychological processes involved in understanding or in using language, spoken or written, which may manifest itself in an imperfect ability to . . ."*

Note the key terminology: *disorder, psychological processes,* and *manifest itself in an imperfect ability.* The implication is that a disorder in one or more psychological processes, depending on what is meant by *disorder,* results only in an imperfect ability to do arithmetic, not in the inability to do arithmetic. This interpretation seems to present learning disability as a discrepancy, a factor that suggests a degree of progress on the part of the individual. No explanation is given as to how the disorders in basic psychological processes result in imperfect abilities in areas such as arithmetic, nor is there any indication of which processes are involved.

The definition of learning disabilities, as proposed by the National Joint Committee on Learning Disabilities (NJCLD) (Hammill, Leigh, McNutt, & Larsen, 1981), makes no reference to basic psychological processes.

Rather, this definition indicates that learning disability is a heterogenous group of disorders that are intrinsic to the learner and presumed to be due to central nervous system disorder.

Note, also, that disorders are presumed to be due to central nervous system dysfunction. No attempt is made to differentiate between central nervous system disorders due to insult or brain damage, those caused by inefficiencies in the integration or utilization of neural mechanisms (e.g., exchanges across the corpus callosum; Kinsbourne, 1983), and those due to developmental variations (e.g, maturation in hemispheric specialization). The implications of nervous system information relative to assessment and instruction for most school-based mathematics problems are less than clear (Cawley & Richstone, 1984).

One of the studies reported by Strauss and Lehtinen (1947) focused on concept formation. The children were given a number of objects and instructed to put together those objects that go together. The brain-injured children chose more objects and formed more groups than the non-brain-injured children. Brain-injured children used unusual and uncommon reasons for grouping. Their approaches to classification follow:

- sorting according to form or color (a sunglass and a wheel went together because they were round)
- sorting according to unessential detail (sandpaper and matchcovers grouped because the matchcover had sandpaper glued to it where the match was struck)
- sorting according to relationships that were vague or far-fetched (stamp and razor blade, because the razor blade could cut the stamp)
- sorting according to hypothetical or imaginary situations (whistle and sunglasses, because they are found on the face of a policeman)

In another study, children were given a set of objects and pictures. They were instructed to place the objects in front of the picture appropriate to each object. The case of a 9-year-old child with a mental age of 8-2 and an IQ of 88 illustrates the performance of the brain-injured child.

Part of the responses on the picture-object test were as follows: objects chosen for picture of "drowning boy": boat, life preserver, ambulance, nurse, male nurse, stewardess ("she takes care of the little boy"); woman with pail ("that's the old cleaning lady on the boat"); man running ("he is running to get a doctor"); Santa Claus ("he brings something to the little boy to play with"); spring ("that he can sit on it and bounce up and down"); soap ("for him to wash on the boat"); light ("that's a light for him to see in the dark"); birds ("they keep him company and they are in a cage, I wish I could eat them up); button ("if he lost a button he could sew it on"); pencil ("for him to write with. I surely would like to keep this but I got two hundred at home"); small tray with cup ("coffee, coffee, tray of coffee, give it to the drowning boy"); tree ("another tree, a tree grows in Brooklyn"); letter ("that's a letter from his mother because he is away on a farm and swimming"); key ("that's to go in his own room when he wants to"); nails ("when something is wrong on the boat he can give it to the skipper"). In a similar way he chooses the objects for the "fire picture" and comments about them. (Strauss & Lehtinen, 1947, p. 62)

The approach to arithmetic proposed by Strauss and Lehtinen (1947) emphasized the role of visual spatial organization, the need to devote the necessary time and experiences to ensure that concepts are developed and understood, the use of concrete and semiconcrete materials in association with symbols, and the need to modify instruction and materials consistent with personal attributes such as perseveration and distractibility.

A major effort by Cruickshank, Bentzen, Ratzeburg, and Tannhauser (Cruickshank et al., 1961) initiated the transition to what may be considered the modern era of learning disability. This project, commonly referred to as the Montgomery County Project, was designed to demonstrate teaching methods for brain-injured and hyperactive children of average or near average intellectual ability.

The six basic psychological processes on which this project focused were:

1. distractibility
2. motor disinhibition
3. dissociation
4. figure-ground disturbance
5. perseveration
6. inadequate self-concepts and body image

Four elements made up the essentials of the teaching methods recommended for these children:

1. reduced environmental stimuli
2. reduced space
3. structured school programs and life space
4. increased stimulus value of teaching materials

For the most part, the attributes on which Cruickshank and his colleagues focused in the Montgomery County Project fall in the category of mediational factors, as the terms are defined for this text. For example, the child who is distractible—that is, unable to refrain from reacting to irrelevant stimuli or to focus attention on relevant stimuli—will be less able to perform specific cognitive acts upon these stimuli.

The Montgomery County Project contained an arithmetic component. Primary attention was directed to the establishment of number concepts and the development of approaches to instruction that would reduce the negative influence of individual mediational difficulties (e.g., distractibility).

Approximately two decades later, Glennon and Cruickshank (1981), listed the following characteristics of the learning disabled and discussed their implications for mathematics programming:

- attention disturbances and attention span
- figure–ground pathology
- dissociation
- memory dysfunction
- sequencing difficulties
- discrimination
- directionality and body parts
- spatial and temporal disorientation
- obtaining closure
- perseveration
- intersensory disorganization

The preceding highlight the need to consider perceptual-cognitive attributes in planning mathematics programs for the learning disabled.

Any presentation of cognitive attributes of the learning disabled in general, and in mathematics specifically, must acknowledge the following limitations:

- lack of sufficient comparisons across age levels and concurrent lack of longitudinal data
- lack of research relative to divers mathematics topics
- lack of research relative to specific cognitive attributes

The most widely studied cognitive attributes of the learning disabled are those researched within the framework of intelligence. It seems as though just about every kind of comparison (e.g., verbal versus nonverbal patterns) has been undertaken. The results of these comparisons vary, and no definitive conclusions are possible.

Intelligence per se is not a primary topic in this book. It is acknowledged that learning disabilities can exist across the intellectual spectrum. Intellectually bright and less bright children can demonstrate severe discrepancies between expectancy and achievement and, therefore, can meet the rule-based criterion for learning disability (Cawley, 1985).

The relevance of selected intellectual behaviors (e.g., defining words, arranging blocks into designs) to arithmetic operations, such as division, or to the development of quantitative concepts (e.g., part–whole relations, equivalence classes) is anything but specific.

It seems reasonable to assume that those scoring high on performance scales would also have high spatial scores and thus be able to arrange and organize the elements of a task such as division. Whether one could predict that these same individuals are able to perform the symbolic comparisons and operations of division has yet to be determined.

What may be more relevant to an understanding of learning disability is information about intelligent behavior, rather than information about behavior that is defined as intelligence.

Sternberg and Wagner (1982) offer one possibility. These authors view intelligence, in part, as information processing involving the following components:

- metacognition or processes that control what to do or how to do it
- performance or competence to conduct the tasks once they have been chosen
- learning components to provide the means for acquiring, retaining, and transferring information about tasks

Swanson (1982) presents an information-processing model to assess the intellectual performance of the learning disabled. Stress is put on the distinction between assessment of basic intellectual skills and the cognitive strategies of intelligence. This model consists of five planes with different components in each plane. These are shown in Figure 1-4.

The purpose of the strategy plane is to inquire about the relationships between hypothesis testing and performance.

Figure 1-4 Multidirectional Component Analysis of Intellectual Behavior

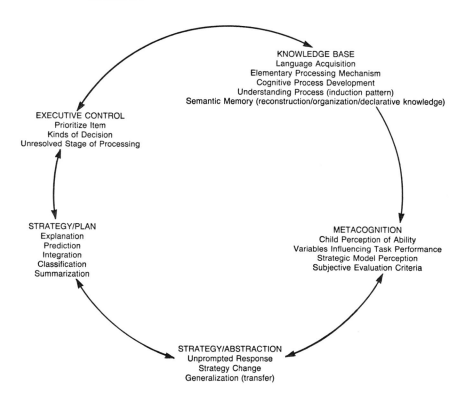

KNOWLEDGE BASE
Language Acquisition
Elementary Processing Mechanism
Cognitive Process Development
Understanding Process (induction pattern)
Semantic Memory (reconstruction/organization/declarative knowledge)

EXECUTIVE CONTROL
Prioritize Item
Kinds of Decision
Unresolved Stage of Processing

STRATEGY/PLAN
Explanation
Prediction
Integration
Classification
Summarization

METACOGNITION
Child Perception of Ability
Variables Influencing Task Performance
Strategic Model Perception
Subjective Evaluation Criteria

STRATEGY/ABSTRACTION
Unprompted Response
Strategy Change
Generalization (transfer)

Source: Reprinted with permission from "A multidirectional model for assessing learning disabled student's intelligence: An information processing framework" by H.W. Swanson in *Learning Disability Quarterly,* vol. 5, ©1982.

The strategy/abstraction plane seeks to determine how extensively a child's strategy scheme is directed toward meeting the critical demands of problem solving.

The knowledge plane determines one's capacity to produce specific information.

The metacognition plane evaluates how well the individual understands his or her own behavior in relationship to the tasks and problems.

The executive function plane assesses the strategy used to select strategies. Exhibit 1-1 provides an example of Swanson's planes using the topic of multiplication.

Exhibit 1-1 A Sample of Swanson's Planes Using the Topic of Multiplication

Strategy Plane	26 × 3		Write the item; examine the item. Recognize the act as multiplication. Do 6 × 3 and hold in memory if remaining is required. Do 2 × 3 and add remaining factor.
Strategy/Abstraction Plane	26 × 3	38 × 8	Generalize 26 × 3 to 38 × 8.
Knowledge Plane	26 × 3		Proceed if known. If not known, do 2 × 3 and 6 × 3. Reconstruct to 20 × 3 and 6 × 3. Teach renaming.
Metacognition Plane	26 × 3		Subject says, "I haven't learned this yet. I'll ask for help." *OR* "I've had this before. It is simple, but I have to remember to carry." Subject is aware that he or she knows or does not know. If helped by teacher, subject might prompt self to pay attention.
Executive Plane	26 × 3		Plans what to do before doing it. Recognizes symbolism of ×. Activates selection of operation.

Reid and Hresko (1981) have analyzed learning disabilities and selected approaches to appraisal and instruction from a cognitive perspective. The following are selected examples of what Reid and Hresko consider the primary characteristics of a cognitive approach:

- Control processes exist that guide the learner's selection of what will be learned—how what is learned and then understood depends on what the learner already knows.
- There is a substantial need to understand that cognitive processes, such as strategy utilization and problem solving, are interrelated.
- Effective instruction provides activities that enhance the learner's ability to construct meaning from experience.

It is important for the learner to be cognizant of a responsibility to be active in learning. The program elements suggested by Sternberg and

Wagner, by Swanson, and by Reid and Hresko are essential in any comprehensive approach to mathematics programming for LD children. In the main, it would be my choice to employ a cognitive or discovery-oriented program with children whose difficulties are projected to be developmental and of a long-term character. In this sense, curriculum or knowledge decisions must be made first and compatible instructional procedures then implemented. Project MATH (Cawley et al., 1976) is an example of such an approach.

By contrast, the problems of some children are specific and may require a more behavioral or direct instruction program (Blankenship, Chap. 3, this volume). These individuals may have extreme difficulty changing from one topic to another. They may experience difficulty in mastering a single operation. The explicitness of instruction and the amount of time devoted to the task may require a concerted effort by the teacher. Multi-Modal Mathematics (Cawley et al., 1980) was designed to meet the needs of such children.

Error analysis is an insufficient diagnostic step for instructional purposes. For any given aspect of mathematics, a relatively small number of conceptual misunderstandings are the likely source of error. Blankenship (1985) might suggest that elaborate schemes are not necessary for instruction. Instead, direct instruction of a data-based nature can ameliorate item difficulty and increase performance to high levels of percent correct. Instruction should probably focus more explicitly on a given topic for a much longer period of time than it now does.

Cognition is referred to as the discovery, awareness, rediscovery, or recognition of information in various forms and to the comprehension of said information (Torrance, 1965).

Exhibit 1-2 lists a set of cognitive terms, all and any of which can be used in quantitatively based activities, both to solve problems and to enhance cognitive growth. As extensive as this listing may be, it is only representative of the universal set of cognitive functions. Yet these and others may be part of the life space of the learning disabled, and some or all may be important to success in school and to survival as an adult. It is important, therefore, that plans be made to allow these behaviors their natural opportunity in mathematics activities. At the very least, they should not be deliberately excluded because they are thought inappropriate or too difficult for LD children.

A difficulty might not be due to the absence or lack of a specific cognitive function. To illustrate, Cermak (1983) studied information-processing deficits in children with learning disabilities. Prior research indicated that short-term memory performance among the learning disabled was somewhat specific. Retention of monosyllabic words was measured across

Exhibit 1-2 Cognitive Terms

Knowledge
Comprehension
Application
Analysis
Synthesis
Evaluation

Convergent Thinking
Divergent Thinking
Evaluative Thinking

Extending
Extrapolating
Elaboration

Serial Learning
Discrimination Learning
Associate Learning
Incidental Learning
Concept Learning
Principle Learning

Sequencing
Seriation
Conservation
Class Inclusion
Categorization
Multiple Classification
Clustering
Concept Formation
Sorting

Syllogisms
Transitivity
Logical Reasoning
Argument
Cause–Effect

Reversals
Intradimensional Shifts
Extradimensional Shifts

Oddity
Opposite

Absurdities
Humor
Riddles

Calibration
Tolerance
Estimation
Approximation

Synonyms
Multiple Meanings
Antonyms
Oddities
Relations
Analogies
Transformations

Transfer
Generalization

Thinking
Reasoning
Problem Solving
Comprehension

Collecting
Organizing
Summarizing
Inferring
Hypothesizing
Criticizing
Decision Making

different time intervals into which distractors were interpolated. When the distracting information was different from the standard, the effect upon retention was minimal. When the distractors were similar to the standard, the effects were more significant among LD children than among non-LD children. Cermak pursued these earlier findings with tests to assess the ability to analyze semantic features. Findings indicated that LD children could analyze information, although at a depressed rate. In effect, when given sufficient time, performance was accentuated.

Information processing requires the individual to attend to the relevant dimensions of stimuli, extract various content from these stimuli, summarize the content, isolate the cognitive functions needed to make decisions about the information, and then respond to this information. With simple stimuli (e.g., $2\overline{)6}$), processing the information may take place so rapidly that an "all or none" effect appears to occur. With complex stimuli (e.g., $213\overline{)4,714}$), the processing must be broken down into a sequence of ordered events and specific actions must be performed on each event. Non-LD children tend to respond automatically or habitually to the simple tasks and more sequentially and methodically to the more complex tasks. The learning disabled child may have to interpret the simple task by designating $\overline{)}$ as "goes into," then stipulate that 2 goes into 6, and finally activate 3 as the proper response. If the 3 is not activated immediately, the individual may go through a series of steps (e.g., 2 goes into 2; 2 goes into 4; 2 goes into 6) or resort to some alternative representation (i.e., get 6 blocks and group them into sets of 2). These steps require considerable sophistication in that the learner recognizes that $2\overline{)6}$ is not known but that certain understandings exist (i.e., it is a division task in which the number of 2s in 6 is sought). Further, there is the implementation of a set of steps to develop the answer.

In reality, recall is the easiest and most expedient way to deal with the simple problems. For that reason, LD children should habituate the basic facts of the four operations of arithmetic.

Case (1982) raises some interesting questions in a discussion of the role of central processing capacity. M-Space, or M-Capacity, is a construct used to describe central processing capacity. What this construct suggests is that individuals have an amount of mental space or capacity to deal with tasks, their components, and the mechanisms by which they are processed. Case suggests that the development of central processing capacity plays an important role in determining the rate of children's cognitive development in a variety of domains. It is suggested that automatization is an essential consideration. Some children may perform less efficiently than others even though they use the same basic strategies. This inefficiency at one level may take up more processing capacity than is necessary and make it difficult for the individual to perform satisfactorily at higher levels. Ineffective or inefficient strategy use and cognitive functioning may be attributed to a lack of processing capacity. The instructional implication may be to reduce the workload, distribute the workload over a longer period of time, or remain with the item until it has been automatized or habituated.

What happens when $213\overline{)4,714}$ is encountered by an individual who is inefficient with $2\overline{)6}$? Is there sufficient M-Space to integrate the more complex task? Clearly, this points out one of the reasons why an individual confronted with $213\overline{)4,714}$ should be someone who is proficient with all previous steps. This means intactness for subtraction, multiplication, and all prior division.

Swanson (1982) notes that the performance of learning disabled children on different tasks is fragmented and inconsistent. One must be cautious, therefore, when attributing information-processing difficulties in one domain to those in another, a factor observed in a study by Saxe and Shoheen (1981).

A combination of Piagetian tasks and Gerstmann syndrome was studied in two 9-year-old children with numerical difficulties (Saxe & Shoheen, 1981); IQs of 100 and 81 were reported for the two youngsters. The tasks studied were as follows:

Gerstmann Syndrome:
　　Left–right orientation
　　Finger agnosia
　　Graphic skills
　　Mathematics behavior
　　　rote knowledge of number systems
　　　applying the rote system
　　　　counting accuracy
　　　　counting to compare arrays
　　　　counting to reproduce arrays: drawing task
　　　　counting to reproduce arrays: rewrite placement task
　　　numerical calculations
　　　　single digits addition and subtraction
Piagetian Tasks:
　　Concrete operational tasks
　　　number conservation
　　　class inclusion
　　　seriation
　　　liquid quantity conservation

Both youngsters showed persistent deficits in all Gerstmann tasks. Performance on rote number tasks was deficient. For example, in writing numbers, B wrote 63 as 32 as he vocalized, "Three, six."

Neither youngster was able to count, nor was either able to use counting to demonstrate number. Both showed an awareness of the arithmetic symbols, but they could not do the addition or subtraction tasks.

Performance on the Piagetian tasks was limited. Both children believed that changing the configuration changed the amount in the conservation task. Neither could arrange items in order. Both failed the class inclusion item.

The overall pattern of numerical, neurological (Gerstmann), and developmental deficits suggests that academic arithmetical difficulties and cognitive limitations may not be isolated phenomena.

In another inquiry on cognitive development, Cherkes (1983) examined task characteristics in the processing of transitivity problems among four age groups of LD children. Transitivity was examined from both linguistic and spatial perspectives.

Transitivity is a relational process with many implications for mathematics. In a task such as, *Mary is faster than Fred; Mary is slower than Charles,* the measurement concept of speed serves as the basis for comparison.

Cherkes's data showed continuous increases in performance across the age groups. Task data showed higher scores on linguistic input–spatial output combinations, on cross-modal combinations, and on spatial output tasks. Measurement comparisons exceed quantity comparisons. LD children seem to formulate transitivity inferences, although performance is influenced by task characteristics (e.g., tasks requiring linguistic output produced lower scores). Task characteristics influenced performance more than cognitive development or cognitive style did.

MODALITY

Mathematics, at least at entry into new topics or during the developmental years, is a subject that involves the use of divergent types of stimulus presentations and response modes. Simply illustrated, one combination would have the instructor state a number and then have the youngster select that many items. This would involve auditory–manipulative combinations. Zendel and Pihl (1983) studied auditory–visual matching in LD and non-LD children. Modality integration was studied using a variety of visual and auditory stimuli in combination with one another. Visual stimuli consisted of dot patterns. Auditory stimuli consisted of four or five tones. Learning disabled children performed more poorly on all auditory–visual combinations.

Additional data on the WISC-R and the Halstead-Reitan Battery were analyzed and then correlated with visual–auditory performance. Arithmetic and Digit Span loaded heavily on one factor among the learning disabled, but this factor did not correlate with any visual–auditory combination. No single psychological process seemed related to visual–auditory integration.

Webster (1980) contrasted the performance of three groups of children. Two groups were mathematically disabled. A third group was mathematically proficient. Each group was given a short-term memory task consisting of 14 strings of 7 upper-case letters and 14 strings of 7 digits. Half the children received visual input first, and the other half received aural input first. Half the total group received verbal output first, and half received graphic-symbolic output first.

Significant differences were found between nondisabled and severely disabled children. A significant effect for modality occurred, with visual input superior to aural input.

It was noted that both groups of deficient children relied heavily on visual encoding and that at the sixth-grade level, no group had stabilized a modality-specific learning strategy.

STYLES AND SELF-DIRECTION

Cognitive styles and learning styles have significant implications for the field of learning disability. The basic approaches to these phenomena differ substantially. Cognitive style is approached through the direct measurement of selected student traits. Two examples of this are the use of embedded figures to measure field dependency or independency and using figure matching to measure impulsivity or reflectivity.

Learning styles, by contrast, tend to be measured by some form of self-rating or prioritizing through the use of questionnaires or observations.

In either case, we seem faced with the "chicken or egg" question in that we have only a limited basis for predicting which comes first—style or performance—and we remain limited with respect to our understanding of aptitude-by-treatment effects (Frederico, 1984). To illustrate, Figure 1-5 sets forth three conditions of style. Under Condition I, the children who manifest one style are grouped together, as are those with the other styles. Each group, according to its learning style, is taken through a program of mathematics in which each reaches an equivalent and similar

Figure 1-5 Examples of Intervention Options

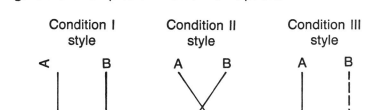

Condition I   Condition II   Condition III
style   style   style

A   B   A   B   A   B

Source: Reprinted from "Commentary" by J.F. Cawley in *Topics in Learning and Learning Disabilities,* vol. 3, p. 90, with permission of Pro-Ed, ©1982.

level of proficiency. That is, when finished, one group is essentially the same as the other in mathematics.

Under Condition II, children who manifest one style may convert to another as the properties of mathematics change (e.g., performance in arithmetic and algebra associated with verbal; performance in geometry associated with spatial). Do educators know how and when to attempt this crossover?

Under Condition III, children with different learning styles learn different mathematics topics.

In the present context, both learning styles and cognitive styles are grouped within the set of mediators.

Blackman and Goldstein (1982) reviewed literature relative to cognitive styles, processing deficits, and hyperactivity. These authors conclude that the cognitive styles of field dependence and reflectivity–impulsivity do relate to achievement among LD children. Much of the literature cited by these authors reflects a perceptual orientation. For example, they refer to work showing that visual information-processing training has an impact on performance. Yet this type of training has been extensively criticized in the special education literature over a number of years. What probably has to be recognized is the need to be cautious about the results of any single investigation.

Gerber (1983) found different theoretical and applied approaches to strategy use with the learning disabled. He grouped them as follows:

- information-processing models that focus on cognitive control processes

- developmental models that focus on the emergence of age-related changes
- behavioral perspectives that describe problem-solving techniques for controlling problem-solving responses
- social learning theories that accept self-statements and images as modifiable behavior
- educators who design generalizable instructional strategies

Gerber focused upon three topics: cognitive styles, cognitive behavior modification, and metacognition. He concluded that LD children did not lack strategies; rather, (1) their strategies are inefficient or inflexible, (2) the usefulness of strategies such as cognitive behavior modification in academic remediation is questionable, and (3) findings relating metacognition to strategy enhancement are disappointing.

Hallahan and Sapona (1983) conducted a review of self-monitoring of attention among the learning disabled. They noted that self-monitoring of attention during academic work leads to increases in attentional behavior, with a resulting effect upon academic productivity. Their most salient observation follows:

> It is our opinion that the self-monitoring techniques work when children are working on tasks for which they already have the skills. In other words, we are skeptical about how successful the procedure would be for children when they are in the acquisition stage of learning. (p. 619).

Given the continuous introduction of new mathematics topics in the regular grades and the fact that LD children lack skills and knowledge, a basic question remains about how to use mediators to go about competency development in the skills, concepts, and problem-solving demands of mathematics.

Attention has long been regarded as essential in acquisition (Zeaman & House, 1963). It seems, therefore, that the instructional or experimental procedure employed during acquisition will have to stimulate or control attending for mastery to occur. Personal observations over the years clearly indicate that manipulatives have a significant role to play in this regard, for every action or move by the learner is observable and capable of being monitored. The learner cannot properly manipulate the materials without focusing on them. The key is for the instructor to create the proper cognitive demand so that information processing is conducted simultaneously with the action. In an indirect sense, this was a key element in the VAKT procedure of Fernald (1943). It was not the fact that tracing letters and words sent the messages up the arm to the brain. The key factor was that the instructor was able to observe the synchronization with which letter-sound relationships were operative.

Self-monitoring, it seems, should be implemented during overlearning— to stimulate rehearsal and for practice. In effect, failure to implement self-monitoring, metacognition, or any of the self-directed tactics may be due, not to processing or mediational difficulties, but to knowledge. My own summaries of the literature indicate that most of the processing activities take place within the topics of addition and subtraction and that none, to the best of my knowledge, has taken place with complex multiplication or division. Thus, we have yet to determine the true extent to which self-directed and monitoring tactics can facilitate growth in knowledge, skills, and concepts.

VERBAL PROBLEM SOLVING

There are many types of problem solving, and within each type there are numerous dimensions and qualities that distinguish subcomponents from one another. Verbal problem solving in mathematics is a vital topic for two reasons. First, these skills are among the most demanding in the educational problem-solving domain; all math texts include verbal problem solving, and many of the activities in other subject areas (e.g., science) are predicated on verbal problem solving. Second, verbal problem solving is a cognitive activity that is subject to inquiry in heterogeneous samples across the developmental span, from preschool through adulthood.

Special education has not developed any relevant data base, nor has there been any substantive theoretical interpretation of problem solving relative to the learning disabled. O'Loughlin and Fleischner (1980), in a technical report from the Columbia University Research Institute for the Study of Learning Disabilities, discussed story problem solving and its implications for the learning disabled. However, the report has not a single reference that cites work relative to the learning disabled and word problem solving. In fact, the sources tend to come from general education, and over 25 percent of them are European.

During the late 1940s, a series of studies focusing on arithmetical performance of the mildly retarded (e.g., Cruickshank, 1948a; 1948b) showed that these children have difficulty in many areas, and particularly in solving verbal problems that contain extraneous information. Professionals erroneously concluded from these studies that, because the children were unable to do the problems, this meant they could not learn to do them.

Henceforth, problems of this type were excluded from educational programs. About 20 years after the Cruickshank efforts, however, Cawley and Goodman (1969) demonstrated that mildly retarded children could learn to do problems of the extraneous number type. In the 1970s, as part of Project MATH, the group at the University of Connecticut completed some 20 studies of verbal problem solving among the mildly retarded (Cawley, et al., 1976). These studies indicated that the extraneous information difficulty might not be due to the influence of extraneous information per se, but rather to the influence of computational rules when applied in problem-solving situations (Goodstein, et al., 1974); and that performance could be enhanced through the use of indefinite quantifiers (Schenck, 1973). Difficulty with problems of the extraneous information type were studied by Velez (1974), who tested retarded, bilingual Hispanic children in both English and in Spanish, and by Bessant (1972), who contrasted the performance of educable mentally retarded children (EMRs) on meaningful and nonmeaningful stimuli (problems composed of such words as *pawsill,* in contrast to words such as *apple*). In both these studies, the results were similar. The children missed the problems with extraneous information under either condition but got the nonextraneous information problems correct. DeVard (1973) gave us some insight into this phenomenon in a study in which mildly retarded children were asked to read a set of problems one week and then do the problems the next week. DeVard found that extraneous information problems were missed whether the child read them accurately or not, and that nonextraneous information problems were correct regardless of reading performance.

Boyd (1974) and Mayer (1974) conducted comparisons between problems of the direct type and the indirect type. Boyd included extraneous information in her problems but used only one age group. Mayer took a cross-sectional approach and studied children of different ages. In the main, indirect problems proved more difficult than direct ones.

Levy (1980) contrasted the performance of children who were learning disabled in mathematics with children who were not disabled. He used different formats and arrangements of the arithmetic subtests of the WISC-R and found that the WISC-R test did differentiate between these samples, although less so when it was administered in some kind of written format.

Goodstein and Sedlak (1972) contrasted the performance of average, retarded, and LD children on a verbal problem-solving task built around Piaget's idea of class inclusion. The problems were administered aurally. The investigators found it necessary to repeat the problems many times to the LD children, but once they gathered the information, the problem was solved correctly. The mildly retarded did not take as many repetitions to store the information but did not respond correctly when they did.

Average children were accurate and quick to store. To the best of my knowledge, this is the only comparative study of word problem solving contrasting these three groups of children.

The general literature in learning disabilities fails to show any significant attention to verbal problem solving. Blankenship and Lovitt (1976) conducted one study in which it was noted that the children did not read the problems carefully. The investigators trained the children to reread problems and then observed their performance. Rereading was recommended as a teaching tactic. In another study, Trenholme, Larsen, and Parker (1978) evaluated performance on problems consisting of varying syntactical arrangements. Problems with more complex syntactical arrangements were more difficult. Breault (1983), of the University of Connecticut, followed up the Trenholme study by adding the conditions of extraneousness to the syntactic arrangements. The latter study showed that extraneous information was a much more difficult problem than syntactic variation.

Cawley, Fitzmaurice, Shaw, Kahn, & Bates (1979) have proposed matrix formats to develop and teach problem solving to the handicapped. Essentially, what the matrix format does is allow the teacher to control the characteristics of the problem in such a way that any single variable can be manipulated when necessary. If, for example, the child cannot read the material, a lower level reading channel can be followed through the matrix. All other problem characteristics will be constant (e.g., computational difficulty, problem type).

An analysis of performance from the National Assessment of Educational Progress (NAEP) (Carpenter, Corbitt, Kepner, Lindquist, & Reys, 1983) indicates that most students across the three age ranges of 9, 13, and 17 years could solve routine, one-step word story problems but experienced considerable difficulty with problems that went beyond the routine (e.g., problems that contain extraneous information). The NAEP panel of experts recommends in-service training for regular class teachers so they can learn effective ways to teach problem solving.

DeCorte (1984) has examined the semantic influences in verbal problem solving by rewording problems. DeCorte's results support those of the American investigators (i.e., when more difficult problems were reworded to make them easier, scores were higher and performance characteristics changed), although he feels that other task variables have important effects (e.g., sequencing information, the degree to which semantic relations are made explicit between given and unknown relations). A key element in rewording problems is to reword them so that the problem level is maintained. Cohen and Stover (1981) had children rewrite extraneous problems to make them easier. When, for example, a problem contained extraneous information, the children eliminated it. In effect they changed a problem to a nonproblem.

Space limits the extent to which the research in verbal problem solving can be reviewed. National and international efforts, however, can be summarized. Verbal problem solving is an area of relatively high difficulty for both handicapped and nonhandicapped children. Verbal problem solving is a multifaceted phenomenon that is being studied extensively among nonhandicapped children. Attention is being directed toward many topics, such as the interrelationships among reading, computation, and problem solving (Ballew & Cunningham, 1982); semantic factors (Greeno, 1983; Riley, Greeno, & Heller, 1983); structural characteristics of problems (DeCorte, 1984); characteristics of approaches to the solution of problems (Carpenter & Moser, 1982); and the development of problem-solving capability (Carpenter, et al., 1980).

Arithmetic word problems are problems in which the words, their attributes, and the manner in which they are structured and used create problems. Word problems are not computational tasks embedded in words. To solve a word problem, the individual must analyze and interpret the information that is transmitted by the words and their structure and then use this information to make decisions. This is not quite the same perspective used to guide the writers of curriculum materials or texts that stress the use of *cue words* (Mercer & Mercer, 1983). Generally, these individuals are more interested in using word problems to provide computational practice and, in fact, use the cue words to encourage the individual to bypass the information set the words provide. Reducing the information set to dependency upon a single word (e.g., *divide*) and then suggesting that the word implies only one meaning or decision is both harmful to the child and inaccurate, as shown below:

> A boy planned to divide all his apples so that each of his 6 friends would get 2 apples. How many apples did the boy have to divide?

Nesher (1982) has conducted several studies of word problems in addition and subtraction. Independent of calculation, addition problems are significantly easier than subtraction problems. Extraneous information adds an element of difficulty, probably because of the need to clarify types of agreement in quantitative arguments.

An understanding of problems with extraneous information requires comprehension of the logical structures of arithmetic. When logical structures are controlled and semantic and syntactic factors are studied, semantic variables are influential. The logical relations, provided the learning disabled understand these as logical relations, can be linguistically encoded in many ways. These might involve statements relative to agents, location, time, and verbs. For example, *had, gave,* and *have* are verbs in the following:

> Victor *had* five stamps and *gave* two of them to Joe. How many stamps does Victor *have* now?

Rearrangement into indirect formats (i.e., Victor had five stamps after he gave two stamps to Joe. How many did Victor start with?) requires a different conceptualization of the semantic features.

Consideration also needs to be given to Shaw's distinction (1981) between the problem, an example, and an exercise. Shaw indicates that a problem exists when the individual has to search his or her repertoire of experience, knowledge, and skills—and possibly those of others (e.g., teachers) or other resources (e.g., books)—to provide the basis upon which an appropriate analysis, interpretation, and decision can be made. For example, the problem

> What is the voltage drop in 1,000 feet of No. 4 copper wire carrying 40 amperes?

should pose a problem to us and, given the absence of a teacher as a source, we would likely go to a book. We would look at a table to determine the resistance of No. 4 wire (i.e., .028 ohms per 1,000 feet). Next, we would identify the relevant formula, $E = IR$, and proceed. If we were in school and we knew how to solve problems, we would likely be given a number of similar items. These would become progressively easier and, instead of retaining their status as *problems,* they would become *examples.* The example level is the stage most individuals reach in school because a new topic is soon introduced and the individual is returned to the problem level for the new topic. Shaw suggests that the new topic should not be introduced until the individual has reached the exercise stage. This is the stage at which the learner proceeds speedily and automatically to produce decisions. This seems to be a state that handicapped children seldom reach. Failure to reach the exercise stage produces two difficulties, I believe.

One difficulty is that the learning disabled never become good enough to generalize and to return efficiently to the example stage when items are reintroduced at a subsequent time. The individual returns later to similar items at the problem stage, I think, and must begin all over again as though this were the initial introduction.

The second difficulty is the inability to reinterpret information after it has been rearranged in a related item, such as:

What size wire is required to send 40 amperes through 1,000 feet of copper wire if the voltage drop is 12 volts?

Again, we have $E = IR$ rearranged to $R = E/I$. The mathematics involved in $E = IR$ is nothing more than the *factor* $\times$ *factor* = *product* relationship the child learned in $2 \times 3 = 6$. If taught properly, this would have enabled the child to generalize to $2 \times \square = 6$ or $\square \times 3 = 6$ where the individual would have transposed the combinations to $2\overline{)6}$ and $3\overline{)6}$. As one can see, the arithmetic is not particularly complex. What creates the difficulty is the words (our knowledge of them) and their arrangements to signal the appropriate decision (multiply or divide, and which combination).

SUMMARY

Cognitive functioning is an important consideration in mathematics programs for the learning disabled. Cognitive functioning is involved in all types of problem solving, reasoning, and thinking. Situations involving the use of mathematical stimuli can be structured to include many types of cognition. These seem reasonably easy to do. What seems more difficult at the time is to make explicit the cognitive acts that are involved in mathematics performance. Given that we have little information about just what cognitive acts are involved in mathematics and even less information specific to cognitive performance among the learning disabled, we must proceed with caution. Nonetheless, we must proceed.

REFERENCES

Ballew, H., & Cunningham, J. (1982). Diagnosing strengths and weaknesses of sixth-grade students in solving word problems. *Journal for Research in Mathematics Education, 13,* 202–210.

Bessant, H.P. (1972). *The effects of semantic familiarity and information load on the arithmetical verbal problem solving performance of children in special classes for the educable mentally retarded.* Unpublished doctoral dissertation, University of Connecticut, Storrs.

Blackman, S., & Goldstein, K. (1982). Cognitive styles and learning disabilities. *Journal of Learning Disabilities, 15,* 106–115.

Blankenship, C.S. (1985). Linking assessment to curriculum and instruction. In J.F. Cawley (Ed.), *Practical Mathematics Appraisal of the Learning Disabled* (pp. 59–80). Rockville, MD: Aspen Systems.

Blankenship, C.S., & Lovitt, T.C. (1976). Story problems: Merely confusing or downright befuddling? *Journal for Research in Mathematics Education, 7(5),* 291–298.

Boyd, F. (1974). *The effect of extraneous and nonextraneous information in direct and indirect type problems in the arithmetical verbal problem solving performance of the educable mentally retarded.* Unpublished doctoral dissertation, University of Connecticut, Storrs.

Breault, M.A. (1983). *The effects of selected variables in the arithmetical verbal problem solving performance of learning disabled children*. Unpublished doctoral dissertation, University of Connecticut, Storrs.

Capobianco, R. (1957). Quantitative and qualitative analyses of endogenous and exogenous boys on arithmetic achievement. *Monograph of the Society of Research in Child Development, 19*, 101.

Carpenter, T., Corbitt, M., Kepner, H., Lindquist, M., & Reys, R. (1980). Results and implications of the second NAEP mathematics assessment: Elementary school. *Arithmetic Teacher, 27*, 10–47.

Carpenter, T., Moser, J., & Romberg, T. (1982). *Addition and subtraction: A cognitive perspective*. Hillsdale, NJ: Lawrence Erlbaum.

Case, R. (1982). General developmental influences on the acquisition of elementary concepts and algorithms in arithmetic. In T. Carpenter, J. Moser, & T. Romberg (Eds.), *Addition and subtraction: A cognitive perspective* (Chap. 11). Hillsdale, NJ: Lawrence Erlbaum

Cawley, J.F. (1981). Commentary. *Topics in Learning and Learning Disabilities, 1*, 89–95.

Cawley, J.F. (1984a). An integrative approach to the needs of learning disabled children: Expanded uses of mathematics. In J. Cawley (Ed.), *Developmental teaching of mathematics for the learning disabled* (pp. 88–94). Rockville, MD: Aspen Systems.

Cawley, J.F. (1984b). Learning disabilities: Issues and alternatives. In J. Cawley (Ed.), *Developmental teaching of mathematics for the learning disabled* (pp. 1–28). Rockville, MD: Aspen Systems.

Cawley, J.F. (1985). Learning disability and mathematics appraisal. In J. Cawley (Ed.), *Practical mathematics appraisal of the learning disabled* (pp. 1–40). Rockville, MD: Aspen Systems.

Cawley, J.F., Cawley, L.J., Cherkes, M., & Fitzmaurice, A.M. (1980). *Beginning education assessment, levels 4, 5, & 6*. Glenview, IL: Scott-Foresman.

Cawley, J.F., Fitzmaurice, A.M., Goodstein, H.A., Lepore, A., Althaus, V., & Sedlak, R. (1976). *Project MATH, level II*. Tulsa, OK: Educational Progress.

Cawley, J.F., Fitzmaurice, A.M., Shaw, R.S., Kahn, H. & Bates, H. (1979). Math word problems; Suggestions for LD students. *Learning Disability Quarterly, 2*, 25–41.

Cawley, J.F., Fitzmaurice, A.M., Shaw, R.S., Norlander, K., Bates, H., & Schunmann, J. (1980). Multi–Modal Mathematics. Unpublished material, Storrs, CT.

Cawley, J.F., & Goodman, J. (1969, October). Arithmetic problem solving: A program demonstration by teachers of the mentally handicapped. *Exceptional Children, 36*, 83–90.

Cawley, J.F., & Richstone, E. (1984, December). Brain, mathematics and learning disability. *Focus on Learning Problems in Mathematics*.

Cermak, L. (1983). Information processing deficits in children with learning disabilities. *Journal of Learning Disabilities, 16*, 599–605.

Cherkes, M. (1983). Cognitive development and cognitive style. *Journal of Learning Disabilities, 16*, 95–101.

Cohen, S.A., & Stover, G. (1981). Effects of teaching sixth-grade students to modify format variables of math word problems. *Reading Research Quarterly, 16*, 175–200.

Cruickshank, W.M. (1948a). Arithmetic ability of mentally retarded children. I: Ability to differentiate extraneous materials from needed arithmetical facts. *Journal of Educational Research, 42*, 161–170.

Cruickshank, W.M. (1948b). Arithmetic ability of mentally retarded children. II: Understanding arithmetic processes. *Journal of Educational Research, 42,* 279–288.

Cruickshank, W.M., Bentzen, F., Ratzeburg, F., & Tannhauser, M. (1961). *A teaching method in brain-injured and hyperactive children.* Syracuse, NY: Syracuse University Press.

DeCorte, E. (1984). *The influence of rounding verbal problems on children's problem representations and solutions.* Paper presented at the annual convention of the American Educational Research Association,

DeVard, A.J. (1973). *Oral reading of arithmetical problems by educable mentally retarded.* Unpublished doctoral dissertation, University of Connecticut, Storrs.

Fernald, G. (1943). *Remedial techniques in basic school subjects.* New York: McGraw-Hill.

Frederico, P. (1984). *Individual differences in brain event-related potentials and concept acquisition.* Paper presented at the annual meeting of the American Educational Research Association, New Orleans.

Gerber, M. (1983). Learning disabilities and cognitive strategies: A case for training or constraining problem solving. *Journal of Learning Disabilities, 16,* 255–260.

Glennon, V., & Cruickshank, W.M. (1981). Teaching mathematics to children and youth with perceptual and cognitive processing deficits. In V. Glennon (Ed.), *The Mathematical Education of Exceptional Children and Youth* (Chap. 3). Reston, VA: National Council of Teachers of Mathematics.

Goodstein, H., Cawley, J., Gordon, S., & Helfgott, J. (1971). Verbal problem solving among educable mentally retarded children. *American Journal of Mental Deficiency, 76,* 238–241.

Goodstein, H.A. (1974). Individualizing instruction through matrix teaching. *Education and Training of the Mentally Retarded, 9,* 189–190.

Goodstein, H.A. (1981). Are the errors we see the true errors? Error analysis in verbal problem solving. *1981 Topics in Learning and Learning Disabilities, 1,* 31–46.

Goodstein, H.A., & Sedlak, R.A. (1972). *The role of memory in the VPS of average educable mentally retarded and learning disabled children.* Mimeographed manuscript, University of Connecticut, Storrs.

Greeno, J.G. (1983, March). *Processes of solving arithmetic word problems.* Paper presented at the annual meeting of the American Educational Research Association, New York.

Hallahan, D., & Sapona, R. (1983). Self-monitoring of attention with learning disabled children: Past research and current issues. *Journal of Learning Disabilities, 16,* 616–620.

Halpern, N. (1981). Mathematics for the learning disabled. *Journal of Learning Disabilities, 14,* 505–506.

Hammill, D.D., Leigh, J., McNutt, G., & Larsen, S. (1981). A new definition of learning disabilities. *Learning Disability Quarterly, 4,* 336–353.

Kinsbourne, M. (1983). Brain basis of learning disabilities. *Topics in Learning and Learning Disabilities, 3,* 1–13.

Levy, W. (1980). *WISC-R Arithmetic subtest performance of mathematically handicapped and non-handicapped learning disabled students as a function of presentation/response behavior and vocabulary interactions.* Unpublished doctoral dissertation, University of Connecticut, Storrs.

Mayer, M. (1974). *An investigation of the problem solving performance of EMR students with direct and indirect problem using an action sequence presentation of arithmetic verbal problems.* Unpublished doctoral dissertation, University of Connecticut, Storrs.

McLeod, T., & Armstrong, S. (1982). Learning disabilities in mathematics—Skill deficits and remedial approaches at the intermediate and secondary level. *Learning Disability Quarterly, 5,* 305–311.

Mercer, C.D., & Mercer, A.R. (1981). *Teaching students with learning problems.* Columbus, OH: Charles E. Merrill.

Nesher, P. (1982). Levels of description in the analysis of addition and subtraction word problems. In T. Carpenter, J. Moser, & J. Romberg (Eds.), *Addition and subtraction: A cognitive perspective* (Chap. 2). Hillsdale, NJ: Lawrence Erlbaum.

O'Loughlin, M., & Fleischner, J. (1980). *Story problem solving: Importance of research for teaching children with learning disabilities* (Tech. Rep. No. 12). Teachers College.

Reid, K., & Hresko, W. (1981). *A cognitive approach to learning disabilities.* New York: McGraw-Hill.

Resnick, L., & Ford, W. (1981). *The psychology of mathematics for instruction.* Hillsdale, NJ: Lawrence Erlbaum.

Riley, M.S., Greeno, J.G., & Heller, J.I. (1983). Development of children's problem-solving ability in arithmetic. In H.P. Ginsburg (Ed.), *The development of mathematical thinking* (pp. 153–200). New York: Academic Press.

Saxe, G., & Shoheen, S. (1981). Piagetian theory and the atypical case: An analysis of the developmental Gerstmann syndrome. *Journal of Learning Disabilities, 14,* 131–135.

Schenck, W. (1973). Pictures and the indefinite quantifier in verbal problem solving among EMR children. *American Journal of Mental Deficiency, 78,* 272–276.

Sedlak, W. (1973). *Performance of good and poor problem solvers on arithmetic word problems presented in a modified cloze format.* Unpublished doctoral dissertation, Penn State University.

Sharma, M. (1984). Mathematics in the real world. In J.F. Cawley (Ed.), *Developmental teaching of mathematics for the learning disabled* (Chap. 8). Rockville, MD: Aspen Systems.

Shaw, R. (1981). Diagnosing and using non-word problems as aids to thinking and comprehension. *Topics in Learning and Learning Disabilities, 1,* 73–80.

Sternberg, R., & Wagner, R. (1982). Automatization failure in learning disabilities. *Topics in Learning and Learning Disabilities, 2,* 1–11.

Strauss, A.A., & Lehtinen, L.E. (1947). *Psychopathology and education of brain-injured children.* New York: Grune and Stratton.

Swanson, H.L. (1982). A multidirectional model for assessing learning disabled students' intelligence: An information processing framework. *Learning Disability Quarterly, 5,* 312–326.

Thurstone, L.L., & Thurstone, T.G. (1941). *Factorial studies of intelligence.* Chicago: University of Chicago Press.

Torrance, E.P. (1965). *Constructive behavior: Stress, personality and mental health.* Belmont, CA: Wadsworth Publishing.

Trenholme, B., Larsen, S.C., & Parker, R. (1978). The effects of systematic complexity upon arithmetic performance. *Learning Disability Quarterly, 1,* 80–85.

Velez, D. (1974). *Effects of extraneous information on the solving of arithmetic word problems by the Spanish speaking mentally handicapped.* Unpublished doctoral dissertation, University of Connecticut, Storrs.

Webster, R. (1980). Short-term memory in mathematics-proficient and mathematics-disabled students as a function of input-modality/output-modality pairings. *Journal of Special Education, 14,* 67–78.

Zeaman, D., & House, B. (1963). The role of attention in retardate discrimination learning. In N. Ellis (Ed.), *Handbook on mental deficiency.* New York: McGraw Hill.

Zendel, I.H., & Pihl, R.D. (1983). Visual and auditory matchings in learning disabled and normal children. *Journal of Learning Disabilities, 16,* 158–160.

Chapter 2

Techniques for Determining Cognitive Qualities

Paulette J. Thomas

A prerequisite to teaching youngsters anything is first to determine what they know. An assessment performed to ascertain whether or not a pupil qualifies for special education intervention typically involves the administration of norm-referenced instruments. While it is important, and in many states required, to determine that students deviate significantly in achievement from their peers or their own individual projected ability, this knowledge gives little direction to the teacher (Hargrove & Poteet, 1984). The classroom teacher is, therefore, faced with students about whom he or she knows a grade level achievement score and possibly some of the errors they committed. This is hardly enough information around which to design a program of instruction for each individual learner. The teacher must investigate thoroughly what the students know (content and rules) and how they solve problems (mode). Chapters 3 through 9 detail cognitive considerations of specified learning theories. Those chapters include examples of specific content to be tested related to the particular cognitive learning theory. The purpose of this chapter is to describe the process of classroom assessment of the mathematically learning disabled (LD) pupil regardless of selected cognitive theory. The chapter is organized as follows: review of certain measurement principles, planning for the test, item construction and scoring, and evaluation of the administered test.

REVIEW OF CERTAIN MEASUREMENT PRINCIPLES

All educational and psychological measures of mental processes are said to be indirect, incomplete, and relative. We measure behavior that is thought to reflect a cognitive trait or process. We cannot measure the target trait or process directly (Bertrand & Cebula, 1980). Consequently, there must be a clear relationship between the behavioral tasks of the test (which can be directly measured) and the underlying trait or process the test presumes to measure. Educational and psychological measures are also described as incomplete. The implication of this characteristic is that there is no way to test everything an individual knows or can do. Rather, the teacher must sample from the universe of items the student is expected to be able to do. Caution must be exercised to sample fairly and representatively from the pool of appropriate tasks for the mental process being measured. (See the discussion of the Table of Specifications in this chapter.) Finally, educational and psychological measures are relative. That is, for test scores to be meaningful, they must be interpreted in terms of some reference group. For example, if you were told that your IQ was 150, you would probably be pleased. If you were told, on the other hand, that your GRE score was 150, you might fall into the depths of depression. Why might you have these different reactions? You are probably aware that the average score for an IQ test is 100 and your score is more than three standard deviations above that average. You are probably also aware that the average GRE score is 400, which places your performance significantly below average. In other words, you are informed of the reference group or "yardstick" against which your scores are measured.

Another very important principle is that the measurement of all types of data contains error (Brown, Amos, & Mink, 1975). It is possible to calculate the range within which an individual's true score is likely to fall. The statistic that estimates the standard deviation of error scores is called the standard error of measurement (SEm). The standard error of measurement should always be applied to obtained scores.

Before using test results, a teacher should always ascertain that the test is relevant to the intended use. To be relevant, a test must first measure consistently. The quality of consistency is technically referred to as reliability (Carmines & Zeller, 1979). The combination of consistency and relevancy yields a concept known as validity. It is as important for a teacher-made instrument to demonstrate reliability and validity as it is for a standardized test (Goodstein, 1984). Use of the Kuder-Richardson Formula 21 is a relatively painless method of determining the reliability of an objective test in which the items can be scored 1 or 0. Of course, there are other methods of determining reliability. The reader can consult any educational measurement textbook (e.g., Anastasi, 1976) for other formulas.

A quick review of the interpretation of reliability follows. (Those of you who still remember reliability from your college days may skip this paragraph.) A high positive reliability coefficient indicates that the teacher can be reasonably confident in a set of test scores. A reliability coefficient near zero indicates little relationship between what the students know and what is being tested. That is, it is likely that scores represent little more than chance results. Teacher-made tests should demonstrate reliability coefficients of at least + .60.

A statement was made earlier to the effect that the standard error of measurement should always be considered when interpreting test scores. It is interesting to examine the interrelationship of the standard error of measurement and the reliability coefficient. Recall that the standard deviation is a measure of variability—or "spread-out-ness" from the mean. If the standard deviation is "large," then the scores vary quite a bit from the mean. If the standard deviation is "small," the scores tend to cluster around the mean score. To illustrate the relationship of the standard error of measurement, the standard deviation, and the reliability, four situations are presented.

> Let "large" standard deviation (*sd*) = 15
> Let "small" *sd* = 5
> Let "high" reliability (*r*) = .90
> Let "low" *r* = .30

1. Large *sd*, low *r*　　SEm = 12.55

   In this example, the standard error of measurement is almost as large as the standard deviation. To identify the range within which a particular student's true score probably lies, it is necessary to add and subtract 12.55 to the obtained score. Knowing that the student's score falls within a 25-point spread is virtually useless.
2. Large *sd*, high *r*　　SEm = 4.74

   A reliable test, on the other hand, reduces the point spread in this example to approximately 9.
3. Small *sd*, low *r*　　SEm = 4.18

   Again, the low reliability of this test results in a standard error of measurement that is nearly equal to the standard deviation. Test scores become meaningless in this situation.
4. Small *sd*, high *r*　　SEm = 1.58

   These results indicate that the scores did not vary very far from the mean, the test was reliable, and we can estimate the students' true scores within about 3 points.

Obviously, it is desirable to have a small standard error of measurement in interpreting test scores. An example of interpreting IQ test scores using the standard error of measurement is pertinent. IQ tests typically report a mean of 100 and a standard deviation of 15. If an IQ test reported a standard error of measurement of 13 and a student's observed score was 85, we can be reasonably sure (applying the standard error of measurement) that this student's IQ falls somewhere between 72 and 98. What do we conclude about this student's IQ? Should we say that his IQ ranges from borderline retarded to average intelligence? It sounds a bit ridiculous, doesn't it? If, on the other hand, the student obtained a score of 85 on an IQ test with a standard error of measurement of 3, his score would range from 82 to 88. Now we can conclude that this student's IQ is approximately one standard deviation below the mean. The IQ information is now usable.

For test results to be useful, the test must demonstrate both consistency and relevancy. This combination of characteristics describes validity. The commonly asked question associated with validity is, "Does the test measure what it purports to measure?" If a test is to be valid, it must first demonstrate reliability. Given that an acceptable reliability coefficient has been obtained, the teacher must examine the question of relevancy. Criterion-related validity is concerned with predicting behavior from the results of a test. While the merits of computing predictive or concurrent validity cannot be disputed, it is simply not practical to attempt this for every test administered in the classroom. Therefore, (even though it goes against my professional grain to state this), it is probably more realistic to expect most classroom tests to exhibit curricular (i.e., content) validity. Curricular validity can usually be ensured by adhering to a table of specifications (described later in this chapter) in designing items for the test. This activity will at least establish the relationship between the content and goals of the class and the examination.

PLANNING FOR THE TEST

The first stage of planning for a test is to determine the purpose of testing. The purpose for testing will, in turn, guide the teacher in designing the makeup of the test—that is, what kind of items to include, what subject matter to test, how many items to present, and so forth. If that purpose is to assess how well the students have learned the material, then a test should be constructed that touches all aspects of the material and the items should be of medium difficulty. If the purpose of the test is to rank order the students on the magnitude of their differences, then the teacher should construct a test that touches critical aspects of the material and contains items that are medium to hard in difficulty. If the purpose is to diagnose strengths and weaknesses, then items should be constructed that measure all aspects of the subject and range in difficulty from easy to hard. It is often useful to administer a test constructed for the first purpose in order to create a "yardstick" against which to measure student achievement. For instructional purposes, however, to design effective instructional programming, the third purpose is more appropriate. After the purpose for testing has been decided, the teacher is ready to construct a blueprint for the test.

Table of Specifications

This blueprint, formally known as a Table of Specifications, outlines the levels of the cognitive domain to be tested, specific objectives to be examined, and the length of the test. Although this illustration uses Bloom's taxonomy for the column weights, any of the cognitive learning theories can be substituted. Begin by drawing a grid such as the one shown in Table 2-1.

In test construction, the levels of the cognitive domain that are tested typically include *knowledge, understanding,* and *application* (a combination of application, analysis, synthesis, and evaluation). The knowledge level can be described as recall of factual information, such as knowledge of multiplication tables. The understanding level tests the student's ability to translate, reword, or rephrase learned information. The application level measures the pupil's ability to use learned facts and understanding of mathematical concepts to solve problems. By way of example:

Knowledge   correctly answering *2* to the problem *1 + 1 =*
Understanding   correctly answering ½ to the problem ¼ + ¼ =
Application   correctly answering ½ to the problem, *If the Coney family eats ¼ of the pie for lunch and ¼ of the pie for dinner, how much of the pie did they eat?*

The test constructor must decide which of the three levels of the cog-

Table 2-1 Table of Specifications Grid

Weight	Content	Know-ledge ____ %	Under-standing ____ %	Appli-cation ____ %	# of items by con-tent area
____ %	Objective I				
____ %	Objective II				
____ %	Objective III				
					Total # of items ____

nitive domain to include on the test. It is acceptable to use one, two, or all three levels, depending on what information the teacher wants to learn about the pupil. If the teacher wants to measure all three levels, he or she may decide to distribute the weightings as follows: knowledge—30 percent, understanding—40 percent, and application—30 percent. This distribution is subject to the discretion of the teacher. However the weightings are distributed, the percentages must, of course, equal 100 percent.

The rows under the column heading "Content" represent the instructional objectives to be tested. These objectives can be as broad or narrow as the situation requires. Notice that each of the objectives carries a space for a weighting to be inserted. The test generator determines the relative weight of each objective based on three factors: the amount of time spent on the material to be tested, the relative importance of the material, and/or the amount of material presented. Again, the percentages must add to 100 percent.

Thus far, the Table of Specifications may look something like Table 2-2.

The next step in constructing a Table of Specifications is to decide how many items will be presented on the test. This decision should be based on the age of the examinee, the time available to answer the test, the extent to which the teacher wishes to "test the limits," and any other pertinent factor. For illustrative purposes, we insert *50* as the total number of items to be included on the sample test. The blueprint now appears as shown in Table 2-3.

The next task is to determine the number of items in each cell. The result will specify the number of items to be constructed at each level of

Table 2-2 Table of Specifications, Next Stage

Weight	Content	Know-ledge 30%	Under-standing 40%	Appli-cation 30%	# of items by content area
22%	Objective I				
37%	Objective II				
41%	Objective III				
					Total # of items ___

Table 2-3 Table of Specifications Blueprint, Next Stage

Weight	Content	Know-ledge 30%	Under-standing 40%	Appli-cation 30%	# of items by con-tent area
22%	Objective I				
37%	Objective II				
41%	Objective III				
					Total # of items 50

Table 2-4 Completed Table of Specifications

Weight	Content	Know-ledge 30%	Under-standing 40%	Appli-cation 30%	# of items by con-tent area
22%	Objective I	3.3	4.4	3.3	11
37%	Objective II	5.55	7.4	5.55	18.5
41%	Objective III	6.15	8.2	6.15	20.5
					Total # of items 50

the cognitive domain for each objective to be tested. The number of items per cell is obtained by multiplying the row weight by the column weight by the total number of items. For example, to fill the cell that intersects the "Knowledge" level and Objective I, multiply *.22 × .30 × 50*. The product is *3.3*. To fill the cell at the intersection of "Understanding" and Objective I, multiply *.22 × .40 × 50*. This product is *4.4*. The product in the cell intersection of "Application" and Objective I is, of course, *3.3*. The total "# of items by content area" (add the products in the row) is *11*. The remainder of the Table of Specifications can now be completed (see Table 2-4).

This completed Table of Specifications indicates that the teacher should create 3.3 items to measure Objective I at the "Knowledge" level of the cognitive domain. Of course, it is not possible to administer 3.3 items. The situation dictates that each cell be filled with a whole number. It is now the job of the test creator to round the fractional numbers in each cell to whole numbers. It also becomes apparent that rounding cannot follow the usual mathematical rule. Examine the cells in the Objective I row. Following the usual mathematical rule, *3.3* would be rounded down to *3* and *4.4* would be rounded down to *4*. This rounding would result in a total "# of items by content area" of only *10* when there should be *11*. Therefore, the teacher must round fractional numbers in such a way that the total number of items remains constant. Inspection of the column "# of items by content area" reveals that rounding may be necessary in this column, too. If rounding is necessary, the row totals must add to the "Total # of items." The final completed Table of Specifications for the example, then, would be as shown in Table 2-5.

The task of creating a 50-item test has now been reduced to creating a series of minitests. The teacher's task seems quite a bit easier if he or she has to generate only four items, for example, that measure factual knowledge of whatever subject matter is in Objective I. An added benefit of developing a Table of Specifications is knowledge that the pupil is being tested over a fair representation of items. The composition of the test will reflect actual instruction, rather than being composed of easily constructed items that may weigh more heavily on easily tested constructs or facts. For example, it is more difficult to generate items that measure the higher levels of the cognitive domain. It is a great temptation to sling together a test that simply measures knowledge of facts when, in fact, all math instructional units, even at the most elementary level, include application of learned facts.

Table 2-5 Table of Specifications after Rounding

Weight	Content	Knowledge 30%	Understanding 40%	Application 30%	# of items by content area
22%	Objective I	4	4	3	11
37%	Objective II	5	7	6	18
41%	Objective III	7	8	6	21
					Total # of items 50

ITEM CONSTRUCTION AND SCORING

The following types of items are discussed: multiple choice, completion (fill-in-the-blank), true–false, matching, and essay. Do's and don'ts are listed for each type of item. Scoring hints are outlined and examples presented where pertinent. The teacher should keep in mind that principles of item construction and scoring apply regardless of content or the particular cognitive theory embraced.

Multiple-Choice Items

There are three parts in a multiple-choice item: stem, keyed response, and distractors (or foils or alternatives). The stem should pose a clear, central problem and should be complete enough to make one answer justifiable. Wording should be as concise as possible. Each item should be independent of all other items. The example illustrates what happens when one item depends on a correct answer from a previous item. The youngster has no chance of getting the second problem correct if he or she misses the first one.

Don't

Sue ate 1/6 of the pie. George ate 1/3 of the pie. How much of the pie was left?

a. 2/9
b. 1/3
c. 1/2
d. 2/3

Theresa ate 1/4 of the remaining pie. How much was left then?

a. 1/3
b. 1/4
c. 1/2
d. 2/3

Vocabulary should be appropriate to the group for whom it is intended. Avoid sentence structure that is confusing. State the stem in positive form if possible. Emphasize negative wording whenever used in the stem either by underlining the negative word or by writing it in all capital letters. The example given next could easily be stated in the positive. It is given only to demonstrate emphasis of the negative wording.

Do

Which of the following is NOT a mixed fraction?

a. 6/4
b. 1/8
c. 3 1/7
d. 9 11/12

Do *not* quote textbook or instructional material. Avoid giving clues in the stem.

Don't
An eight-sided figure is called an
a. octagon.
b. hexagon.
c. pentagon.
d. triangle.

A better way to write this item, so that grammatical clues do not automatically give away the answer, follows.

Do
An eight-sided figure is a(n)
a. octagon.
b. hexagon.
c. pentagon.
d. triangle.

The keyed response is the choice the teacher has selected as *the answer*. The keyed response should be grammatically and logically consistent with the stem and should appear with approximately equal frequency in all response positions. The keyed response should be different from the distractors only in meaning, with no superficial verbal clues (e.g., specific determiners "never," "always," etc.) Use special alternatives (e.g., "all of the above," "none of the above") sparingly, if at all. There are specific rules to be followed if the teacher elects to use special alternatives. Use the special alternative early in the test as the keyed response. (This alerts the examinee to consider seriously that "none of the above" may, indeed, be a correct response.) If the format is a four-option multiple choice, then the special alternative should be the keyed response one-fourth of the time and an incorrect choice three-fourths of the time. Thus, if there are 100 multiple-choice items and all the items contain a special alternative, the special alternative should be correct 25 times and incorrect 75 times. (This illustration violates the rule of using the special alternative sparingly, but the math was easy.)

The distractors must be plausible. The distractors and the keyed response should be similar in length, parallel in construction, and equally precise in expression. It is advisable to construct distractors from common misinformation and feasible but erroneous conclusions.

Do
The area of a rectangle whose sides measure 2 inches by 4 inches is
a. 12 inches.
b. 12 square inches.
c. 8 inches.
d. 8 square inches.

Completion Items

A completion item should be able to be answered with a word, phrase, symbol, formula, or short sentence for paper/pencil tasks. A problem-solving exercise, such as Piaget's conservation of liquid task, is considered a completion item. In this case, a response may take the form of an action or oral explanation. Use direct questions where feasible, or place the blanks near the end of the sentence. This allows students to begin formulating their responses after they have received all the relevant information from the test item. Each item should be specific, clear, and unambiguous. Avoid excessive mutilation; omit only key words (or formulas or the like).

Don't
The _____of the _____is the _____ .

Do
The formula for the area of a circle is _____ .

Make sure that this is the most efficient item format for testing the objectives. Prepare a scoring key before the test is administered. Technical difficulties can often be avoided by taking this precaution.

True–False Items

True–false items are essentially multiple-choice items for which only two choices are possible. The chance of selecting the correct answer by guessing is 50 percent. It is, therefore, quite difficult to ascertain whether students really do demonstrate mastery of the test material or whether they are good (or lucky) guessers. If, however, it is determined that this is the best way to test certain objectives, there are certain guidelines that should be followed in composing items. Express each item in clear, simple language. Refrain from lifting verbatim statements from instructional material. Avoid specific determiners and double-barreled items (i.e., part true, part false). Avoid negative statements where possible. Consider this item:

A right triangle does *not* have at least one 90-degree angle.

How might a learning disabled youngster answer? "Yes, a right triangle *does* have a 90-degree angle." or "No, that's not right. A right triangle does have a 90-degree angle." Which answer does the student record—yes or no? Given the explanatory statements (which do not appear on the answer sheet), the child clearly knows the concept being tested.

There should be approximately the same number of true and false items. Directions must clearly indicate the type of response desired. (For example, "Circle *true* if the statement is correct, *false* if the statement is wrong.") The test maker should take all precautions necessary to discourage cheating on true–false items since it is relatively easy to change a *T* to an *F*. Perhaps the wisest course is for the teacher to grade true–false items rather than the easier change-papers-with-your-neighbor method.

A slight variation of the true–false item is the correction-type true–false item in which the examinee must correct any statements that are false. If the test constructor elects to use this type of true–false item, there are a few pointers to learn. Be sure to provide space for correcting the statement for all items, even the ones that are true. Highlight the words to be corrected. Note this sample.

T   F   The square root of 6 is 2.

The examinee might circle *F* and write, "The square root of 6 is not 2." How do you score this response? Do you give the student credit? Her answer is technically correct. If you expect her to give the exact square root of 6, then you must indicate that by underlining the part of the statement to be corrected. The improved item is now written as follows:

T   F   The square root of 6 is 2̲.

Now the examinee must enter "2.45" to receive credit. The teacher now has a better idea of whether or not the student really knows how to obtain a square root.

A final word about true–false items is in order. Make sure this is the best way to test the objective. The preceding example would really be best written as a completion item.

Matching Items

A matching exercise is another case of a multiple-choice item in which there are numerous stems and shared alternatives. The stem in a matching item is called the premise list, and the alternatives are called the response list. It is not difficult to construct good matching items if certain rules are followed. The response and premise lists should be homogeneous and should contain between 5 and 12 entries. If an answer can be used more than once, that should be clearly stated in the directions. The response list should typically be longer than the premise list. This discourages students from guessing by elimination. Both lists in the matching exercise should appear on the same page. All suggestions for constructing multiple-choice items also apply to constructing matching items. It might be helpful to view poorly constructed and well constructed matching exercises.

Don't

Matching
_____ 1. addition   a. −
_____ 2. subtraction   b. ×
_____ 3. multiplication   c. +
_____ 4. division   d. ÷

Do

Directions: Match the symbol to the function described. Each answer may
    be used only once.
_____ 1. addition   a. √
_____ 2. division   b. %
_____ 3. multiplication   c. −
_____ 4. square root   d. +
_____ 5. subtraction   e. #
                                                         f. ×
                                                         g. ÷

It is advisable to construct the scoring key before administering the test to avoid "cute" response patterns (e.g., patterns that spell a word) and to detect any technical errors that might spoil an item.

EVALUATION OF THE ADMINISTERED TEST

The final step in test construction is to evaluate the test that has been administered. This process is called item analysis and can be performed easily via computer program. Since most classrooms do not yet have computer facilities, a simple method of performing item analysis manually is described step by step. (For a fuller description of a similar method of performing item analysis by hand, consult Anastasi, 1976.) Construct a blank chart similar to Table 2-6.

Table 2-6 Item Analysis Chart

Item	H	L	H + L	H − L	Flag?
1	10	10	20	0	*
2	9	5	14	4	
3	3	7	10	−4	*
.					
.					
.					
50	8	5	13	3	

1. Score the papers, and select the ten highest-scoring papers and the ten lowest-scoring papers.
2. Under the column in Table 2-6 headed "H," enter the total number of the high-scoring papers that answered the item correctly. Under the column marked "L," enter the total number of the low-scoring papers that answered the item correctly.
3. Determine the index of difficulty by adding the H and L columns. The index of difficulty provides an indication of the difficulty of each item. An item that has an index of difficulty ranging from 13 to 17 can be considered of medium difficulty. It follows, then, that an item with an index of difficulty of 20 would be considered "easy" and an item with an index of difficulty of 5 would be termed "hard." The decision of whether to aim for a test that contains "easy" or "hard" items should be governed by the designated purpose of the testing (see "Planning for the Test" in this chapter).
4. Compute the index of discrimination by subtracting L from H. An item is deemed to be a "good" discriminator (i.e., separates the better prepared from the less well prepared students) if the index is 3 or more. An index of discrimination of 0 indicates no separation among students.
5. Designate those items that fall outside the desired ranges either on the index of difficulty or the index of discrimination. It is now the task of the teacher to determine why those items were flagged. Is the item defective? Did I not teach the material well? Is the item too difficult for this level of students? Unfortunately, there are no stock guidelines to assist the teacher in answering these questions.

Item 1 is flagged because it is easy and does not discriminate among students. Item 3 is flagged because it is of more than medium difficulty and indicates that the less well prepared students tended to answer the item correctly more often than the better prepared students.

Once the teacher determines the reason for the defective item, he or she may then modify the item, reteach the material, or discard the item.

SUMMARY

This chapter has detailed the process of assessing the mathematically learning disabled student via teacher-constructed instruments regardless of which cognitive theory is embraced. Measurement terms have been reviewed, and examples of their application to classroom tests have been presented. The nuts and bolts of planning for the test, constructing the items, and evaluating the items have been described in easy-to-follow guidelines. The chapters that follow discuss certain cognitive theories as applied to mathematically learning disabled youngsters. Each theory dictates content that can easily be translated into test items by following the framework of this chapter.

REFERENCES

Anastasi, A. (1976). *Psychological testing* (4th ed.) New York: Macmillan.

Bertrand, A., & Cebula, J.P. (1980). *Tests, measurement, and evaluation: A developmental approach*. Reading, MA: Addison-Wesley.

Brown, A.L., Amos, J.R., & Mink, O.G. (1975). *Statistical concepts: A basic program* (2nd ed.). New York: Harper & Row.

Carmines, E.G., & Zeller, R.A. (1979). *Reliability and validity assessment*. Beverly Hills, CA: SAGE Publications.

Goodstein, H.A. (1984). Assessment: Examination and utilization from pre-K through secondary levels. In J. Cawley (Ed.), *Developmental teaching of mathematics for the learning disabled* (pp. 55–81). Rockville, MD: Aspen Systems.

Hargrove, L.J., & Poteet, J.A. (1984). *Assessment in special education: The education evaluation*. Englewood Cliffs, NJ: Prentice-Hall.

Chapter 3

A Behavioral View of Mathematical Learning Problems

Colleen S. Blankenship

Behaviorists and cognitivists are often depicted as being on opposite ends of a continuum, disagreeing vehemently at times, about such basic issues as how learning occurs and how students are best taught. Eloquent arguments have been made for both sides. Behaviorists have questioned the necessity of using inner causes to explain behavior and have expressed doubt concerning the verifiability of cognitive theories of learning. Similarly, cognitivists have called behaviorists to task for reducing all the complexities of inner mental processes to observable behaviors, relying on external reinforcement, and for advocating "teaching by telling," which, in their view, results in rote learning.

At times, the division between cognitive and behavioral psychology has prompted "manifesto papers, acrimonious controversy, [and] mutual rejection" (Krantz, 1971). Special education, particularly learning disabilities, has provided a convenient testing ground for evaluating learning theories. The debate is obviously over for some, with victory being proclaimed, curiously enough, by proponents of both sides! Others appear to have opted out entirely, stating that a combined cognitive, neuropsychological, and behavioral approach holds the greatest promise for educating learning disabled (LD) students (Gaddes, 1983). For some, the controversy rages on (Brophy, 1983; Greer, 1983), while still others explore the potential of melding cognitive and behavioral orientations (Hallahan et al., 1983; Meichenbaum, 1977).

The split between cognitive and behavioral psychology has led some to ask, "Can the two views ever be reconciled?" The answer is, probably not. Reconciliation may not even be desirable, since more progress may be made with each camp pursuing separate lines of inquiry. Perhaps a better question is, "Can cognitivists and behaviorists learn any lessons from each other?" In terms of improving mathematics instruction for students with learning problems, the answer to that question is, decidedly, yes. Proponents of both views could profit from a thorough examination of each other's research. Little overlap exists between sources cited in behavioral and cognitive studies on the teaching of mathematics. Consequently, adherents of both perspectives are not well informed about each other's research.

This chapter presents a behavioral view of mathematical learning difficulties and summarizes research related to improving the acquisition, generalization, and maintenance of mathematical skills among LD students. As such, it stands in marked contrast to the other chapters in this text and provides an alternative view of learning difficulties and procedures for their remediation. Following the review of research, discussion focuses on assessing the contribution of the behavioral approach to mathematics instruction. Research directions are proposed that address some of the criticisms cognitively oriented mathematics educators have made about the behavioral approach to teaching mathematics.

MATHEMATICAL LEARNING PROBLEMS

Many students experience difficulties in learning mathematics. Some students lack accuracy, while others may be very accurate but compute problems too slowly. Other students behave inconsistently—solving problems correctly one day, but not the next. Still other youngsters fail to maintain learned skills for extended periods of time or have difficulty applying their knowledge in new situations. Behaviorists attribute pupils' mathematical difficulties to such factors as failure to master prerequisite skills, lack of instruction, inadequate stimulus control, insufficient reinforcement, use of inefficient procedures, and limited opportunities for practice. In this section we examine how these factors can produce students who have difficulty acquiring, maintaining, generalizing, and demonstrating proficiency in mathematics. Later, research is reviewed supporting the views presented in this section.

Consistently low accuracy often indicates lack of knowledge. Suspicions are aroused that a student cannot, or at least does not know how to, respond correctly when assessment data reveal deficient performance on prerequisite skills. Daily written work also provides clues to aid in pinpointing learning problems. Students who perform at very low levels of accuracy often make the same errors day after day, such as subtracting the minuend from the subtrahend ($37 - 9 = 32$) or failing to rename ($46 + 8 = 414$). Sometimes students indicate that they do not know how to respond correctly, often making comments such as, "But I don't know how to multiply" or "Teach me how to do the line and the two dots" (referring to division). Other tip-offs signaling a possible lack of knowledge include papers littered with tally marks, excessive interest in a fellow classmate's paper, or failure to complete assignments.

The behavior of some students is inconsistent; they solve problems correctly one day, but not the next. Possible explanations include ineffective consequences for accurate performance, poor stimulus control, and counting errors. The typical reinforcers used in classrooms, such as grades and feedback, simply are not sufficient to motivate all pupils to perform at consistently high levels. Inadequate stimulus control can also result in inconsistent performance. For example, consider a student whose accuracy in computing subtraction problems is high when the teacher reminds the pupil to "remember to rename" but low when helpful prompts are not provided. In this instance, the behavior is not under the control of the relevant stimulus—namely, the problem itself. Rather, it is being controlled by the supplementary stimulus (prompt) provided by the teacher. Accuracy can also fluctuate from day to day when students rely on counting to determine answers to problems. Unless care is taken to start and stop the count on the appropriate numbers, careless errors may result.

While accurate and consistent performance is important, computational speed is also desirable. Some pupils compute problems accurately but much too slowly. Barring motor impairments, low computational rates may be due to reliance on time-consuming strategies such as counting, lack of practice, or insufficient reinforcement for rapid responding.

Some students have difficulty maintaining skills for extended periods of time. A variety of factors may contribute to poor maintenance. Because arithmetic texts provide few opportunities to acquire new skills before advancing to other topics, some students never master the skills presented. Even when students do achieve criterion levels, poor maintenance can result if opportunities to review previously mastered skills are provided infrequently. Last, some students may fail to maintain high levels of accuracy simply because it is not sufficiently reinforcing to do so.

One of the primary goals of mathematics instruction is to equip students with sufficient skills to apply their knowledge to solve problems encountered in daily life. Frequently, very little is done to encourage students to demonstrate their skills in different settings. Instead, real-life word problems are presented in the hope that students will apply what they learn in the classroom to solve a variety of problems encountered in daily life. Some students have difficulty generalizing their skills from one classroom to another, let alone applying their knowledge to solve real-life problems.

Another type of difficulty with generalization consists of failure to apply previously mastered skills to solve related problems. For example, a student may correctly solve problems of the type [ ] + 3 = 5, but be unable to solve more complex problems, such as [ ] + 30 = 50. Failure to generalize from one setting to another or from one problem type to another can be due to a number of factors, including: (a) inability to perform all components of the behavior, (b) failure to recognize the similarity between stimuli, and (c) insufficient reinforcement for correct responding.

To illustrate how applied behavior analysts remediate the types of learning difficulties described here, research related to improving the mathematical performance of LD students is presented. First, however, a brief discussion of applied behavior analysis (ABA) research methodology is presented to acquaint the reader with the general characteristics of the approach.

ABA RESEARCH ON MATHEMATICS INSTRUCTION

Characteristics

Applied behavior analysis research is characterized by direct measurement, daily measurement, experimental control, individual analysis, and replicable teaching procedures (Lovitt, 1981). After carefully defining the behavior under study, the performance of each subject is assessed daily, or at least very frequently. Typically, data for each pupil are charted. During the initial, or baseline, stage, the aim is to determine each student's level of functioning prior to treatment. Measurement often takes the form of counting discrete behaviors, such as the number or rate of problems computed correctly and incorrectly.

Applied behavior analysts study the effects of what may appear to be simply teaching techniques, such as demonstration, modeling, knowledge of results, and various reinforcement schedules and contingencies. Interventions are usually described in sufficient detail to allow researchers to replicate them and to assist teachers in implementing promising techniques in their own classrooms. Reliability checks are typically conducted by an independent observer to determine whether the procedures were administered precisely as described. The emphasis on reliability applies to dependent measures as well; in mathematics research, an independent observer recorrects a sample of each student's work and verifies the accuracy of the charted data. By quantifying dependent measures and precisely describing independent variables, applied behavior analysts can scientifically assess the effects of different teaching techniques on pupil performance.

A variety of within-subject designs are available; each is appropriate for demonstrating experimental control in certain situations (Hersen & Barlow, 1976; Kazdin, 1982). For example, to assess the effects of reinforcement on computational errors, a researcher might choose to use a withdrawal design. By continuously measuring performance while alternating baseline and intervention conditions in separate phases over time, one can determine whether or not performance varies as a function of altering conditions.

Although withdrawal designs provide dramatic evidence of functional relationships, the irreversibility of some behaviors precludes the use of designs that rely on the reinstatement of baseline conditions to establish experimental control. For example, after instruction on a previously unknown skill, such as renaming in subtraction, students frequently maintain high levels of accuracy. By anticipating the nonreversibility of behavior in such cases, a researcher can select a more appropriate design, such as a multiple baseline design. Using this design, instructional effectiveness is assessed by simultaneously measuring two or more behaviors, then systematically applying the intervention to each behavior in turn. Provided that each successive application of the intervention is accompanied by a change in the behavior to which it was applied, experimental control can be demonstrated. Later, studies are reviewed that used multiple baseline designs to assess the effects of treatment on (a) different mathematical skills within individual students, (b) the same skill across several students, and (c) the transfer of skills from one setting to another.

Research Focus

ABA research on mathematics has focused primarily on two areas—arithmetic computation and word problems. With respect to computational arithmetic, several different types of learning problems have been investigated. The computational research has been grouped according to its focus on increasing accuracy, consistency, proficiency, maintenance, and generalization. This classification scheme was adopted to illustrate the range of problems that have been investigated and to highlight the types of techniques used to remediate different types of learning difficulties. While considerably less research has been conducted in the area of problem solving, studies focusing on this important topic are discussed after the review of computational research.

Arithmetic Computation

Accuracy

Applied behavior analysts have studied the effects of two types of events on the computational performance of students performing at very low levels of accuracy. Events that occur prior to a response are known as antecedents; whereas those that follow a response are referred to as consequents. Tactics such as instructions, demonstrations, and modeling are examples of some of the antecedent events that have been investigated. Some of the consequent events that have been studied include providing feedback, reinforcing correct responses, and arranging contingencies for errors.

Lovitt and Curtiss (1968) conducted one of the first studies to investigate the effects of an antecedent event on behavior. The subject in their study was an 11-year-old boy whose accuracy in computing subtraction problems was very low. The study, which consisted of three experiments, assessed the effects of self-verbalization on the pupil's ability to compute subtraction problems of the type $[] - 2 = 6$, $[] - 20 = 60$, and $4 - 3 = 9 - []$. During the first phase of each experiment, no verbalization was required. In the second phase, the student was asked to verbalize each problem and answer before solving the problems. During the last phase, the pupil was directed to refrain from verbalizing the problems and answers. Accuracy increased when the student was required to verbalize before responding. While no generalization occurred from one problem type to another, the student maintained his accuracy on all three problem types following the termination of instruction.

Lovitt and Curtiss's study marked the beginning of a series of investigations examining the effects of different types of antecedent events on mathematical performance and led to eventual comparisons between the effects of antecedent and consequent events. It predated cognitive behavior modification studies on the role of self-verbalization in learning and highlighted the importance of assessing for the generality of behavior change.

Other antecedent events, shown to increase the accuracy of low-performing students, include demonstration and modeling. Smith and Lovitt (1975) conducted three related studies with seven LD students whose accuracy in computing various types of subtraction and multiplication problems was near zero. In Study 1, the effects of demonstration and modeling were assessed. Study 2 replicated the first study and examined the effects of a consequent event (feedback) on performance. In the third study, a component analysis of the demonstration and modeling technique was undertaken to determine the relative effects of each component of the procedure.

The results of Study 1 indicated that demonstration and modeling were clearly effective in improving the pupils' computational accuracy. Prior to the intervention, the students' accuracy was near zero. Accuracy increased when they were provided with a verbal explanation of the correct procedure, shown how to perform the necessary steps, and given a completed problem to refer to as they computed their problems. During the intervention condition, each pupil's accuracy increased to 90 percent correct or better. Figure 3-1 presents data for one pupil and illustrates the dramatic effect that demonstration and modeling had on his performance. Even though the intervention was directed toward only one set of problems, (Set la), accuracy also increased on Set 1b, problems of comparable difficulty.

The component analysis of the demonstration and modeling condition revealed that not all pupils required both conditions to achieve mastery. For one pupil, the permanent model alone was effective, whereas demonstration alone was sufficient to enable the other two subjects in Study 3 to achieve mastery.

In comparing the effects of feedback to demonstration and modeling, Smith and Lovitt (1975) found that telling pupils which answers were correct and incorrect was not effective in improving their accuracy. As the data for a representative subject shown in Figure 3-2 indicate, accuracy was not affected by feedback. Similar results were found in studies that compared the effects of demonstration and modeling to reinforcement contingencies on the computational performance of students functioning at very low levels of accuracy (Blankenship & Korn, 1980; Smith & Lovitt, 1974).

In conducting their research, Smith and Lovitt (1975) distinguished between generalization to problems of difficulty comparable to those demonstrated (within-class generalization) and generalization to more complex problem types than those taught (across-class generalization). Within-class generalization occurred in all 14 experiments in which it was assessed. Across-class generalization occurred less frequently; in 7 out of 12 cases, students were able to solve more complex problems than those that were taught.

In pursuing the issue of across-class generalization, Blankenship (1978) studied the performance of nine elementary-school-age LD students, all of whom were making systematic errors. Eight pupils subtracted the minuend from the subtrahend ($37 - 9 = 32$), while one boy simply recorded a zero in columns requiring renaming ($37 - 9 = 30$). During baseline, the students made the same types of errors on nine different types of problems, ranging in complexity from $37 - 9 = []$ to $953 - 487 = []$.

The intervention consisted of the experimenter verbally explaining the correct procedure while working a sample problem of the type $37 - 9 = []$ on an index card. Following the demonstration, each pupil was required to solve a problem of comparable difficulty. Usually, only one demonstration was required before a student could solve the practice problem cor-

Figure 3-1 Percentage-Correct Data for Sets 1a and 1b Problems for Kenny

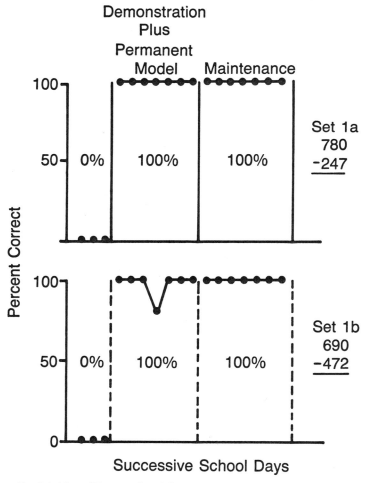

WITHIN CLASS GENERALIZATION

Source: Reprinted from "The use of modeling techniques to influence acquisition of computational arithmetic skills in learning-disabled children" by D.D. Smith & T.C. Lovitt in E. Ramp & G. Semb (Eds.), *Behavior analysis: Areas of research and application,* p. 299, with permission of Prentice-Hall, Inc., © 1975.

Figure 3-2 Percentage-Correct Data for Kenny's Set 1a Problems During Study 2

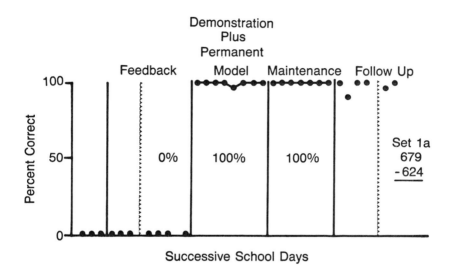

STUDY 2

Source: Reprinted from "The use of modeling techniques to influence acquisition of computational arithmetic skills in learning-disabled children" by D.D. Smith & T.C. Lovitt in E. Ramp & G. Semb (Eds.), *Behavior analysis: Areas of research and application,* p. 294, with permission of Prentice-Hall, Inc., © 1975.

rectly. In a few cases, the demonstration and practice cycle was repeated using additional problems until the student solved the sample problem correctly. Completed problems were removed after the demonstration. Each student was presented with a work sheet containing 45 problems, 5 problems of the demonstrated type and 5 each of 8 other types of subtraction renaming problems. Following completion of the day's assignment, the experimenter corrected the first row of problems (demonstrated problem type) and returned the papers to the students with correct and incorrect answers marked. The experimenter pointed out each correctly and incorrectly solved problem of the demonstrated type but made no comment concerning the pupils' responses to the more complex problems.

All nine pupils rapidly acquired the ability to compute correctly the demonstrated problem type; five generalized to most of the other problem types; and seven maintained a high level of accuracy up to one month after the termination of instruction. The data presented in Figure 3-3 indicate the rapid change in performance that occurred once students were provided with demonstration and feedback.

Taken together, the previously discussed studies illustrate that techniques such as demonstration and modeling are effective in improving the accuracy of students who are performing at very low levels. Using these techniques, students rapidly acquired new skills and most were able to maintain and apply their knowledge to solve more complex types of problems. Feedback and reinforcement alone were not effective in the initial acquisition stage when students did not know how to respond. In cases where demonstration and modeling resulted in improvement but not mas-

Figure 3-3 Percent Correct Scores on All Problem Types for Joe During Baseline (B), Intervention (I), and Maintenance (M)

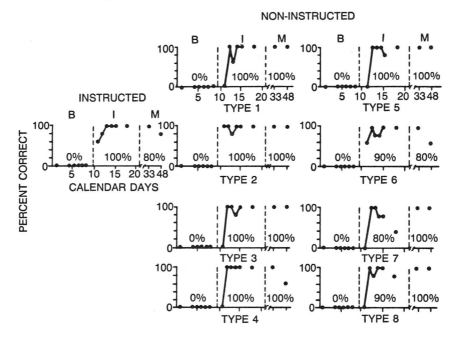

tery, reinforcement, feedback, or contingencies for errors provided the extra boost some students needed to attain criterion levels (Blankenship & Korn, 1980; Smith & Lovitt, 1975).

Consistency

In contrast to the studies discussed previously, in which pupils' accuracy was quite low and stable, the performance of some students tends to be erratic. To encourage students to perform at consistently high levels of accuracy, consequent events are used. The following studies illustrate the effects of using positive reinforcement and a response-cost contingency to increase accuracy in cases where students can respond correctly but fail to do so consistently.

Hasazi and Hasazi (1972) documented the effects of teacher attention on the digit-reversal behavior of an 8-year-old boy. The pupil often pointed out reversals on his papers that the teacher failed to catch and sometimes erased correctly ordered digits and wrote them in reverse order. Bob's reversals drew a good deal of attention from the teacher, who provided him with extra help to correct problems with mistakes.

The data in Figure 3-4 indicate Bob's performance throughout the experiment. During baseline, Bob's corrected papers were returned with correct and reverse-ordered digits noted. The teacher pointed to each reversal and commented that it was incorrect because the pupil had reversed the numbers in the answer. Using a variety of manipulative aids, the teacher carefully explained the correct computational procedure to the student. During the intervention, no extra assistance was provided and all answers were marked as correct whether or not they contained reversed digits. Attention was drawn to correctly written answers by providing positive comments to the student, smiling at him, or patting him on the back.

Bob's charted data clearly reveal the effects of teacher attention on digit reversals. Although some educators believe that reversals are symptoms of a neurological dysfunction, Hasazi and Hasazi—by not making such an assumption—were able to identify an environmental cause to explain the student's troublesome behavior. Lest the reader assume that the results of this study are atypical, other researchers have reduced letter and number reversals using similar procedures (Smith & Lovitt, 1973; Stromer, 1979).

Lovitt & Smith (1974) also worked with a student whose performance was described as very erratic. A multiple baseline design was used to assess the pupil's accuracy in computing three types of subtraction problems ranging in difficulty from $18 - 9 = []$ to $34 - 16 = []$. During baseline, no instruction or feedback was provided to the student. On the

Figure 3-4 Number of Digit Reversals per Day Under Baseline and Experimental Conditions

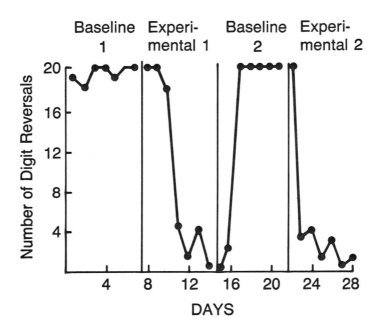

Source: Reprinted from "Effects of teacher attention on digit-reversal behavior in an elementary school child" by J.E. Hasazi & S.E. Hasazi in *Journal of Applied Behavior Analysis,* Vol. 5, p. 160, with permission of Allen Press, Inc., © 1972.

first day of the intervention, the student was told that one minute of recess time would be subtracted for each incorrect answer. The contingency was successively applied at 5-day intervals to each problem set and remained in effect on all three problem sets for an additional 12 days. Later, the contingency was sequentially withdrawn from two of the three sets. When the response-cost contingency was applied to the first set, accuracy on that set improved; however, performance on the other two sets was not affected. Similarly, when the intervention was directed toward the second set, accuracy increased on that set, but no improvement was noted on the last set until the contingency was finally applied to it. Although generalization did not occur, once the contingency had been applied to each problem set, the student maintained a high level of accuracy on all sets when the contingency was withdrawn.

The studies reviewed in this section, as well as similar research on the effects of consequent events on academic performance (Haring, Lovitt, Eaton, & Hansen, 1978), illustrate the effectiveness of using positive reinforcement to encourage students to attain consistently high levels of achievement. Mathematics teachers have a vast number of potentially reinforcing activities to motivate students, including praise, allowing them to play math games, and granting access to calculators and microcomputers. Although the aim should be to try positive procedures first, occasionally it is necessary to arrange contingencies for errors, such as writing wrong answers x number of times or requiring students to complete additional exercises.

Proficiency

A variety of techniques have been used to improve students' fluency in performing mathematical calculations. Perhaps the simplest technique involves requesting that students "go faster." Lovitt (1978) reported that directions to work faster resulted in increasing pupils' computational rates. A related tactic involves establishing a desired aim based on the performance levels of normally achieving students, encouraging low-performing pupils to strive to attain the aim, then informing them of their computational rates (Blankenship & Lovitt, 1974; cited in Blankenship & Lilly, 1981).

Various forms of positive reinforcement have also been shown to increase computational proficiency. Kirby and Shields (1972) documented the effects of using praise and feedback to improve the computational rates and attending behavior of a 13-year-old boy. The opportunity to earn free time contingent upon achieving high response rates has also been associated with increases in computational proficiency among students classified as behaviorally disordered and learning disabled (Lovitt & Esveldt, 1970; Smith & Lovitt, 1976). Daily practice, self-correction, praise, and public posting of pupils' highest correct rate scores have also yielded increasing computational rates (Van Houten, Morrison, Barrow, & Wenaus, 1974).

Generalization and Maintenance

Although many of the previously discussed studies monitored generalization and maintenance, relatively few investigations have focused on identifying techniques to promote long-term retention and transfer of previously learned skills in situations in which they did not spontaneously occur.

Blankenship and Baumgartner (1982) conducted an investigation designed to assess the extent to which nine elementary-school-age LD students could acquire, generalize, and maintain their accuracy in solving subtraction renaming problems. All the pupils were making systematic errors of some type—either subtracting the minuend from the subtrahend or recording a zero or random digit in columns where renaming was required. The study assessed acquisition of the demonstrated class of problems ($37 - 9 = []$), generalization to problems of comparable difficulty, and generalization to 12 different types of subtraction renaming problems. Following a baseline period during which no instruction or feedback was provided, all pupils received demonstration-and-modeling plus feedback, using the procedure described in the review of an earlier study (Blankenship, 1978). In contrast to the previous study, the students received feedback on all problem classes rather than just on the demonstrated problem type. The results indicated the following:

- Demonstration-and-modeling plus feedback was sufficient to enable three pupils to acquire, generalize, and maintain a high level of accuracy in computing subtraction renaming problems.
- Increased generalization was noted for three students when they were given the opportunity to earn points and exchange them for school supplies; three other pupils required additional instruction on several problem types before they were able to generalize.
- Maintenance was enhanced by reinforcing accurate responding on an intermittent basis.

Lack of prerequisite skills and failure to apply previously learned strategies can also produce difficulties in generalizing computational skills. Lloyd, Saltzman, and Kauffman (1981) demonstrated the importance of preskills and strategy training on the ability of LD students to generalize a multiplication skill. Preskills training for multiplication facts consisted of teaching students to perform rote counting sequences for six fact tables and to write missing numbers for multiplication chains (e.g., 0, 2, __ , 6, __ , __ , 12, __ , __ , __ , 20). Strategy training involved requiring students to: "(a) point to a number you can count by; (b) make hash marks for the other number; (c) count by the number you pointed to once for each hash mark; and (d) write in the answer space the last number you said" (Lloyd et al., 1981, p. 207).

The results indicated that both preskill and strategy training contributed to students' ability to generalize. The pupils did not use the strategy adequately on problems for which instruction on preskills had not been provided, but were able to apply it successfully to solve problems once they had mastered the necessary prerequisite skills.

The previously reported studies focused on generalization from one class of problems to another. A second type of generalization involves applying learned skills in different settings. The ability to generalize from one setting to another was investigated by Baumgartner (1979). One facet of her dissertation involved assessing pupils' abilities to apply a skill acquired in a resource room setting to the regular classroom (cited in Blankenship & Lilly, 1981). Following direct instruction on renaming in subtraction in the resource room, 14 of 19 elementary-school-age LD students successfully transferred their newly acquired computational skill to their regular classrooms.

Five students did not automatically generalize from the resource room to the regular classroom. Data for one pupil who had difficulty generalizing are shown in Figure 3-5. Four of the pupils were able to generalize once their regular classroom teacher provided the following reminder, "What was the borrow rule you learned in the resource room; do that here" (Baumgartner, 1979, p. 49). The remaining student was able to generalize when the reminder was coupled with a reinforcement contingency. The students maintained a fairly high degree of accuracy after the reminder was no longer provided.

Word Problem Research

Many students experience difficulties in solving word problems (Carpenter, T.P., Corbitt, M.K., Kepner, H.S., Lindquist, M.M., & Reys, R.E., 1980). Factors that have been associated with poor performance include failure to read and comprehend the information presented, compute the required calculations, and identify an appropriate solution strategy. Although accuracy can be affected by varying the level of complexity of the vocabulary used or by including extraneous information (Blankenship & Lovitt, 1976), pupils' poor performance on word problems can rarely be attributed to reading difficulties. Often, students who fail to solve problems can accurately read as well as restate problems in their own words (Knifong & Holtan, 1976). Many mathematics educators believe that "deciding which operation to perform (addition, subtraction and so on) is the major stumbling block to successful problem solving" (Zweng, 1979, p. 2).

A recent ABA study focused on investigating the use of a pictorial aid to assist students in selecting appropriate operations for solving word problems (Blankenship & Black, 1985). Pupils were presented with word problems that contained words they could correctly read and combinations they could calculate with a fairly high degree of accuracy. To ensure further that reading and computational difficulties would not impair their perform-

Figure 3-5 Student's Percent Correct Scores on Math Problems Computed in a Resource and Regular Classroom

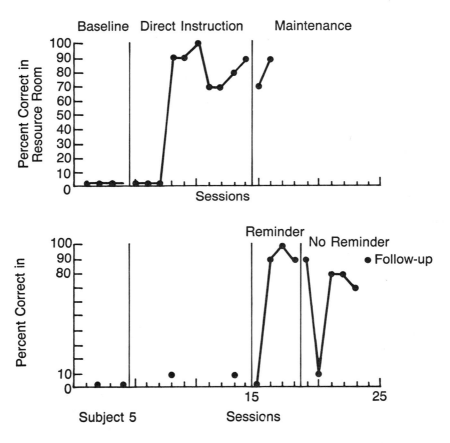

Source: Reprinted from "Generalization of improved subtraction regrouping skills from resource rooms to the regular class" by M. Baumgartner. Unpublished doctoral dissertation, University of Illinois.

ance, students were allowed to ask for assistance in reading troublesome words, and a subtraction fact sheet was provided to help them find answers to unknown combinations.

Nine elementary-school-age students, identified by their teachers as low achievers, participated in the study. Based on initial assessment data, work sheets were developed that contained comparison subtraction problems that individual students were unable to compute. Table 3-1 shows a representative set of problems used in the project.

A multiple-baseline, across-subjects design was used. During baseline, the pupils were presented with Set 1 (no pictorial aid). Once the intervention was underway, performance on problems comparable with the pictorial aid (Set 2) was also assessed. Throughout the experiment, performance on problems not scheduled for instruction (Set 3) was occasionally probed to assess for across-class generalization.

During baseline, students were directed to write number sentences to solve the problems and to put their answers in the spaces provided on the

Table 3-1 Description of Problem Sets

Problem Set	Number of Problems per Set	Sample Problems
Set 1 No Pictorial Aid	4	Pat has 11 "E.T." posters. Jack has 9 "E.T." posters. How many more posters does Pat have than Jack?
	4	Sue has 7 cookies. Jerry had 4 cookies. How many fewer cookies does Jerry have than Sue?
	2	*Nancy had 3 cats. Lisa gave her 7 more cats. How many cats does Nancy have?
Set 2 Pictorial Aid	Same number and types of problems as Set 1, but accompanied with a pictorial aid.	
Set 3 No Pictorial Aid	1	Linda has 487 stickers. Tim has 135 stickers. How many more stickers does Linda have than Tim?
	1	Eric has 347 rocks. Paul has 23 rocks. How many fewer rocks does Paul have than Eric?
	2	Mary has 5 crayons. Cindy has 3 more crayons than Mary. How many crayons does Cindy have?
	2	Pat has 8 comic books. He has 3 fewer comic books than Connie. How many comic books does Connie have?
	2	John has 8 stamps. He has 3 more stamps than Lisa. How many stamps does Lisa have?
	2	Jerry has 9 marbles. Sue has 2 fewer marbles than Jerry. How many marbles does Sue have?

*Addition problems served as foils to detect students who might rotely subtract all problems presented, hence obtaining the right answers but for the wrong reason.

work sheet. Pupils were told that they could put a question mark next to any problem they were unable to solve. No assistance was given other than reading troublesome words, and no feedback was provided.

The intervention consisted of the experimenter demonstrating a procedure for constructing pictorial representations for each problem type contained in Set 2. Using a grid similar to the one shown in Figure 3-6, the experimenter:

- read each sentence of the problem aloud and asked the student to color in the appropriate amount;
- drew a line across the columns to indicate the point at which both parties in the problem had an equal amount;
- stated the correct subtraction number sentence to solve the problem; and
- directed the student to write the appropriate number sentence in the boxes provided, compute the answer, and check it by counting up from the lesser to the greater quantity shown on the columns.

Throughout the intervention, students were presented with Set 2 problems and directed to color in the columns to represent the information contained in the problems before solving them. Following completion of the day's assignment, students were informed of their scores and given extra help to correct inaccurate pictorial representations or incorrect number sentences. No instruction or feedback was provided on Set 1 or Set 3 on days on which performance on these problems was probed.

The charted data presented in Figure 3-7 show the performance of two students throughout the experiment. During baseline, the students' average accuracy on the problem types targeted for instruction was 1.9 problems correct out of 10. An analysis of the students' errors revealed that they were making a large number of wrong operation errors—that is, adding instead of subtracting. The accuracy of all pupils was positively affected by the intervention condition. Average accuracy increased to 7.7 problems correct during the instructional phase, and operational errors were significantly reduced. Probes collected during the intervention period indicated that students could solve the demonstrated set of word problems without pictorial aids (average 7.3 problems) almost as well as with pictorial aids (average 7.7 problems). Slight generalization was noted to the noninstructed problem types (Set 3), indicating that further direct instruction would be needed to master other types of comparison problems.

Two aspects of the study deserve comment. First, the technique used in this research attempted to systematize procedures for teaching students

Figure 3-6 Description of Teaching Procedure

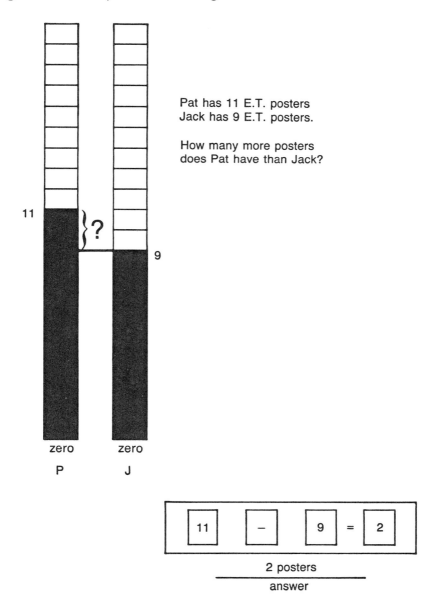

Pat has 11 E.T. posters
Jack has 9 E.T. posters.

How many more posters
does Pat have than Jack?

Source: Adapted from *Using student-constructed pictorial aids to increase accuracy in solving word problems* by C.S. Blankenship and M. Black from manuscript submitted for publication, with permission of the authors, 1985.

Figure 3-7 Number of Word Problems Computed Correctly by
Subjects 1 and 2

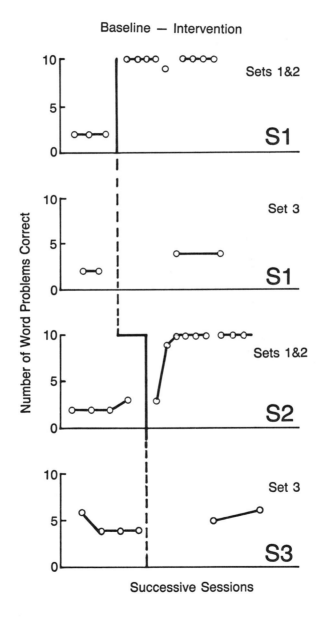

Source: Adapted from *Using student-constructed pictorial aids to increase accuracy in solving word problems* by C.S. Blankenship and M. Black from manuscript submitted for publication, with permission of the authors, 1985.

to relate pictorial representations to number sentences. Cognitively oriented mathematics educators have long advocated that through pairing pictorial aids to the production of number sentences, children come to understand the meaning of mathematical operations. Second, the technique lends itself to both small and large group instruction. Using an overhead projector, teachers can easily demonstrate the correct representations for problems using columns and then relate them to writing number sentences. Similarly, students can be provided with work sheets containing columns to color in to represent the situations presented in word problems. Following up on this theme, research in progress is investigating the use of computer-generated pictorial aids to improve performance in solving word problems.

ASSESSING THE BEHAVIORAL CONTRIBUTION TO MATHEMATICS INSTRUCTION

Implications for Instruction

Although the research reviewed in this chapter illustrates the effectiveness of using particular techniques to remediate various types of mathematical learning difficulties, the behavioral approach offers teachers far more than a collection of teaching strategies. First and foremost, the behavioral approach assists teachers in assessing pupil performance, pinpointing learning problems, and evaluating instructional effectiveness based on pupil progress. Suggestions for applying the approach to assess mathematical performance, individualize instruction, and make instructional decisions have appeared in companion volumes to this text (Blankenship, 1985a; 1985b) as well as in other sources (Haring, Lovitt, Eaton, & Hansen, 1978; Idol-Maestas, 1983).

Equally important, the behavioral approach provides teachers with a framework for viewing learning problems as arising from environmental causes rather than as the result of hypothesized internal deficits. Teachers who adopt a behavioral approach plunge ahead to remediate learning problems rather than waiting for students to reach a hypothesized level of appropriate cognitive functioning or lamenting deficits due to presumed central nervous system dysfunctions. By precisely defining behavior problems in observable terms and arranging appropriate antecedent and consequent events, while continuously measuring pupil performance, teachers can successfully remediate a variety of learning problems.

In applying the behavioral approach, teachers are not limited to using a circumscribed set of techniques. While the research reviewed in this chapter documents the importance of using both antecedent and consequent events to remediate mathematical learning problems, the specific techniques mentioned (e.g., demonstration, modeling, reinforcement, feedback) merely illustrate the kinds of procedures that have been found effective in improving performance. Teachers are certainly free to use techniques that they or others have developed. Suggestions for teaching abound in publications such as *The Arithmetic Teacher* and *The Mathematics Teacher*. Using the behavioral approach, teachers can easily establish the effectiveness of their favorite techniques and evaluate those suggested by others.

While many of the studies reviewed in this chapter delivered instruction on a one-to-one basis, they frequently required only a few minutes of teacher time. Some techniques have been adapted for teaching small groups of students (Smith & Fleming, 1976). In addition, DISTAR instruction (Engelmann & Carnine, 1975), which embodies many behavioral procedures (e.g., demonstration, modeling, reinforcement, feedback), is appropriate for both small and large group instruction.

Finally, the behavioral approach provides teachers with a means of documenting their effectiveness. By charting pupil performance data, teachers can easily gauge pupil progress and share the information with students, parents, and other school personnel. Very often, pupils become motivated to improve their performance once they see that they are indeed making progress.

Research Directions

Cognitively oriented mathematics educators acknowledge the contribution of behaviorism to mathematics instruction, often citing its simplicity, effectiveness in producing short-term learning gains, and the extent to which it provides data on accountability (Reys, Suydam, & Lindquist, 1984). It is argued, however, that higher level cognitive processes, such as problem solving, are deemphasized while undue stress is placed on mastery of lower level computational skills. While this appraisal is justified based on previous research emphasizing computational arithmetic, it signals a need for applied behavior analysts to refocus their efforts by investigating other mathematical topics.

With the exception of an isolated study on the acquisition of fraction concepts (Carnine, 1976), behaviorists have not addressed themselves to the teaching of mathematical concepts. Traditionally, mathematics educators have stressed the importance of understanding concepts such as place value; however, specific procedures for assessing students' knowledge of concepts and proven techniques for teaching them lag far behind efforts in teaching computational arithmetic. Behavioral models for teaching concepts (Becker & Engelmann, 1978; Markle, 1983) provide a basis for conducting research on the attainment of mathematical concepts by students with learning problems and for the eventual development of curriculum materials. Work in this area could serve to (a) operationally define behaviors that may be said to indicate conceptual understanding, (b) identify some effective techniques for teaching concepts, and (c) determine the extent to which concept attainment enhances generalization and maintenance of mathematical skills.

Behavioral research in mathematics education has tended to focus on the use of consequent rather than antecedent events. The research reviewed in this chapter highlights the importance of distinguishing between different types of learning problems in order to select appropriate teaching techniques. While continuing to focus on identifying the relative effects of antecedent and consequent events on the acquisition, generalization, and maintenance of behavior, applied behavior analysts might well broaden the types of antecedent events studied to include the use of manipulative aids and pictorial representations.

Another important area for behavior analysts deals with investigating techniques to facilitate generalization and maintenance. Many of the studies reviewed in this chapter assessed generalization and maintenance. Often, students were able to apply learned skills to solve related problems and to use their newly acquired skills in different settings. In addition, studies that assessed maintenance often found that following the termination of instruction, students maintained high levels of accuracy over a period of at least several weeks. Too few studies, however, have focused on investigating techniques to enhance generalization and maintenance in situations in which they did not spontaneously occur.

Finally, behavioral researchers might make greater use of the oral interview method that predominates much of the research in mathematics education. Research efforts on normally achieving children's solution strategies (Carpenter, Moser, & Romberg, 1982), which are based on verbal report data and direct observation of behavior, should be extended to investigate the strategies used by students with learning problems. Given that some LD students use time-consuming counting strategies to obtain answers to basic facts (Myers & Thornton, 1977), research is needed to identify techniques to teach them to use more efficient strategies.

REFERENCES

Baumgartner, M. (1979). *Generalization of improved subtraction regrouping skills from resource rooms to the regular class.* Unpublished doctoral dissertation, University of Illinois, Champaign.

Becker, W.C., & Engelmann, S. (1978). Systems for basic instruction: Theory and applications. In A.C. Catania & T.A. Brigham (Eds.), *Handbook of applied behavior analysis: Social and instructional processes* (pp. 325–377). New York: Irvington.

Blankenship, C.S. (1985a). Individualizing mathematics instruction for students with learning problems. In J. Cawley (Ed), *Secondary school mathematics for the learning disabled* (pp. 61–82). Rockville, MD: Aspen Systems.

Blankenship, C. S. (1985b) Linking assessment to curriculum and instruction. In J. Cawley (Ed.), *Practical mathematics appraisal for the learning disabled* (pp. 59–79). Rockville, MD: Aspen Systems.

Blankenship, C.S. (1978). Remediating systematic inversion errors in subtraction through the use of demonstration and feedback. *Learning Disability Quarterly, 1,* 12–22.

Blankenship, C.S., & Baumgartner, M.D. (1982). Programming generalization of computational skills. *Learning Disability Quarterly, 5,* 152–162.

Blankenship, C.S., & Black, M. (1985). *Using student-constructed pictorial aids to increase accuracy in solving word problems.* Manuscript submitted for publication.

Blankenship, C.S., & Korn, J. (1980). *The differential effects of antecedent and consequent events on two types of arithmetic errors.* Unpublished manuscript, University of Illinois, Champaign.

Blankenship, C.S., & Lilly, M.S. (1981). *Mainstreaming students with learning and behavior problems: Techniques for the classroom teacher.* New York: Holt, Rinehart, & Winston.

Blankenship, C.S., & Lovitt, T.C. (1974). *Computational arithmetic data collected in Curriculum Research Classroom.* Seattle: University of Washington, Experimental Education Unit.

Blankenship, C., & Lovitt, T.C. (1976). Story problems: Merely confusing or downright befuddling? *Journal for Research in Mathematics Education, 7,* 290–298.

Brophy, J.E. (1983). If only it were true: A response to Greer. *Educational Researcher, 20,* 10–13.

Carnine, D.W. (1976). *Comparing a DISTAR strategy and a practice only treatment in teaching three fraction skills* (University of Oregon Follow Through Model). Eugene: University of Oregon.

Carpenter, T.P., Corbitt, M.K., Kepner, H.S., Lindquist, M.M., & Reys, R.E. (1980). Implications of the second NAEP mathematics assessment: Elementary school. *The Arithmetic Teacher, 27,* 44–47.

Carpenter, T.P., Moser, J.M., & Romberg, T.A. (Eds.). (1982). *Addition and subtraction: A cognitive perspective.* Hillsdale, NJ: Lawrence Erlbaum.

Engelmann, S., & Carnine, D. (1975). *DISTAR Arithmetic I* (2nd ed.). Chicago: Science Research Associates.

Gaddes, W.H. (1983). Applied educational neuropsychology: Theories and problems. *Journal of Learning Disabilities, 16,* 511–514.

Greer, R.D. (1983). Contingencies of the science and technology of teaching and prebehavioristic research practices in education. *Educational Researcher, 20,* 3–9.

Hallahan, D.P., Hall, R.J., Ianna, S.O., Kneedler, D., Lloyd, J.W., Loper, A., & Reeve, R.E. (1983). Summary of research findings at the University of Virginia Learning Disabilities Research Institute. *Exceptional Education Quarterly, 4,* 95–115.

Haring, N.G., Lovitt, T.C., Eaton, M.D., & Hansen, C.L. (1978). *The fourth R: Research in the classroom.* Columbus, OH: Charles Merrill.

Hasazi, J.E., & Hasazi, S.E. (1972). Effects of teacher attention on digit-reversal behavior in an elementary school child. *Journal of Applied Behavior Analysis, 5,* 157–162.

Hersen, M., & Barlow, D.H. (1976). *Single case experimental designs: Strategies for studying behavior change.* New York: Pergamon Press.

Idol-Maestas, L. (1983). *Special educator's consultation handbook.* Rockville, MD: Aspen Systems.

Kazdin, A.E. (1982). *Single-case research designs: Methods for clinical and applied settings.* New York: Oxford University Press.

Kirby, F.D., & Shields, F. (1972). Modification of arithmetic response rate and attending behavior in a seventh-grade student. *Journal of Applied Behavior Analysis, 5,* 79–84.

Knifong, J.D., & Holtan, B. (1976). *A search for reading difficulties among erred word problems* (Report No. SE 021 965). West Virginia University: Morgantown, WV. (ERIC Document Reproduction Service No. ED 134 464).

Krantz, D.L. (1971). The separate worlds of operant and non-operant psychology. *Journal of Applied Behavior Analysis, 4,* 61–70.

Lloyd, J., Saltzman, N.J., & Kauffman, J.M. (1981). Predictable generalization in academic learning as a result of preskills and strategy training. *Learning Disability Quarterly, 4,* 203–216.

Lovitt, T.C. (1978). *Managing inappropriate behaviors in the classroom.* Reston, VA: The Council for Exceptional Children.

Lovitt, T.C. (1981). Graphing academic performances of mildly handicapped students. In S.W. Bijou & Ruiz (Eds.), *Behavior modification: Contributions to education* (pp. 111–143). Hillsdale, NJ: Lawrence Erlbaum.

Lovitt, T.C., & Curtiss, K.A. (1968). Effect of manipulating an antecedent event on mathematics response rate. *Journal of Applied Behavior Analysis, 1,* 329–333.

Lovitt, T.C., & Esveldt, K.A. (1970). The relative effects on math performance of single- versus multiple-ratio schedules: A case study. *Journal of Applied Behavior Analysis, 3,* 261–270.

Lovitt, T.C., & Smith, D.D. (1974). Using withdrawal of positive reinforcement to alter subtraction performance. *Exceptional Children, 40,* 357–358.

Markle, S.M. (1983). *Designs for instructional designers* (2nd ed.). Champaign, IL: Stipes.

Meichenbaum, D. (1977). *Cognitive-behavior modification.* New York: Plenum.

Myers, A.C., & Thornton, C.A. (1977). The learning disabled child—Learning the basic facts. *The Arithmetic Teacher, 25,* 46–50.

Reys, R.E., Suydam, M.N., & Lindquist, M.M. (1984). *Helping children learn mathematics.* Englewood Cliffs, NJ: Prentice-Hall.

Smith, D.D., & Fleming, E.C. (1976). *A comparison of individual and group modeling techniques aimed at altering children's computational abilities.* Unpublished manuscript, George Peabody College for Teachers, Nashville.

Smith, D.D., & Lovitt, T.C. (1973). The educational diagnosis and remediation of b and d written reversal problems: A case study. *Journal of Learning Disabilities, 6,* 356–363.

Smith, D.D., & Lovitt, T.C. (1974). Using withdrawal of positive reinforcement to alter subtraction performance. *Exceptional Children, 40,* 357–358.

Smith, D.D., & Lovitt, T.C. (1975). The use of modeling techniques to influence acquisition of computational arithmetic skills in learning-disabled children. In E. Ramp & G. Semb

(Eds.), *Behavior analysis: Areas of research and application* (pp. 283–308). Englewood Cliffs, NJ: Prentice-Hall.

Smith, D.D., & Lovitt, T.C. (1976). The differential effects of reinforcement contingencies on arithmetic performance. *Journal of Learning Disabilities, 9,* 32–40.

Stromer, R. (1979). Remediating academic deficiencies in learning disabled children. In B.B. Lahey (Ed.), *Behavior therapy with hyperactive and learning disabled children* (pp. 188–196). New York: Oxford University Press.

Van Houten, R., Morrison, E., Barrow, B., & Wenaus, J. (1974). The effects of daily practice and feedback on the acquisition of elementary math skills. *School Applications of Learning Theory, 7,* 1–16.

Zweng, M. (1979). The problem of solving story problems. *The Arithmetic Teacher, 27,* 2–3.

Chapter 4

A Three-Dimensional Developmental Model for Math Instruction of the Learning Disabled

Miriam Cherkes-Julkowski

A developmental model of how a child thinks and learns provides valuable information for planning classroom instruction. It specifies the steps through which a child progresses while maturing or following a concept from its most basic to its most abstract level. It specifies, further, the order in which these steps occur, so that later concepts are delineated as outgrowths of earlier, more fundamental ones. Such a model is clearly useful for designing curriculum and presenting it at the cognitive level that is appropriate for the learning disabled (LD) child or any child. This kind of developmental model has been used in studying the nature of learning disabilities (Bender, 1938; de Hirsch, Jansky, & Langford, 1966), in planning special curricula for LD children (Yselldyke, 1973), and as a basis for diagnosis to identify the instruction that appeals most effectively to those forms of cognition that Piaget calls structures. Since the learning disabled are defined as having a disorder in the learning process, a useful model of development for them should include not only an account of the sequence of cognitive steps but also a careful analysis of the processes that enable a child to move from one set of cognitive forms or schemes to the next (Resnick & Glaser, 1976). It is in the concentration on transitions between cognitive levels that carefully planned instruction is likely to have its greatest effect. Such a model is provided by a group that Case (1978) calls the neo-Piagetians and that is discussed here in its special applicability for LD youngsters. A further critical consideration for an adequate developmental approach to instruction for the learning/cognitively disordered (in addition to the Piagetian and neo-Piagetian ones) is the distinction between the development of natural, involuntary systems for learning, on one side, and arbitrary or voluntary systems on the other. Each of these factors is discussed individually as theory (only briefly), and then they are used together to formulate some principles and some examples for the mathematics instruction of the learning disabled.

Since so much has been written about the Piagetian cum Genevan view of development (Cherkes, 1979; Flavell, 1963; Furth, 1970), no detailed reiteration is necessary here. Instead, those aspects of the model are emphasized that are most important to building a mathematics curriculum. The essence of the developmental position is that children at different developmental levels are able to think and learn in *qualitatively* different ways. Younger children and those who are developmentally less advanced have structures or ways of viewing their world that are limited and less complex compared with those of the mature person who has achieved the final steps in the developmental continuum. It is the specific forms of cognition that a person can command that determine what that person can or cannot learn. If a situation occurs for which the individual does not have the required cognitive set, the information contained in that situation is not only not learned; it is not even recognized. The child must therefore be presented with a curriculum that is within his or her cognitive grasp. As children develop along the developmental continuum, their ways and forms of learning change to enable them to learn further and more complex things.

In actual practice, then, it becomes important for the classroom or resource room teacher first to diagnose the level at which a child is functioning in mathematics and then to gear instruction appropriately to that level. It would certainly be convenient for the teacher if mathematics were one homogeneous, undifferentiated process. If this were so, then the teacher or diagnostician would need only to establish the mathematics developmental level or the mental mathematics age of a youngster. He or she would administer a math test, such as the Wide Range Achievement Test; compute a grade equivalent score; and presumably know the functioning level appropriate for the student. Unfortunately, such a utopian case does not exist. First of all, mathematics is not one thing. It is number and number operations, but is also geometry and measurement and logic and language and more. What typifies a child at, for example, a developmental or mental age of 10 in each of these areas is different.

The 10-year-old child has a math curriculum that requires him or her, most likely, to perform division and computations with fractions and to understand the concepts of area in geometry and equivalent amounts in measurement (5 feet = 1 yard and 2 feet, for example). A child's proficiency in each of these areas is not measurable and cannot be reflected by a single age equivalent. Furthermore, the LD child is characterized by the very fact that he or she is likely to show proficiency in one area and deficiency in another, seemingly related one. For this kind of child, a single developmental level is especially uninformative.

Add to this Piaget's notion of horizontal decalage. In our example, this means that even an average child cannot be expected to be at the same developmental level in all things. Although he may have mastered the principle of equivalence in computations (4 + 3 = 5 + ____) and in fractions (¼ = ⅜), he may not have applied this rule to geometry and to the awareness that two equilateral triangles of the same size are equivalent

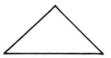 is equivalent to

or, more abstractly, that two widely different shapes might conceivably have the same area.

What we are faced with, then, is a child who does not grow in nice, neat, consolidated steps and a curriculum that is not perfectly integrated in terms of what principles are being applied in all aspects of mathematics at the same time. Nevertheless, to instruct an LD child effectively, we will have to know what cognitive structures the child has available in the context of all aspects of mathematics. Suppose that we are able to discern that our 10-year-old LD child can compute equivalent measurements and that she actually understands this process. She has not yet learned anything about equivalent fractions or equivalent shapes. The Piagetian school establishes that the only effective level at which to design instruction is that which works only with the cognitive structures the child has already developed. What, then, is appropriate instruction for this LD child? Clearly, we are obligated to begin with her set or structure for equivalence. Piaget's belief is that the goal of instruction should be to apply this principle to as many circumstances, examples, or situations as possible. This is a worthy end in itself, since it provides for horizontal transfer or application of a rule, at the same level, to more and more instances. It is also a critical factor, however, in helping a child to grow from her present developmental level to the next step in the hierarchy. Since the child cannot learn anything beyond her present level, she cannot benefit from any instruction that teaches the next step. The only way to help a child ascend the hierarchy is to provide more and more experience at her present level.

Instruction for this child, then, might begin with a lesson that accentuates the basic principles of equivalence. The most effective instruction to this end will avoid the use of any novel or obscure information. Instead, it will utilize any context that the teacher is reasonably sure is very familiar to the child. Any other approach would compound the difficulties of dealing with new information while concentrating on the underlying rule system.

An appropriate lesson might include having the child actually measure the same substance using various units of measurement. Thus, a container of water can be measured in cups, pints, quarts, and liters. Likewise, linear distance and weight can be compared using various units. Each measurement can be recorded on a record sheet like the one suggested in Exhibit 4-1.

As a follow-up, whereas the original measurements were made separately for each unit of measurement, this time the conversions can be worked arithmetically. At the end of this introductory session, the child should be asked to verbalize the concept of equivalence as it applies in all these situations. Sample questions or probes to elicit such a response might include:

- You have written here that ___ cups, ___ pints, ___ quarts, and ___ liters all describe the amount of water in this container. How an all these different measurements describe the same thing? How do you know?
- How are these measurements the same? How are they different?
- Can you explain what equivalent measurements are?
- What is meant by equivalence? Can you give one example from addition? One from outside math?

Once the preceding introduction is completed, instruction on equivalent fractions and equivalent geometric shapes can begin. This sequence should

---

Exhibit 4-1 Sample Work Sheet for Equivalent Measurement

NAME _____

1)
          ___ Cups
          ___ Pints
          ___ Quarts
          ___ Liters

2) Distance from cafeteria to Principal's office
          ___ Feet
          ___ Yards
          ___ Meters

3) Weight of reading book
          ___ Pounds
          ___ Kilograms
          ___ Ounces

draw upon the now explicit concept of equivalence, with the immediate goal of applying it to fractions (which is a nearer transfer or more similar application than the geometry one). To encourage the analogy with measurement and to use the child's existing cognitive set or frame of reference, the form of instruction should parallel that used in the previous example. The student can be asked to "measure" a fractional piece using various "standards of measurement" or fractional units. For example, a pie-shaped piece equivalent to one-fourth of a circle might be given to the student. This piece can be "measured" using pieces cut from another circle of the same size but cut in units of eighths, sixteenths, and possibly even halves. Readings can be recorded in a fashion similar to the one described in Exhibit 4-1. Exhibit 4-2 provides the example.

Transfer of the equivalence principle to geometry should be fairly automatic based on the "measurement" principle combined with the shape-based fractions experience. If instruction up until this point was effective (if not, the student should not be allowed to progress to this point), no concrete, manipulative experiences should be necessary. Perhaps the best way to begin is to start at the most abstract, verbal level to test the depth of the child's understanding of equivalence. Instruction might begin with the following questions and probes:

Exhibit 4-2 Sample Work Sheet for Equivalent Fractions

NAME		
1)	_____ Eighths	(1/8)
	_____ Sixteenths	(1/16)
	_____ Fourths	(1/4)
	_____ Halves	(1/2)
2)	_____ Eighths	(1/8)
	_____ Sixteenths	(1/16)
	_____ Fourths	(1/4)
	_____ Halves	(1/2)
3)	_____ Eighths	(1/8)
	_____ Sixteenths	(1/16)
	_____ Fourths	(1/4)
	_____ Halves	(1/2)

Materials: Three 1/4 pieces, three 1/8 pieces, six 1/16 pieces, one 1/2 piece

- Can you describe what "equivalence" meant when we used measurements (showing the child the work sheet depicted in Exhibit 4-1 might be helpful)?
- Can you describe what "equivalence" meant when we talked about fractions (refer to the work sheet as shown in Exhibit 4-2)?
- Can you tell me what equivalence might mean in *any* situation? What about equivalent chairs? What would be true of equivalent chairs?
- What other kinds of things might be equivalent?
- Now think of equivalent shapes. Can you draw two equivalent shapes? Draw two equivalent triangles. Three equivalent circles.

If the child does not demonstrate a certain ease with this transfer, the teacher is presented with a series of possibilities. He or she must question whether the student has truly mastered the previous lessons, truly understood the concept of equivalence, or whether the pupil has difficulty with the generalization process itself. The answer to these questions determines the next step in instruction. It is more likely, however, that such a student as the one in this example will have learned each of these things with relative ease. If this were in fact so, what would the next step be? This depends partly on the exact nature of the curriculum and partly on the speed with which the child makes the vertical transfer that comes next.

The preceding has been an extended example of what a developmental curriculum implies for the form and sequence of instruction. This notion of sequential continuum (the Genevan's hierarchy) is not to be passed over lightly. Some horizontal transfer must precede vertical transfer. Vertical transfer, however, is the essential component of development. By vertical transfer or vertical continuum, a true developmental mode does not mean Step 1, followed by Step 2, which is easier than Step 3, which is usually followed by Step 4. The idea of continuum is a lot less casual. That is, Step 2 arises *out of* Step 1, Step 2 cannot exist without Step 1, and so on and on. Herein lies the basis for the use of vertical prerequisites in designing a curriculum. A fully mature understanding of cardinality, for example, grows out of an earlier facility with object constancy and one-to-one correspondence (among other things). The child who has not accomplished both of the former will pass through none of the later steps along the developmental continuum.

A great deal of the LD literature has characterized the LD child as one who develops through the same continuum as other children typically do, but with a delay in at least one area (Hallahan, Kaufman & Ball, 1974). With the exception of the problem area, the LD child can develop normally or perhaps in an above-normal way; that is, after all, the definition of LD.

There is some evidence, for example, that 9-year-old LD children who can already read at least at age and grade level have only just begun to move from preoperational mathematics to the concrete operational stage that is associated with a mental age of 6. It is the delayed or impaired area that requires special and careful instruction. The basic procedure for providing such instruction is identical to the one discussed thus far: identify, for each child, the exact aspect of mathematics in which the problem lies. Begin at this point, and build the appropriate hierarchy of steps that comprise a full development in that area. For many children labeled LD, this is enough. The simple recognition that some part of the hierarchy was never thoroughly mastered and the careful plan to remediate the problem area are a quick and effective intervention (Blankenship, 1978). (Here "hierarchy" is used, quite loosely, to mean the sequence adopted by curriculum—add, substract, multiply, divide—which may or may not be a *true* hierarchy in natural development.) For the more difficult LD cases, the hierarchy must be even more cleverly constructed. This kind of LD child is characterized by some disorder in learning that has interfered with his normal ascent through the steps of development. The actual nature of the disorder may vary from child to child. Reported disorders include problems in memory, attention, and impulsivity. What is important to the present developmental discussion is the implication that a hierarchy of steps for the LD child must capture the essence, the critical aspects, of what needs to be learned. Such critical aspects have the quality not only of being stripped of extraneous, possibly distracting, or—worse—misleading cues but also of not being overly narrow and thus losing the essence of what is to be learned. The previous series of equivalence lessons illustrates this point. A more narrow approach to instruction might have presented equivalent measurement as a single, unique arithmetic procedure. In fact, this approach would be likely to bring about a greater number of correct answers in a lesser amount of time. It would not, however, have placed these procedures in the context of the principle of equivalence. Consequently, the more narrow approach to instruction inhibits, if not prohibits, first horizontal and eventually vertical transfer. Eventually, the apparent speed that has been gained turns out to be, not an acceleration, but a deceleration. Without the advantage of transfer, each related procedure requires the same amount of instructional time rather than an ever-decreasing amount. Consider another example. Although it might be efficient and nondistracting to teach division as an isolated process, it belies the concept and inhibits generalization of the principle not to include its relationship to multiplication as well as to fractions and proportions. At this point the reader might like to try to create a series of lessons on this theme.

CONCEPT OF NUMBER OR CARDINAL PROPERTY

With these principles in mind, consider more closely another example with a wider range of implications—the concept of number and number notations as it evolves from infancy through adolescence. Figure 4-1 presents the proposed development sequence. Since cardinal property is a central component in the continuum, the procedure will be to begin at that point and trace the routes first back through earlier stages and then to more advanced levels.

The concept of number or cardinal property evolves in normal development around the age of 6. The critical components of the concept of cardinality have been defined by Piaget and Inhelder (1969) as classification—specifically, class inclusion—and seriation. What is critical in any classification process is recognition of the specific qualities that characterize members in the group. For example, young children eventually learn which animals are included under the rubric "doggie" and, a little later, which are excluded from the group (Brown, 1958). In the classes of numbers, what defines membership is quantity and none of the other possibly confounding features of size, configuration, or amount of space occupied. A group of LD youngsters probably could enumerate more distractors. Thus, the direct precursor of cardinal property is conservation: the ability to focus on and to discern quantity even in the presence of distractors.

Since learning disorders can be characterized as problems in attending to the critical features in a situation, the need to ignore irrelevant information and to focus only on the aspect of number can prove a problem for LD youngsters. What can make it more difficult for the teacher is the pattern so often described: sometimes the child seems to know her numbers; the next day she seems to have forgotten the whole thing. She has probably never learned or forgotten. At one time, she does focus on the clues that help her discern number. At the next, she has switched her focus to something else. She is no longer answering the number question. Her answer may reflect comparisons based on size or shape or color or some other commonality.

To help a child with such a problem, it can be helpful to provide redundant cues. That is, rather than presenting materials that represent the number 5 with five differently colored blocks or five different objects, use five identical objects. Sets to be compared in a conservation task should make the same use of object similarity. Only after the conservation notion is mastered in this way should sets of different objects be compared.

Figure 4-1 Developmental Sequence for Understanding Number and Numeral Notation.

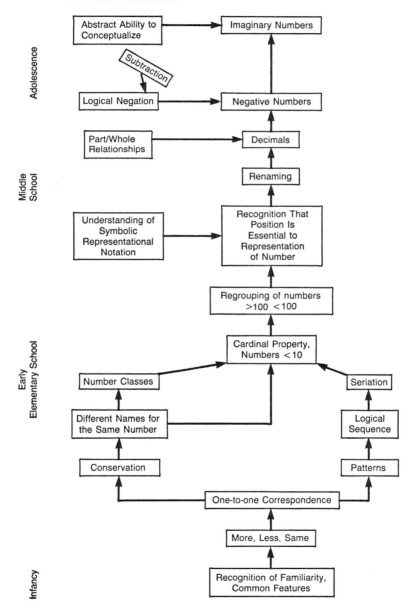

One-to-One Correspondence

The prerequisite to conservation, in turn, is not counting, as it might seem, but rather one-to-one correspondence—the ability to "tick off" the members in one group against those in another in order to make a systematically derived judgment of more, less, or same. (There is some argument in the recent literature that counting, rather than one-to-one correspondence, is a prerequisite to the understanding of cardinal property [Fuson & Richards, 1979].) This needs to be preceded, however, by the concepts of *more, less,* and *same.* The beginning levels of these concepts appear quite early in development. Infants 4 to 7 months old (Fagan, 1982) are making familiar/unfamiliar discriminations. Roger Brown's (1958) toddlers are dealing with commonalities when they develop their early generalizations. *More* and *less* also occur early in the child's development of vocabulary and as a way to express needs and desires. These concepts are, admittedly, vague at this stage, but they are sufficient for understanding the basic concept of cardinality. Piagetians trace the routes of cardinality back to the age of 18 months and the acquisition of object constancy. Since our example brings us back to a mental age well below the beginning of school and even preschool entry, it suffices for our curriculum-planning purposes.

The LD child may have difficulty with one-to-one correspondence even though his general developmental level is a mental age of 4 or 5 (by this developmental age, a child should have mastered this concept). His problem could be a simple horizontal decalage. If this were the case, the instructor would be able to observe other skills that are close in developmental level to this one and not abilities that indicate far more advanced development, such as classification or equivalence. It is more likely that a disorder in learning is interfering with the LD child's ability to demonstrate his level of development. A likely source of difficulty in the case of one-to-one correspondence would be problems in attention maintenance and deployment. The larger the amount and the longer the one-to-one matching procedure, the more likely a child with such a learning disorder would be to lose concentration or be unable to manage the amount of incoming information.

A technique to use with such a child might include the teacher's verbal monitoring of the sort, "Yes, that one goes with the red one." Or verbal monitoring from the child, "First I put this one with this one, then I put. . . ." It is good to have the teacher or child use exact descriptors of objects so as not to slip into an automatic recitation without being aware of what is actually going on. The important part of any intervention is to maintain active attention to the materials and the concept being demonstrated. A more basic approach is to decrease the demands made on attention maintenance. This can be done simply by using smaller amounts. Any activity using sets of three or fewer will reduce significantly the stress on any processing system (further discussion in the section in this chapter on neodevelopmental theory).

Seriation

The essence of seriation, the second component in cardinal property, is the logical sequence that exists between things or events. From the perspective of cardinal property, the important consideration is the gradation of amounts and sizes. This might well be preceded by an understanding of order based on patterns either temporal (rhythms) or topological (square, circle, square, circle). Eventually, this must be traced back to the careful analysis of individual items within a sequence or collection and a comparison among them. At this point seriation converges with the one-to-one correspondence mentioned earlier (see Figure 4-1).

The LD child who manifests difficulty with seriation may be evidencing problems with organization, with recognizing patterns or the underlying rule system that generates a pattern. She can perform one-to-one correspondence procedures because they are one step at a time and do not require an understanding of the entire situation in advance. Although she is developmentally ready for seriation, her disorder presents her with an obstacle to its acquisition. Instruction should be aimed at helping this child recognize the pattern or rule system in a seriated sequence. A simple beginning might include the use of two identical sets of materials—that is, three red rods of differing lengths. These can be ordered from shortest to longest by the teacher. The child can use one-to-one correspondence techniques to copy the model. Nevertheless, to do it correctly, what must be matched is the pattern of lengths. Gradually, the teacher can place more of a demand on the child's recognition of the pattern by giving her, first, objects of different colors and, eventually, objects of different absolute sizes.

Understanding of the basic concept of number, therefore, relies on two prerequisite forms of understanding that *develop, at some points, independently of each other and, at other points, simultaneously.* The system, then, is not a simple, step-by-step, linear one. A true understanding of numbers depends upon the interweaving of various factors with the appropriate timing. A glance back to Figure 4-1 will help demonstrate this point.

The LD child may not be able to accomplish this interweaving independently. There can be several reasons for difficulty at this point. The most likely one relates to the LD child's difficulty in managing large amounts of information at once. To understand any complex concept or relationship, a great deal of information has to come together for a child at a single moment in time. Thus, the relationship can be recognized. The LD child who tends to be overloaded easily is likely to lose some of the important information and achieve a faulty notion of cardinal property, or just be overwhelmed and confused. It becomes necessary to provide some special assistance for this kind of child. The primary goal of instructional assistance is to bring, in our example, the two critical conceptualizations about classification and seriation together for the child and to make explicit how they both relate to the concept of number. Such instruction might begin with an emphasis on classification as sets or groups of things. For example, the student can be asked to make a series of sets of four elements each: four chairs, four pennies, four leaves, four coins (one dime, one nickel, one quarter, one penny). Some discussion should follow on the theme that each of these differently sized sets have the same amount—4. Some suggestions for questioning follow:

- How many chairs does our group (set) have? How many pennies? Leaves? Coins?
- Which group has the biggest things in it?
- Which group has the smallest things in it?
- Which group has the greater number of things in it? How many? How many things do the other groups have?
- What is the same about each of these groups? What is different?

The same procedure can be repeated with sets of three or five things and more if the student still cannot answer easily questions such as the preceding ones. For additional practice, such a student can be given work sheets of a similar nature, this time with pictured sets rather than constructed ones. The next step is to compare sets of differing amounts as well as sizes. Examples here may include comparisons among the following sets:

3 chairs	4 apples
5 pennies	3 M & M's
4 markers	

Questioning could proceed as earlier, perhaps with the added probe:

- Look how big this group of chairs is. How can this tiny group of pennies (or markers or apples) be *more* than the chairs?

Again, follow-up can include examples of other comparisons and eventually work sheet reinforcement. This procedure helps the LD child recognize the materials as one group of things rather than four separate objects. It also emphasizes sets of relatively few objects. The result is to reduce the probability of overload.

The number classification theme can begin to be merged with the seriation theme by using materials that vary size and number simultaneously. One application might be strips of paper with equally sized "blocks" marked off. Each strip is made up of a different number of blocks and is, therefore, of a different length. For example:

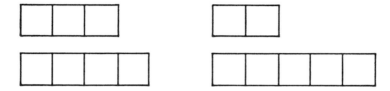

Stacks of blocks consisting of different numbers of blocks would be equally effective. Here the task is to order the stacks or strips first according to size (seriation) and then according to number. Since size and number are directly related to each other, both orderings would be the same. Again, it is good to conclude this portion of the lesson with some discussion:

- Which is biggest? Which has the most blocks (squares)? Count the blocks.
- Rearrange a few of the stacks or strips so they are *not* ordered properly. Then ask if they are still in the right order. Why? Why not?

And, finally, the goal would be to have the child order strips or stacks made of variously sized component blocks:

These should be ordered first according to absolute size and then according to number. The child can be asked the standard battery of questions to see if he can justify the difference in his two sequences. Likewise, such a lesson can be followed with similar activities with slightly different materials and work sheets.

Once children have joined these two systems of thought, seriation and classification, they have not learned all there is to know about number. Clearly, understanding cardinal property does not stop with the understanding of numbers less than 10. Beyond this point, older elementary-school children are asked to comprehend the ideas of place value and unknown numbers. Adolescents are asked to understand negative numbers, and, possibly, imaginary numbers (of the kind $\sqrt{-2}$). Each of these requires its own cognitive, developmental precursors. Consider, for example, the problem of place value. This is another case of converging cognitive systems. Place value begins with the awareness that develops very early on the route to cardinality that there are different ways to represent the same number (e.g., 3 + 4 versus 2 + 5; or 2 tens and 3 ones versus 23 versus 20 + 3 versus 1 ten and 13 ones). This relies on the even earlier ability to formulate and reformulate groups. Add to this the specific understanding of multiples of 10. Finally, the student must be aware that the representation of a number is a symbolic, arbitrarily determined thing that relies on the relative position of numerals.

The understanding of place value, then, requires several abilities that are common sources of difficulty for LD children. The problem of converging concepts already discussed is again an obstacle, but in this context it is a greater problem for two reasons. First, more information must be dealt with at a given instant. Second, the information is at a more abstract level, so it becomes more difficult for the teacher to use clear, concrete examples that reduce the need for the child to create her own mental image. At this stage the LD child will need to take multiple steps to solve a problem. So that she does not lose control of the information, the best solution is to keep careful records of what each step involved and its results.

Another problem that plays a role at this point is the need for flexibility. That is, the relevant prerequisites for place value were learned at another time, in another context, in our example as different names for the same number. The LD child may not possess the cognitive flexibility to extract the concept from its original context and reapply it in this new situation. She can be helped in this by explicit reminders of the original concept and explicit demonstrations of how this kind of grouping and regrouping can be used in units of 10 and, eventually, multiples of 10.

MAKING INSTRUCTION SUITABLE

If we assume that the continuum in Figure 4-1 is a workable representation of development, then we are ready to begin considering another example of how to provide instruction suitable for the LD child so that these steps are learned. Since the LD child is characterized in math (and in other areas) by a variety of disorders in learning, it is important to remember that no single developmental model can incorporate the infinite number of idiosyncratic styles a teacher may encounter. That is, the LD child will need to go through the same developmental steps as other children but will have unusual ways of doing so. The value of the developmental approach is that it clearly defines the essential, relevant components of the *concepts* to be taught, the order in which they occur, and the relationships among them.

Since a carefully detailed program of instruction for the entire sequence presented in Figure 4-1 would require long and boring volumes, it is more effective to extract another slice out of this continuum and construct an example of how a series of lessons might proceed. Let's consider, for example, the understanding of negative numbers. Figure 4-2 displays the selected parts of the original continuum. In Figure 4-2, it can be seen that the understanding of negative numbers rests on three earlier (and, to some degree, distinct) concepts: cardinal property, subtraction, and logical negation. Cardinal property has already been discussed here and in other places as well. From subtraction, a student would need to extract the notion of undoing, reversing, or negating the operation of addition. More specifically, the student would need to realize that the subtracted number has a draining (or negating) effect on the initial number in the equation or in the concrete depiction of the set. Most students who "master" subtraction have only an implicit understanding of all this until they confront their first negative numbers. It is not safe, however, to assume that the LD child who has mastered subtraction has really attended to *these* aspects of subtraction; nor is it a certainty that if the child has only an implicit awareness, he or she will apply it quite naturally and spontaneously in the new context of negative numbers (Brown, 1978). Finally, the student who is to learn about negative numbers will need some understanding of the logical principle of negation. This may appear trivial since even very young children understand forms of *no, not, never,* and the like. There is convincing evidence, however, that these usages do *not* serve a logical function (Cherkes, 1979; Wason & Johnson-Laird, 1972) but rather a loose denial, disapproval kind of function. The logic of negation is in fact difficult to command and includes the ability to exclude certain bits of information

Figure 4-2 Components in the Understanding of Negative Numbers

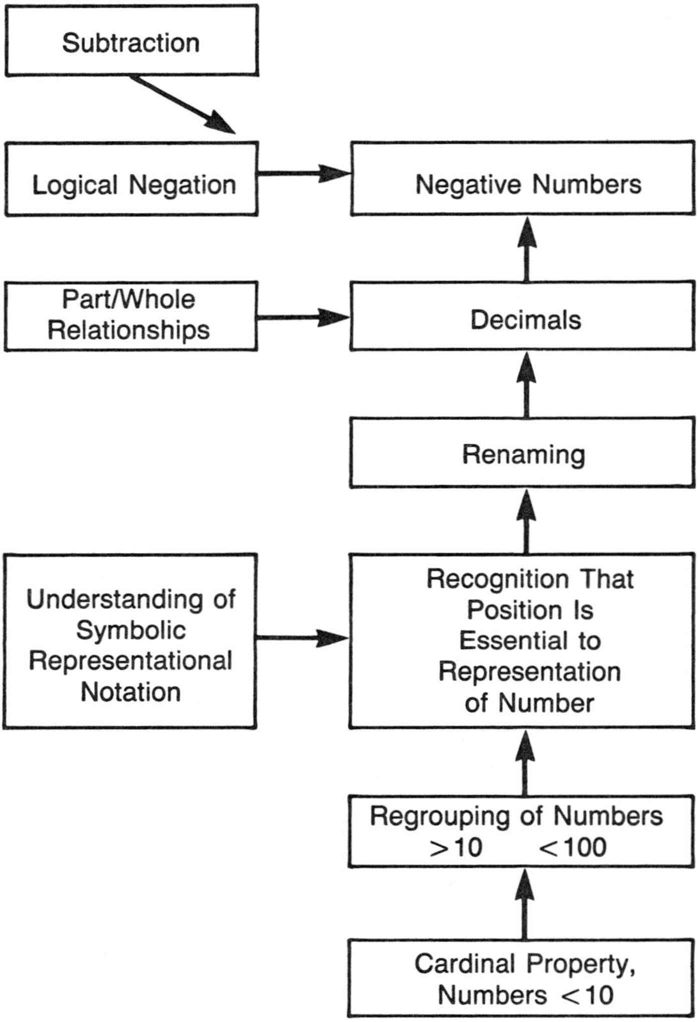

so as to recognize contradictions and opposites. Consider the following problems to appreciate the difficulty:

> Example 1: Either John is intelligent or else he is rich. John is not rich. (Wason & Johnson-Laird, 1972). What can be inferred about John?

Example 2: Either John is intelligent or he is not rich. John is rich. (Wason & Johnson-Laird, 1972). What can be inferred about John?[1]

Artful instruction of negative numbers will not assume that all these prerequisites exist. Even more to the point, however, good developmental instruction will not assume that their existence guarantees that they will be applied individually or together in the proper combinations. Herein lies the challenge, especially for the teacher of the learning disabled. How, then, might negative numbers be taught? First, it seems that the LD teacher should elicit the relevant awarenesses, bring them to the level of explicit understanding, and explain that they will help the student understand a new concept—negative numbers. He or she might begin by doing some exercises around the theme of reversing and finding opposites. Examples around which more complete lessons could be devised are suggested in Figure 4-3.

Figure 4-3 Some Suggestions as a Basis for Understanding Mathematical Negation

Instruct the Child Using Words, Manipulatives, and Demonstrations to:

Take 4, add 2, undo 2
Take 4, undo 4

Find the opposite

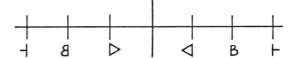

Describe or identify what is meant by: No big ones
                                       None that are not little

Find the opposite

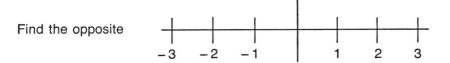

The optimal instruction to reach the goals specified in Figure 4-3 would have been provided early in the child's mathematics education. Since most LD children typically do not receive this kind of well-integrated, longitudinal curriculum, however, it is most likely that these concepts will need to be newly incorporated into the negation lesson. The instructional emphasis is on associating the language of negation with some earlier and very basic principles of subtraction. For example, the teacher might provide a lesson in which the student is asked to create sets and then to undo or do the opposite of what he or she just did. Such a lesson might involve beginning with a set of four objects (pennies, for example). The student can be instructed to put two more objects with the pennies already on the table. Now the pupil is told to do the opposite of what he or she just did. For smaller children, to prepare for later concepts about negative numbers, the lesson might involve instructions such as : "Walk four steps ahead. Walk two more steps ahead. Walk two steps in the opposite direction." Demonstration of the meaning of "opposite" and how it affects the total amount will certainly be necessary. The idea is to introduce the child to the fact that subtraction and opposite/undoing are related concepts. For the older child who is at the point of learning negative numbers, further application of the undoing idea is appropriate. After continuing some work with adding a new amount to a set and doing the opposite, with the result that the set returns to its original size, a more asymmetrical approach may be used. In such a case, the student would be asked to establish one by one, a set of five, for example, and then to undo that set by two (or three, etc.). It is appropriate to begin to associate the + and − signs with the processes they indicate. The student now can be presented with a set of five objects. The teacher can write on the board or on a piece of paper the following commands, one at a time:

$$+5 \qquad\qquad -3$$
$$-2 \qquad\qquad +4$$
$$+1$$

Once this is mastered, some direct instruction about the principles of negation will be necessary. To follow the analogy set up in the previous sequence of lessons, it is useful for the teacher to continue with set formation as the main motif of the lesson and to apply rules, at least at first, of simple negation. Students may then be instructed to make a set or group or pile of all the crayons (or hats or mittens) in the room but *not* the red ones. The language of negation can be varied to include:

Make a group of the girls in the class but *none* with blond hair.

Make a group of red things. *Never* include anything round in the group.
Make a group of round things, and *nothing* should be red.
Make a group of pencils with *no* erasers.

Clearly, the main point in these exercises is to learn to exclude some objects or some information in order to get a correct answer. The next problem involves considering the extent of a negation. That is, a command such as, "Make a group of pencils and pens—*none* of them red," implies no red pencils as well as no red pens. Some exposure to this kind of experience will help the student who eventually has to learn the meaning of $-(-5)$ or $4 - (3 + 2)$.

To ease the transition between these verbal negations and numerical ones, a sign system like the one used in the subtraction example is helpful. For example, *pencils – (red)* might be taught as a symbol for constructing a set of non-red pencils. Complex negation such as *no* non-red pencils or $-(-red)$ would represent the culmination of the lesson.

MAINTAINING MULTIDIMENSIONALITY

Of major importance in these lessons, then, is the maintenance of the richness and multidimensionality of concepts, even at the earliest developmental levels. The tendency to consider development as a purely linear, unidimensional progression leads to "precision" instruction, which in turn leads to an overly narrow understanding (if it is understanding at all). It is little wonder that students with such a narrow view of a concept have the reputation for being unable to generalize and apply what they have learned in novel situations. It is the broad base in which a concept is founded that makes new applications of the idea possible. Concepts are not simple, clearly delineated classification systems (Rosch, 1977). Instead, in their best and richest form, they are vague and multifaceted interweavings of ideas. Rather than extract this complexity in the effort to make the concept easier and clearer, it is important to provide instruction that helps the LD child manage all the necessary aspects of the task. More is said about this in Chapter 5 in the discussion of metacognition.

It is at this point that the neo-Piagetian school of thought has something interesting to add. In the neo-Piagetian view, what changes with development is not the complexity or kind of cognitive structures but the capacity for dealing with increasing amounts of information. Younger children, for example, may be able to handle two or three different bits of information at a time. Older children and adults may be able to cope with five, six, seven, or even nine bits at once. Whereas the traditional developmentalists emphasize that age differences reflect qualitative differences in the way children can think about and structure information, the neo-Piagetians contend that the structures, the ways of thinking, are similar across ages. It is simply that the otherwise adequate thought processes of young or developmentally delayed children are limited by the amount of information they can incorporate. Consider the case of cardinal property as an example. It has become a generally accepted fact that the understanding of number occurs after the ability to conserve, at about mental age 6. Prior to this age, the necessary mental operations (classification, seriation) are not available for such an understanding. Strauss and Curtis (1981), on the other hand, provide convincing evidence that babies as young as 10 months old do have the mental capacity to understand numberness, but babies this age seem limited to the recognition of one-ness, two-ness, and three-ness. According to the neo-Piagetians, their capacity to conceptualize larger numbers will be delayed either until they can increase the amount of information they can process at one time or until some intervention is provided. Since the necessary structures for understanding are there, early intervention becomes possible. The nature of that intervention is to reduce the amount of information a student is required to process at any one time or to decrease the demands made on the child's limited capacity. This can be done by providing background experiences or building on already existing experiences that can act as ways of grouping or chunking and thus compressing information. Or it can be done by presenting information in reduced, preorganized, or precompressed information loads. For the LD student this approach to development promises to be especially useful. The traditional approach would have us wait until the delayed area became ready to learn, for example, cardinal property. If LD students are capable in all other senses of more mature logic, problem solving, and concepts, however, it would be ideal if they could do mathematics problems that are at the level of their individual capabilities and that might be more relevant, challenging, and motivating. Since limited processing span or attention span is a frequently reported learning disorder, an approach to instruction that proposes to deal with it effectively is critical. Under the neo-Piagetian approach, the suggestion is that waiting is not necessary—that, in our example, cardinal property can be taught as long as instruction remains within the bounds of the student's capacity.

In practice this is not an unfamiliar procedure for most teachers of LD children. They are quite accustomed to presenting lessons in small, "broken-down" steps. The challenge, according to this view, is to "break" the concept down into an information load that is small enough for the student but still retains the essence of the concept. It would be difficult, for example, to expect a student to capture the meaning of four-ness if he were asked to view or manipulate one object in isolation, then another in isolation, then another and another. The very nature of the concept depends upon the simultaneous presentation of four things. If the student already knows two, however, a group of two becomes a single unit of information. The teacher who knows this about a student might group a presentation in the way suggested in Figure 4-4.

The examples used thus far have focused on reducing, reorganizing, or compressing information so that it fits within the limited capacity of the young or LD child. There are other interventions that follow from a neo-Piagetian approach to development that emphasize maximizing the capacity of the child. For example, any learner's capacity is taxed when she is confronted with a large amount of new information at any one time or is required to recall and use lots of different processes or strategies to make sense out of a problem. A general principle of good instruction, according to this view, is to free up as much of a child's capacity as possible so she can focus her energy on the lesson at hand. The relative span of a child's capacity to process information depends to a great extent on her previous experience. For example, if a child has had previous experience with logical negation, this is one fewer factor with which she will have to cope when learning about negative numbers. Any child has only a limited capacity for processing information. The LD child is likely to have even greater restrictions on her processing and/or attention span. The more that is brand new and without a frame of reference in any learning situation, the more of a burden is placed on the child's capacity.

The model, then, is a variant of the traditional developmental and task analytic model. The traditional view emphasizes vertical hierarchies and vertical transfer, waiting for readiness and providing necessary help at

Figure 4-4 The Use of Grouping and Simultaneous Presentation To Aid Instruction

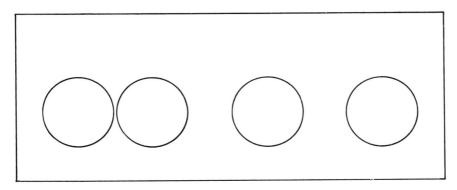

preparatory stages. The modified view emphasizes horizontal transfer, starting from present capabilities and applying them to learn new concepts. In either case, the development of natural learning, of natural forms of cognition, is accounted for quite nicely. That is, given the appropriate experiences, all children of all cultures seem to experience the unfolding of cognitive capacities in a very similar way.

ENVIRONMENTAL DEMANDS

There is reason to believe, however, that some forms of cognition, some ways of thinking and learning, do not occur *naturally* in development at all but, instead, are a result of the kinds of demands made by the environment. There are, then, two different kinds of learning systems. One is the system that occurs naturally in development. The conceptualization of number-ness, of cardinal property, is an example of such a natural evolution in all cultures, regardless of their widely disparate characteristics. It develops whether a child or a people is schooled or unschooled, literate or illiterate. There are, on the other hand, kinds of thinking that occur only when a child or a people is required to experience written symbolic systems (Olson, 1976). It is only when a child must deal with the arbitrariness of a symbol system that he is required to find new techniques for understanding. Prior to this, he has learned all things in context, in ways that make immediate sense and therefore require no active "figuring out" or mediation. Now in the absence of context, of natural meaning, the student needs to find ways of making sense out of what might otherwise be nonsense. Strategies for organizing and retaining information, such as rehearsal, mnemonics, and grouping, become essential.

It is possible, even likely, then, that a child could easily develop through his preschool years, acquiring the awareness of number and logic that comes naturally in the context of experience such as notions of conservation, classification, *more* and *less,* and cardinal property. Some children, however, may begin to show difficulties in development when they begin school. When the kind of learning in school, the learning of symbols, requires completely different strategies, these children might eventually be identified as learning disabled; they will probably be described as having a problem in actively attending or in short-term memory processes. It is interesting that even in normally functioning children, it is not until age 8, third grade, that most children fully understand the role of special strategies for school learning and that in oral cultures these strategies would not evolve at all. They are, then, an outgrowth of demands made on children rather than a natural developmental phenomenon.

A developmental approach to mathematics instruction for an LD child whose problem is adjusting to these new demands might include two major components. First, since there is so much that is natural about the development of mathematical concepts, these can be capitalized on. The obvious implication is to maintain the meaning, the context that normally surrounds unschooled math learning. Manipulatives, direct experience, and discovery methods are examples of just such an approach. Some elements of math, however, are part of the symbolic, abstract, arbitrary association system. The notation system (numerals and place value) is an unavoidable instance. At this point the second component of instruction becomes relevant. LD children may need special instruction in realizing that this kind of learning is different from what they have been used to, and in learning specific strategies for doing so. Strategies appropriate for this kind of learning are discussed more fully in Chapter 6.

There are, then, at least three aspects of development that provide the foundation for mathematics instruction for the learning disabled. First and most basic is the awareness of the order in which cognitive capacities evolve. This includes consideration not only for a step-by-step progression but also for the fact that many concepts depend upon a complex, multifaceted integration of prerequisites. Second is the possibility that the critical factor in development may not be changing cognitive structures but, instead, the increasing capacity to deal with greater and greater amounts of information. Finally there is the necessary distinction between the learning of information that occurs in context, as a result of natural development, and learning that is a result of arbitrary and symbolic systems. For instruction, this suggests an approach that respects the complexity of mathematical concepts and aims to clarify that complexity rather than avoiding or denying it. It suggests the possibility of intervention based on the careful structuring of information to suit the student's limits and previous experience. It suggests, further, the need to recognize that some information will not make immediate sense to a student despite his otherwise adequate development, that school learning often requires strategies for learning that do not evolve naturally but need rather to be elicited. Sound mathematics instruction will include a delicate balance of all these considerations.

NOTES

1. For those interested, the answers to these problems follow. In Example 1, the proposition that John is not rich negates the clause "he is rich." Since that clause is false, the alternative clause must be true (according to the rule of disjunction); therefore, John is intelligent. In Example 2, the fact that John is rich negates the clause "he is not rich," making the clause "John is intelligent" true.

REFERENCES

Bender, L. (1938). A visual motor Gestalt test and its clinical use. *American Orthopsychiatry Association Research Monograph* No. 3.

Blankenship, C.S. (1978). Remediating systematic inversion errors in subtraction through the use of demonstration and feedback. *Learning Disability Quarterly, 1*, 12–22.

Brown A. (1978). Knowing when, where, and how to remember: A problem of metacognition. In R. Glaser (Ed.), *Advances in instructional psychology* (Vol. 1). Hillsdale, NJ: Lawrence Erlbaum.

Brown R. (1958). *Words and things*. Glencoe, IL: Free Press.

Case, R. (1978). Piaget and beyond: Toward a developmentally based theory and technology of instruction. In R. Glaser (Ed.), *Advances in instructional psychology* (Vol 1. pp. 167–228). Hillsdale, NJ: Lawrence Erlbaum.

Cherkes, M. (1979). A preliminary investigation of the role of logic in special class instruction. *Contemporary Educational Psychology. 4*, 67–80.

de Hirsch, K., Jansky, J., & Langford, Q. (1966). *Predicting reading failure*. New York: Harper & Row.

Fagan, J.F. (1982). Infant memory. In T.M. Field, A. Huston, H.C. Quay, L. Troll, & G.E. Finley (Eds.), *Review of human development* (pp. 79–92). New York: Wiley.

Flavell, J. (1963). *The developmental psychology of Jean Piaget*. New York: Van Nostrand Reinhold.

Furth, H.G. (1970). *Piaget for teachers*. Englewood Cliffs, NJ: Prentice-Hall.

Hallahan, P.P., Kauffman, J.M., & Ball, D.W. (1974). Developmental trends in recall of central and incidental auditory material. *Journal of Experimental Child Psychology, 17*, 409–421.

Olson, D.R. (1976). Culture, technology and intellect. In L. Resnick & R. Glaser (Eds.), *The nature of intelligence*. Hillsdale, NJ: Lawrence Erlbaum.

Piaget, J., & Inhelder, B. (1969). *The psychology of the child*. New York: Basic Books.

Resnick, L.B., & Glaser, R. (1976). Problem solving and intelligence. In L.B. Resnick (Ed.), *The nature of intelligence* (pp. 205–230). Hillsdale, NJ: Lawrence Erlbaum.

Rosch, E. (1977). Classification of real-world objects: Origin and representations in cognition. In Q.N. Johnson-Laird & P.C. Wason (Eds.). *Thinking* (pp. 212–222). Cambridge, England: Cambridge University Press.

Strauss, M.S., & Curtis, L.E. (1981). Infant perception of numerosity. *Child Development, 52*(4), 1146–1152.

Wason, P.C. & Johnson-Laird, P.N. (1972). *Psychology of reasoning*. Cambridge: Harvard University Press.

Yselldyke, J.E. (1973). Diagnostic prescriptive teaching: The search for aptitude. Treatment interactions. In L. Mann & D. Sabatino (Eds.), *The first review of special education* Philadelphia: JSE Press.

Chapter 5

Metacognitive Considerations in Mathematics Instruction for the Learning Disabled

Miriam Cherkes-Julkowski

The learning disabled (LD) youngster is often described as having difficulty applying the appropriate strategy to learn or to study. He may not, for example, have a systematic strategy for solving problem information. Or he may not be able to perform mental computations because he does not use appropriate verbal rehearsal strategies. There is a long list of strategies that play a role in learning, and an LD problem can occur in any one or more of them. Failure to use appropriate strategies can be explained in at least two ways. The learning disabled student is either deficient in the strategy itself or in the ability to produce that strategy in the proper situations (Flavell, 1970). It is the more recent, metacognitive view that LD-like problems in thinking and reasoning are more probably due to the inability to call forth the appropriate strategies under appropriate conditions.

THINKING ABOUT THINKING

Metacognition can be described as the plan to have a plan or thinking about thinking. It means, literally, those processes that override the use of particular thinking and learning strategies. The computer analogy is that of the executive function. That is, one can program a computer to perform a series of operations on any given set of information, but which operation should it perform when? The command to select strategy A (or B or C) is the executive function that orchestrates the appropriate use of these strategies and operations. So it is, say the metacognitivists (Brown, 1978; Flavell & Wellman, 1977), with the human mind. There, too, exists a series of strategies such as attention focusing, special and individualistic ways of using algorithms for computing, rules of logic for problem solving. There, too, must be some command or executive branch of mental governing. The learner's task is to select the appropriate strategy for learning the particular task or solving the particular problem at hand.

Much of the work in metacognition has been done with mildly handicapped and LD youngsters (Arbitman-Smith & Haywood, 1980; Brown, 1978). All this work, but primarily Brown's, points dramatically to the fact that LD and LD-like children can be taught to use *exactly* those strategies that they previously lacked and whose absence made learning faulty if not impossible. Although this population can be taught to use these strategies, such as labeling or rehearsal, in a particular situation, the LD youngster tends not to apply the trained strategy spontaneously either in exactly the same situation a little bit later or in a similar, generalized situation. Oddly enough, the child simply needs to be reminded, "Do you remember what we did last time when we tried to learn this?" and can be expected to call forth the strategy and use it again. An even more dramatic example is discussed by Brown (1978). She described a group of mildly handicapped youngsters who were asked to view a series of videotape segments. The segments depicted a series of children studying for a test. Each videotaped child was using one of the following strategies to learn a list: categorizing, rehearsing, labeling, and looking. The handicapped viewers demonstrated that they were quite able to identify the best strategies for learning the list (categorizing and rehearsing)—an encouraging finding. The viewers were then asked to learn a list themselves, however. The unusual finding was that they did not use the effective strategy they had just identified.

Thus far we have identified the metacognitive state of the LD child as one in which strategies for learning/problem solving might exist, one in which those strategies at the very least can be taught. The problem is not in the ability to learn or use strategies or to recognize which is the best strategy, but in the ability or awareness or willingness to evoke it. This problem of not *executing* the appropriate strategy should not be confused with a similar, typical LD problem of executing an inappropriate strategy. For example, the child who has devised a left-to-right adding algorithm may be using an inappropriate strategy. Nevertheless, when she evokes exactly that strategy in all addition problems, at least she is executing a strategy that she associates with a particular situation. The metacognitive problem refers very specifically to deficiencies, not at the strategy level, but at the level of executive function.

At this level of selecting an appropriate strategy, there are at least two conceivable steps to the process. First, to engage in the activity of selecting a strategy, the learner must be aware that he *needs* to do so and he must be willing to do it. Second, once the strategy selection process has been activated, the learner needs to be able to *judge* which of his strategies is best suited to the unique characteristics of this problem situation.

Active Strategy Selection

Consider the first step in the sequence: willingness to activate the selection process. This step requires the learner to acknowledge that his active participation in the learning process is essential and that he must sustain that active involvement until he has found some way to deal with the problem at hand. While this level of involvement may seem a minimal expectation for average learners, it can pose grave difficulties for certain kinds of LD children. Those LD children who are characterized by impulsivity, by a low tolerance for frustration, and by a general passivity in learning may not be able to command the processes at this step. Suppose the youngster has been presented with a word problem in a format or of a kind he has not yet encountered but for which he has all the appropriate strategies for solution. For example:

> Mary started with 4 dolls. She has 10 dolls now. How many did her mother give her?

The impulsive LD child may simply add the numbers to get an answer (Goodstein, Cawley, Gordon, & Helfgott, 1971). The child with a low frustration tolerance may recognize that this is a new kind of problem, make a few stereotyped attempts to solve it, and then give up. Perhaps she will hand in two or three solutions or semisolutions. The passive child may read the problem. When he realizes that he has no instant solution, he replies that he has not yet learned how to do those. For him, there is no other alternative than to sit and wait for the teacher to show him how.

These, however, are examples of purely cognitive explanations for not activating the process of selecting appropriate strategies. There are also more affective, motivational issues to consider. The attribution literature (Cherkes-Julkowski, Guskin, Schwarzer & Okolo, 1982; Heider, 1958, Weiner, 1974) asserts that success or failure in any situation can be attributed to the internal factors of ability and effort or to external factors, luck, and task difficulty. It has been suggested that LD children with histories of failure begin to feel that their efforts do not really make a difference (McGuire, 1982; Short & Ryan, 1982). This same tendency to think that effort is not important has been found in young children. They are likely to learn only incidentally at first. Later they try to learn and remember things by labeling them or repeating them, and later still they recognize the need actively to do something to new information in order to make it their own. In both cases the learner does not attribute successes or failures to effort, leaving things to raw ability or inability or to luck or to task. Such a youngster is unlikely to engage in the metacognitive step that is in essence a purely motivational, effort-exerting stage—the process of searching one's stored-up strategies and deciding which to apply. Activities at this stage do not bear any tangible or recognizable results. They require sheer effort or motivation, with only a delayed reward that is associated, not with this process at all, but with the next one—the application of the strategy that yields the correct answer. If the answer is incorrect and no reward is earned, it becomes difficult for the naive learner to distinguish between the processes of strategy selection and strategy application, to decide which behavior is the appropriate one to alter.

A continued pattern of failure can result, then, in learned helplessness. That is, the LD child can learn that trying is only frustrating or, worse, self-defeating. He therefore consciously decides *not* to exert the effort, *not* to activate his entry into the learning process. The recommended intervention for this problem has been to provide a consistent set of success experiences. Although this is certainly necessary, from the metacognitive perspective, it is also recommended that successes be systematically attributed to effort. In math, a good starting point for this intervention might be computations. As long as the computations are at a level the child can handle, she can earn a great deal of positive feedback for speed and accuracy. Speed is an especially important component in this context because it requires effort and concentration. If the teacher based his feedback on evidence of these rather than on correct responses, it could encourage the student in her awareness that effort counts.

Let us suppose, however, that our youngster has made it through his first, activation step. Now she will need to select the appropriate strategy or strategies to solve the unique problem before her. There are many different strategies that can be used in any process of learning. If a child needs to memorize number facts or mathematical axioms, then rehearsal strategies will be important. If she sees a problem she's never seen before, then generalization strategies are required. When she learns new concepts such as place value or equivalent measurements or geometric rules, she needs to draw upon attention focusing, classification, hypothesis testing, labeling, association, and probably more strategies.

Although there is some belief that LD youngsters are deficient in one or more of these strategies, there is a more recent finding by researchers in metacognition (Arbitman-Smith & Haywood, 1980; Brown, 1978) that the deficiency lies, not in the strategies themselves, but in the process of selecting the proper one at the proper time. Since generalization is the key to real learning, it deserves primary and careful attention. In this context, generalization is the process of applying what has been learned in one situation to very similar, but somewhat different, situations (near generalization) and to increasingly novel situations (far generalization). Generalization, then, is what enables the learner to extend her knowledge, to learn in the absence of direct instruction. Suppose an LD youngster had been taught to derive equivalent measurements, problems of the kind:

$$4 \text{ cups} = \underline{\hspace{1cm}} \text{ pints or } 8 \text{ ounces} = \underline{\hspace{1cm}} \text{ pounds}$$

Suppose, too, that she has been able to do these examples correctly and consistently. A near generalization task that might cause her some difficulty would be the application of this process to linear measurement problems, such as:

$$24 \text{ inches} = \underline{\hspace{1cm}} \text{ feet}; 7 \text{ feet} = \underline{\hspace{1cm}} \text{ yards } \underline{\hspace{1cm}} \text{ feet}$$

The literature suggests (Brown, 1978) that near generalization is facilitated when the teacher reminds the LD youngster of the appropriate strategy. So a prompt as simple as, "Remember how we did it with cups and pints?" is likely to be all that is needed. Nevertheless, without such a prompt, the youngster is at a standstill.

Far generalization is a bit more elusive. Examples are the application of the principle of balancing equations to that of equivalent fractions, finding common denominators, or balancing algebraic equations to find an unknown number. An example of the latter is:

$$(1)\ 2/3x = 20;\ (2)\ 3/2(2/3x) = 20(3/2);\ (3)\ x = 30$$

In the case of the more talented LD student, the principle can also be applied to the process of balancing chemical equations in a high school chemistry class. A basic equation is: $0 + 2 H = H_2 0$ (water). When the student is told that oxygen appears in nature as 0_2, however, she needs to find a way to keep her equation balanced: $1/2\ 0_2 + 2H = H_2 0$.

In either of these two examples the generalization is distant and much more difficult to accomplish than the earlier case of near generalization. In fact, it has been almost impossible in practice to induce mildly handicapped students to make spontaneous far generalizations. This may be due to the problem of "task welding" (Burger, Blackman, Clark, & Gordon, 1982) at the stage of initial learning. That is, when the first principle of finding equivalent measurements was learned, it was learned as a specific procedure attached only to that task, rather than as a general principle with applicability to many situations. This kind of faulty learning can be due to oversimplified instruction that uses very similar problems during the learning stages, thus failing to demonstrate that the principle has wide applicability. It can also be due to metacognitive problems within the LD child. He is perhaps a passive learner who receives the information that if 2 cups = 1 pint, then 4 cups = 2 pints. He might even be able to tell you how he attained the answer 2 pints. He has not attended, however, to the principles involved in the basic notions of *equations* and *balancing* that allow him to change an equation in *any* way as long as he makes his changes equivalently to all parts of the equation. He has not understood the depth or complexity of the principle.

In either case instruction must be carefully planned to emphasize the central, generalizable aspect of the task and to demonstrate a variety of

applications. In geometry, for example, to teach that a triangle is is to imply that all triangles have three equal sides and are symmetrical. An approach to instruction that discourages task welding and avoids overwhelming the LD pupil might begin with a lesson that asks the child to color in four triangles of the sort:

This can be followed by asking the child to cut out the shapes, to draw further attention to contour. Next the child can be asked to paste each on a separate piece of paper and to draw a picture around it. The purpose of this last step is to emphasize the shape in relationship to other shapes and to draw attention to real things that have that shape. Before the lesson is over, some example of what is *not* a triangle will be necessary. Although most children will recognize a circle as a nontriangle, they may have more difficulty discriminating between kites, parallelograms, and triangles.

Another example of anti-task-welding instruction in the area of fractions is to demonstrate that fractions can be parts of whole objects and parts of sets of objects. So ½ can be half of a circle but also half of a group of 4 or 6 or 7 things. Likewise, ½ can be part of different shapes of different sizes.

Likewise, subtraction is not simply the process of take-away. It is also the processes of what's the difference between and how many more do I need? Early problems should reflect all three aspects. So, in addition to the standard take-away approach,

Mary had 3 apples. She ate 1. How many does she have left?

there is also the issue of how many more do I need?

Mary needs 10¢ to buy a balloon. She has 3¢. How much more does she need?

And there is the issue of what's the difference between?

> Mary has 10 apples. Susan has 7. How many more apples does Mary have?

Perhaps it is the notion of complexity that is most important here. Rigid, overlearned, automatic responses are antithetical to an appreciation of complexity in a concept or principle. Kuhn (1977) describes the essential aspect of real problem solving as the imposing or applying of several different frames of reference on the same information. In our equation examples, the LD youngster would need to view balanced equations from the perspective of algebraic equations, different kinds of measurement, equivalent fractions, chemical equations, and so on and on, before he could understand the full richness of the concept. From an information-processing perspective, in each of these varied situations, the learner has a different context in which to view the same or similar information. Each context provides depth and understanding for one idea. And each context provides an opportunity for relating that idea to the knowledge the learner already has. The greater the number of contexts, the greater the number of associations and, thus, the greater the number of stimuli that trigger that idea or principle as relevant and/or critical to understanding. Thus, what seems to be fundamental to strategy selection is the awareness that strategies in general fit in an infinite number of situations that are variations on a theme, and that the specific strategy in question has been viewed in a wide enough series of situations.

Findings from the field of social cognition confirm this view. It is commonly marveled that many LD youngsters are so streetwise at the same time they have so much trouble in school. Research supports this anomaly. It is true that social cognition tends to exceed school-related cognitions in the mildly handicapped (Greenspan, 1979). The question arises, What is different about social situations that make them easier for children to understand? Aside from the fact that social situations may be more immediate and therefore more motivating, there is also a conceptual explanation. Damon (1981) suggests that social learning not only takes place in context but also in a wide variety of subtly changing and not so subtly changing contexts. And, perhaps more critically, the learner is forced to see the same situation from the various perspectives of each of the participants. Another metacognitive function that social, but not academic, learning demands is the constant reformulation of ideas in order to reach compromises, to come to a consensus, or just to make oneself understood. Although these metacognitive aspects occur quite naturally in social contexts and not so naturally in academic ones, there is no reason why they cannot be built into mathematics education for the learning disabled. One technique might be to set up a dialogue between students. For example, the student who has solved a word problem or who has truly understood the principle of balancing equations is paired with a student who—although he seems to have all the subskills—has not really "put it all together" yet. The dialogue between them would be the process of reaching a consensus, a la social consensus style, that would allow the not-yet-ready student to formulate his *own* conceptualizations in his own words. This differs from thorough instruction that imparts the whole package to a passive receiver.

This approach has also taken the form of small groups (four or five) of students at various levels who discuss possible solutions or possible explanations for mathematical problems. It is possible, for example, to ask a group of students to solve a math problem. Their task is to decide on a procedure for finding the solution. Problems that lend themselves to such discussion situations follow:

1. John ate ⅔ of a small pizza. The whole pizza looked like this:

Susan ate ½ of a medium pizza. Her whole pizza looked like this:

Who ate more?

2. Carlos has 2 children. One day he was walking with his daughter Maria. Is his other child a boy or a girl? What are the chances that the other child is a boy?

Note that there is no definitive answer to this. If one approaches the problem by saying the possible combinations are boy/girl   boy/boy girl/girl, then one set of probabilities is generated. One might say more simply, however, that the probability is always 1 in 2 of having a boy at any time (Bar-Hillel & Falk, 1982). This kind of issue lends itself to discussion particularly well. Regardless of the problem, it will be to the teacher's advantage to listen carefully to the discussion. He or she can learn exactly how each child is formulating ideas and how each responds to feedback from the others.

Overgeneralizing

Related to the phenomenon of not generalizing and not selecting the appropriate strategy is the tendency LD youngsters have to overgeneralize. Although the two may seem contradictory, they are really both parts of the same phenomenon. The LD youngster is likely to develop a broad, loosely defined concept or rule that overincludes instances. This should not seem bizarre since it is typical of all children at early developmental levels and of anyone at the beginning stages of learning something new. Only later, at a more sophisticated level, does a learner begin to be precise and know what is excluded from the new concept or what is contradictory to it. The LD youngster demonstrates some difficulty in the transition into this second, more sophisticated stage or recognizing inappropriate situations for the application of a given rule or concept. Probably the most familiar example is the overgeneralization of the commutative property of addition to subtraction, so that the youngster is likely to "problem solve" using his dominant, commutative strategy this way:

$$\begin{array}{r} 890 \\ -327 \\ \hline 577 \end{array}$$ The student says: Seven take-away zero is seven; nine take-away two is seven; eight take-away three is five.

Another example is the effort to impose a simple addition solution on all multiple-number word problems (Goodstein et al., 1971) so that the following type of problem is answered as the sum of 2 + 3 + 1, or 6.

1 boy has 2 cats
1 girl has 3 cats
another boy has 1 cat
How many cats do the boys have? [Cawley et al., 1976]

This tendency may take the form of seemingly rigid or dogmatic thinking. The fact is that the child has only a limited number of rules to choose from if he has not differentiated his broader strategies into smaller, more precise, and more numerous ones. So the LD student is likely to exhibit a high percentage of systematic errors in mathematics (Cox, 1975; Radatz, 1979). He is, after all, applying the same strategy over and over again. When asked why, he is likely to answer that he was told to do it that way. He tends to form loose associations between things. For example, if the first two shapes in a geometric reasoning task are symmetrical, he assumes the rest will be, too (Radatz, 1980). This apparent rigidity or dogmatism may result, not from a cognitive or personal style, but rather from a limited, overly undifferentiated pool of strategies from which to draw. To refine this condition, it will be necessary for the student to self-evaluate; to recognize that there is something wrong with his answer; to return to the original problem, examine it more closely, and modify his strategy or at least recognize that his strategy needs to be modified. But alas, self-evaluation, self-checking, and careful scanning of the problem are other activities that the LD youngster is wont to do.

SELF-MONITORING

Before the child can engage in self-monitoring or self-checking procedures, he first must be aware that a problem exists and must be solved. The LD student (and young children in general) tends to believe that there is one "right" answer and that only it is important (Arbitman-Smith & Haywood, 1980). How that answer is derived or why it is right is of little significance. This fits with the relatively passive nature of an LD child. In interviews with young children about their awareness of problem-solving strategies, Lester and Garofalo (1982) found that elementary-school-age students did not feel compelled to check their work. They would check only their computations if there was ample time, but no mention was made of checking the demands of the original problem.

From a remediation perspective, what seems necessary first is to make the LD child aware of the fact that he is being confronted with a problem. This assumes that previously he has not been encouraged to believe that speed and accuracy are the great gods of mathematics. Perhaps they serve a purpose, but they encourage an orientation toward automaticity, which prohibits awareness that a problem in fact exists. Automaticity means the lack of careful contemplation. At this level students can be asked to paraphrase a word problem or describe a computational procedure with a word problem (i.e., given the exercise $4 \times \frac{1}{2}$, the youngster would create a word problem for which that procedure is the solution). Procedures such as these have been found effective in helping mildly handicapped youngsters to remember and understand story narratives. In story narratives, the task is to have children paraphrase the story for themselves and for the instructor. By doing so, they translate the story into something that is meaningful to them. The process of surrounding computations with self-made problems has the same advantage of having the learner search her experience, her store of knowledge, or her frame of reference and come up with a context that is meaningful to her. This, according to some (Ausuhel, 1968), is the essence of learning.

An approach to instruction that encourages automatic procedures that can get right answers discourages the learner's search through her own reference system; it therefore reduces the probability of her really understanding the process. To discourage the child further from her get-the-right-answer-quick set, the LD child may be given problems with solutions already provided:

$$\frac{2}{3} + \frac{1}{2} = \frac{7}{6}$$

She must describe how the answer was obtained. It is also possible to emphasize techniques to force problem scanning prior to solution finding. In a task similar to the patterns of the Raven Test of Progressive Matrices, Feuerstein, Rand, and Hoffman (1979) asked their handicapped subjects simply to "look at this," "Now, look at this" until they had drawn their attention to all the aspects of the problem. Then they asked the youngsters to find the answer that correctly finished the pattern. This intervention achieved remarkable gains. Its effectiveness lies in the fact that the children had to look at all aspects of the problem and analyze the task carefully. Since LD children are often not conscious of exactly what they need to know to solve a problem and whether they have enough information to do so, forced attention to each aspect of the problem is necessary. In mathematical problem solving, it is useful to ask the child to read the problem and then outline each thing the problem has told him. A typical math problem follows:

> It took 5 hours to drive from John's house to his grandmother's. They traveled 200 miles. How fast were they going?

The child's first response would not be an answer but a list of facts:

> 5 hours = total time
> 200 miles = total distance

From here the teacher can question the student about what it is he needs to find out to begin to find the procedures for solution.

A slightly different approach is to ask the student to look at the problem and plan the steps in its solution (the metacognitive plan to have a plan). If the problem is to find the area of an equilateral triangle and the child knows the length of one side, she can enumerate the rest of the steps:

1. Recall formula: ½ base × height = area.
2. Reassign length of one side to length of base.

3. Find half the length of the base.
4. Use the formula for the hypotenuse of a right triangle: $a^2 + b^2 = c^2$.
5. Plug in the known quantities c and a.
6. Square these.
7. Subtract $c^2 - a^2$ to get b^2.
8. Take square root of b.
9. Assign value of b to the height of the triangle.
10. Plug in known quantities into area formula: ½ base $\times$ height $=$ area.
11. Compute answer.

At this point, if the steps are correct and thorough, she can be allowed to compute her solution.

An example for younger children is to decide the steps needed to figure out how many more dimes they need to buy a toy for $1.00 if they already have 10¢.

In general the goal is to enhance the overall keenness and alertness of the student, with the particular purpose of forcing careful examination of problem demands. To achieve this, it is important to provide novelty in the kinds of problems presented. Once the problems become stereotyped, even a good student will cease to respond to them as if they are problems. Instead, the tasks come to trigger automatic responses that preclude metacognitive functioning. There are techniques to keep LD students "on their toes." One approach is to include one problem for which the student has not yet had instruction. His task is to scan the problems, find the one he is not ready to solve, circle it, and then go back and do the rest. This approach may take the form of varying the format of problem presentation. In computations it may be as simple as:

Twenty-five plus 5 equals   46
32 + 9 =   +   9

18 + _____ = 27
seven plus thirty-six _____43

In word problems this might involve avoiding the use of key words such as *less* or *more* or using them in misleading ways, so that a problem including the phrase *less than* actually requires addition. An example follows:

Tony has 2 marbles. He has 3 less than Susan. How many marbles does Susan have?

(This idea is pursued further in *Project Math* [Cawley et al., 1976].)

In addition to before-solution approaches, some techniques encourage self-monitoring during problem solving and self-checking afterward. To enhance self-monitoring, one simple technique is to have the student talk out loud to describe each procedure he follows. If this is taped, the student can use the tape later to check his procedure and identify the locus of his errors. Other ways to encourage the student to examine her existing strategies in order to select the best one include asking her to find three or four different ways to get the same answer, or asking her to guess how another child (a younger or older child) might have done it. All these techniques have in common the purpose of keeping the child flexible in her application of various strategies. Modeling of monitoring behavior (Reid & Hresko, 1981) by the teacher has been a much-used approach. To set the proper example for the child, then, the teacher may demonstrate how he talks out loud to solve the problem or how he makes a real or mental list of what procedures to follow. For example, faced with the problem mentioned earlier of finding the area of the equilateral triangle or the more basic task of determining how many dimes were needed, the teacher might first model the behavior:

> Now, let me see. What do I need to do to get the answer? Well, first I need to look at what I know. I know *[here he writes something that the learner need not see]*. And I know that [_____].
> What will I need to find out? Well, how much [_____]. Now, I'm going to write down each step I will need to take [_____]. Before I solve the problem, I need to check my steps to see if I've forgotten anything [_____]. OK, first I do this [_____]. Check it. Now I do this [_____]. Check it. Let me see. Does this make sense? One last check [_____].

Such a procedure can take place with the teacher and learner side by side. As he models each step, the teacher can wait for the child to complete his version of that step and then go on. With younger children, this approach is often modified by having the child repeat exactly what the teacher does at each step.

The teacher who opts for this approach will need to be careful. Just because the child can model the correct response does not mean he will be able to generate it on his own, either in response to the original type of problem or to a more distant one. This, after all, is the nature of the problem—failure to generate the appropriate strategies. Nevertheless, with careful plans to fade the modeling out gradually and with applications of the approach in many, varied situations, the teacher can optimize results.

To encourage the learner further in self-monitoring, the teacher can work more directly to instill self-evaluation devices. Self-evaluation techniques can be as simple as telling the student to check her answers. Or the teacher may tell the student that on the ten items she did, she made mistakes on two. Her task is to circle the two that need correction. To make more of a game of this, the student can play teacher. The game involves a work sheet or test that a fictional student has completed. The "teacher" must (1) correct the paper and (2) teach the fictional student how to do it right. A variation on this theme is to give the student a description of another fictional student. Fictional Johnnie, for example, does not understand place value. With which of these problems will he have difficulty?

1)	48	2)	12367	3)	98	4)	65
	+19		+67321		−32		−29

5)	34	6)	23	7)	86
	×21		×12		×59

Note that item 5 may weed out the less analytical type of LD student who does not follow procedures all the way through.

Recognizing Contradiction

Still another way to have the student check or monitor his answers and procedures is through the careful use of contradiction. Piaget has done much to establish that some contradiction (disequilibrium) must be present for any learning to take place. That is, for the learner to go beyond his present level of understanding, some event must occur to make him realize his limitations. One problem with LD-like youngsters is that they often do not recognize the contradictions that might have helped them in the learning process. The goal for the teacher, then, is to design activities that, first, set the child up to encounter a conflict or contradiction, to emphasize its existence, and then to work to a resolution. One teacher of LD adolescents was particularly distressed because the youngsters in her class were so unpleasant to one another. She designed a lesson, originally with the intent of teaching a little cooperation, that turned out to be the basis of a unit in fractions. To begin with, she brought in a bag of candy bars, one for each student, and asked one child to pass them out. This went on for several days until the children grew to expect it. One day, as expected, the teacher reached for her bag of candy bars and asked one child to pass them out. This time, however, there was one fewer candy bar than there were students. The unexpecting student passed a candy bar to each of the others, expecting to take his at the end. He was very disappointed. After much complaining and asking the others, he was still without candy and there was general confusion in the class. The next day, out came the bag and the assigned student began his distribution duties. This time, however, he took his candy bar first and passed around the rest. Thus, one student at the end of the distribution did not receive one because, again, there was one fewer bar. This procedure went on for several days until the students found a way to divide up the existing candy bars evenly. Once this resolution had been achieved, the teacher began varying the number of candy bars even more erratically—sometimes one extra, sometimes two fewer, and so on.

From a metacognitive perspective, the lesson served several functions. First it led the children to expect a certain set of circumstances—a candy bar for each person. Second, the conflict was made, perhaps painfully, obvious. Now the children were forced to examine their previous strategy—blind distribution (Brown [1978] talks about blind rule-following in LD youngsters with metacognitive problems)—and come up with another strategy. The distributor on day 2 found a solution that suited him—taking his first and being happy. But he soon found that others could use that strategy, too, and one day he went without. Eventually the group took to counting all the candy bars first and the number of students second, then tried breaking off the right number of pieces for each person. Of course the inevitable happened, and there was a veritable chorus of "he got more than me." To be sure, at this point some instruction on fractions was needed. With the established "metacognitive set" or readiness to learn and the appropriate information, however, the group had a very good beginning in learning fractions.

What was valuable, metacognitively, about the lesson was not the group activity. That was designed originally for another purpose and in this case was instrumental in establishing the conflict. There are more individualistic ways of doing this, as well, however. Consider an example in computations. The teacher who knows that children have difficulty in their first carrying and borrowing experiences might take these steps. First, even at the earliest levels, have the child estimate the answer:

3 and 4 are about ____

One way to encourage estimation and *not* counting and *not* rote computation is to say the numbers to the child or display some objects, but to take them away again quickly and ask the students to "guess" immediately. Then they can check their guesses computationally and with concrete materials. This way, the teacher sets up the estimating strategy and also encourages a checking procedure. Once this is established, the child can apply the strategy for a while through all kinds of problems:

$$
\begin{array}{cccc}
12 & 9 & 13 & 13 \\
+\ \ 3 & -\ 6 & -\ 1 & +\ 12 \\
\hline
\end{array}
$$

Eventually the learner will confront something like this:

$$
\begin{array}{c}
15 \\
+\ 26 \\
\hline
\end{array}
$$

Left to his own devices, he will probably come up with 311 by adding either from the left or from the right. If he has been following the estimate-check routine, however, he will have seen the contradiction. Now he knows that this problem must call for some other strategy than the one he has applied to all problems until this time. This is the proverbial teachable movement.

Inherent in this approach is the role of conflict or contradiction. This means the children cannot be protected from their errors. Since this is dangerous ground, a few cautions are necessary. Certainly, the previous statement does not mean to imply that children should be allowed to make errors and practice them until they become yet another basis for blind rules or automatic responses. Also, children should *not* be humiliated by defeat. Remember that in our last example, the child had a string of successes before experiencing that first conflict. This is necessary, first, for the emotional and motivational well-being of the child and, second, for the cognitive paradigm we are attempting to create. That is, there would have been no conflict without the prior existence of a strong confidence in the original strategy. Nevertheless, unless the child is allowed to make *some* errors, he never has the personal experience of realizing that his existing set of strategies is not enough and that he needs to figure out, or needs the teacher to help him figure out, what comes next.

SUMMARY

To meet the metacognitive needs of the LD child, then, mathematics instruction should encourage the child to be actively involved in thinking through problems, to be flexible, and to self-evaluate. An appropriate analogy is the way young children often are taught to swim. The swimming instructor stands with her hands held out near the child. But as the child gets closer and closer to his target, the instructor, she moves very gradually away. The child's target is slightly elusive. As a result, there is always a little reaching, a little struggling required of the child. Metacognitively, this is an ideal state for the learner. The teacher, then, needs to strike a delicate balance between keeping the student involved and active but not placing the object of the lesson too far beyond the learner's grasp.

REFERENCES

Arbitman-Smith, R., & Haywood, C. (1980). Cognitive education for learning disabled adolescents. *Journal of Abnormal Child Psychology, 8*(1), 51–64.

Aushuhel, D.P. (1968). *Educational psychology: A cognitive view*. New York: Holt, Rinehart & Winston.

Bar-Hillel, M., & Falk, R. (1982). Some teasers concerning traditional probability. *Cognition, 11*, 109–122.

Brown, A.L. (1978). Knowing when, where and how to remember: A problem of metacognition. In R. Glaser (Ed.), *Advances in instructional psychology* (pp. 77–163). Hillsdale, NJ: Lawrence Erlbaum.

Burger, A.L., Blackman, L.S., Clark, H.T., & Gordon, R. (1982). *The far generalization of visual analogies strategies in impulsive & reflective EMRs*. Paper presented at the Gatlinburg Conference, Gatlinburg, TN.

Cawley, J.F., Fitzmaurice, A.M., Goodstein, H.A., Lepore, A.V., Sedlak, R., & Althaus, V. (1976). *Project Math*. Tulsa, OK: Educational Progress Corporation.

Cherkes-Julkowski, M.G., Guskin, S., Schwarzer, C., & Okolo, C. (1982). *Attitude formation: A case of loose-logic*. Paper presented at the 6th Congress of the International Association for the Scientific Study of Mental Deficiency, Toronto, Canada.

Cox, L.S. (1975). Systematic errors in the four vertical algorithms in normal and handicapped populations. *Journal of Research in Mathematics Education, 6*, 202–220.

Damon, W. (1981). Exploring children's social cognition on two fronts. In J.H. Flavell & L. Ross (Eds.), *Social cognitive development* (pp. 154–175). Cambridge: Cambridge University Press.

Feuerstein, R., Rand, Y., & Hoffman, M. (1979). *The dynamic assessment of retarded performers: The learning potential assessment device, theory, instruments and techniques*. Baltimore: University Park Press.

Flavell, J.H., & Wellman, H.M. (1977). Metamemory. In R.V. Kail & J.W. Hagen (Eds.), *Perspectives on the development of memory & cognition*. Hillsdale, NJ: Lawrence Erlbaum.

Fuson, K.C., & Richards, J. (1979) Children's construction of the counting numbers from a spew to a bidirectional chain. Unpublished manuscript, Northwestern University.

Goodstein, H., Cawley, J.F., Gordon, S., & Helfgott, J. (1971). Verbal problem solving among EMR children. *American Journal of Mental Deficiency, 76*, 238–241.

Greenspan, S. (1979). Social intelligence in the retarded. In N. Ellis (Ed.), *Handbook of mental deficiency, psychological theory and research* (2nd ed., pp. 483–532). Hillsdale, NJ: Lawrence Erlbaum.

Heider, F. (1958). *The psychology of interpersonal relations.* New York: Wiley.

Kuhn, T.S. (1977). A function for thorough experiments. In P.M. Johnson-Laird & P.C. Wason (Eds.), *Thinking* (pp. 264–273). New York: Cambridge University Press.

Lester, F.D., & Garofalo, J. (1982). *Metacognitive aspects of elementary school students' performance on arithmetic tasks.* Paper presented at the meeting of the American Educational Research Association, New York.

McGuire, J. (1982). *An investigation of attributional responses among mildly retarded, learning disabled, low achieving and high achieving students following success and failure on achievement tasks.* Unpublished doctoral dissertation, University of Connecticut, Storrs.

Radatz, H. (1979). Error analysis in mathematics education. *Journal of Research in Mathematics Education, 6*, 202–220.

Radatz, H.R. (1980). *Fehleranalysen In Mathematikunterricht* [Error analysis in mathematic instruction]. Braunschweig/Wiesbaden, West Germany: Vieweg and Sohn.

Reid, O.K., & Hresko, W.P. (1981). *A cognitive approach to learning disabilities.* New York: McGraw-Hill.

Short, E.J., & Ryan, E.B. (1982). *Metacognitive differences between skilled and less skilled readers: Remediating deficits through story grammar and attribution training.* Paper presented at the meeting of the American Educational Research Association, New York.

Weiner, B. (Ed.) (1974). *Achievement motivation and attribution theory.* Morristown, NJ: General Learning Press.

Chapter 6

Information Processing: A Cognitive View

Miriam Cherkes-Julkowski

Learning disabilities are defined as disorders of various kinds that impede the child's reasoning, memory, or achievement of skills and information. To the extent that the teacher understands these disorders, he or she will be effective in helping the youngster compensate and become an efficient learner. Let's assume, for example, that a teacher of youngsters, some or all of whom are learning disabled, is confronted with two children who are having some difficulty with solving word problems. Let us assume, further, that the problems in question all require three steps in their solution. One step requires addition with renaming, one subtraction with renaming, and one simple division. One approach to helping these students is to assume that, since they both have the same problem, they both require the same instruction. Instruction might proceed, then, by demonstrating how such a problem might be approached. This is a task analysis or a task-oriented approach. Another approach is to ask, for each child, "What is the source of the problem?" For one of our youngsters the problem could be at the level of renaming. For the other, it might be difficulty in coordinating so many steps in the solution process. The kind of intervention eventually provided will depend upon the exact nature of the original problem. In our example, one child would receive intensive instruction in place value. The other would receive some help with organizational problems.

STRATEGIES FOR LEARNING

The focus in this chapter, then, is on the various strategies that influence learning, where they can go wrong, and how teachers can begin to help students compensate for strategy problems. This is, however, not the simple task it might appear to be. The teacher will need to consider which strategies or which forms of processing information are required by a given task. If it is a mental computations task, memory processes are required. If it is a problem-solving task, certain forms of reasoning and logic will be required. He or she will also need to recognize that strategies seldom if ever are selected and exercised in isolation. That is, problem solving may require specific forms of reasoning, but it also requires memory of previously learned things as well as attention to the task and motivation, to name a few.

The cognitive view that forms the basis for this chapter and this book suggests that thinking and learning are not processes that proceed in a step-by-step, one-strategy-at-a-time fashion. Instead these processes consist of a more holistic way of conceptualizing and, thus, learning. This chapter, then, needs to begin with some explanation of terminology and a clear statement of what cognitive approaches imply for learning and teaching mathematics. This is a brief but necessary diversion before getting into some specific problems in processing mathematics information and what can be done about them instructionally.

INFORMATION PROCESSING

To begin with, the phrase *information processing,* which names this chapter, needs to be explained. The term was originally applied to early computer simulation models of how the mind works. These models are now more often referred to as artificial intelligence, or AI, models. Regardless of the language, the concept likens the workings of the human mind to the processing mechanisms of a computer. Just as a computer takes in data—one piece of information at a time, albeit very rapidly—so does the human mind, according to this model, receive consecutive, disparate pieces of information. Once "input," the information is processed, again sequentially, according to whatever program is appropriate. So, for example, the human mind or the computer can be fed a list of numbers. The system already has within it, let's assume, a program for adding and for dividing. We can tell our system, then, first to use its program for adding, get a total, then divide by the total number of units added, and thus obtain an average. What characterizes the human or machine approach in this example is the linear, sequential flow of ideas and processes. First, each item of data is considered separately. Second, each operation or strategy is applied separately, one after the other, in step.

Bits, Bytes, and Mind

Among the earliest conceptualizers of the computer simulation, information-processing model were Miller, Galanter, and Pribram (1960). In the past decade they have changed their thinking dramatically. They no longer promote the one-step-at-a-time model that fits machine processing. Instead, they acknowledge that something much more complex happens when the human mind processes information. Pribram (1975), for example, compares the working of the mind to that of holography. Holography creates an image, literally a three-dimensional photograph, through the use of laser technology. An early popular use of holography was to display new model cars. The holograph looks like a small plastic model of a car. When the onlooker stands on one side of the image, he sees the opposing side of the model, a little of the front, and so forth. On the other side, another perspective is evident. Nevertheless, the image is only an image; no solid object exists. Pribram explains that the mind works in a similar fashion. Several processes are activated *at once*. One strategy projects one aspect of the situation, another strategy projects still another aspect, and so on, until various projections create in the mind a whole image similar to the holograph of the model car. The important point for our discussion of information processing in learning disabilities is that although it is essential to tease out separate strategies for learning, to understand them better and to understand their malfunction, this separation is artificial. When the child learns—disabled or not—according to the cognitive view, he or she will not do so by employing separate strategies, each in isolation.

It is possible, though, that a disability lies within only one or within some combination of strategies for any given child. It is important, therefore, for the teacher of the learning disabled (LD) child to be aware of the numerous strategies involved in learning and how they can affect instruction in mathematics. Strategies for learning can be grouped largely into the following categories: selective attention, long-term memory, working memory, sustained motivation, organization, and logical or loose-logical forms of thought. The term *loose logic* and what it means for teaching math to LD youngsters is explained more fully in a later section of this chapter. Briefly, the term refers to forms of logic children typically use that may not be totally valid.

When problems in attention are discussed in terms of the LD child, they often are associated with short attention span or distractibility. Short attention span is the inability to sustain attention to a task over a period of time. Although this can be a problem in itself, it should not be confused with other issues. For example, it is not uncommon for an LD child to do one math problem, get it right, begin the next, and then begin to play with things near his desk or get up and walk around and get involved with something else. If that same child can play in the sandbox or play ball or do a drawing for an extended period of time, his problem is not one of attention span but, perhaps, one of sticking to a math task that he finds either uninteresting or overly challenging. For the child who can pay attention for a while but does not in the context of math instruction, one approach is to begin to present math concepts in areas that are of high interest to the student. Thus, the youngster who likes cars might have the assignment to look at car advertisements in the local newspaper and compare prices of various 1-year-old cars. Or the student who enjoys cooking might learn fractions or measurement in that context. At the same time, however, instruction will need to include some effort to help the child sustain attention even in less motivating situations. Behavior modification programs based on gradually increased attention periods are the most direct approach. It is also useful to vary the kind of activity frequently for this kind of child. So he might be asked to do work sheets for ten minutes, then to construct a model of something, then to move around and take some measurements, and so forth. This way he shifts, not from an assigned task to an unassigned one, but from one assigned task to another.

The child who shifts attention when he finds a problem overly challenging is another kind of problem. This kind of youngster is often described as a passive learner or a learner with a low tolerance for frustration. Rather than attempt to process information in various ways, he is more likely to wait until someone explains how to do it. In more extreme cases the child can refuse even to attempt to do any kind of task or enter into any kind of situation that could potentially cause discomfort. This can occur even in cases where the child is quite able to do what is asked of him. Nevertheless, if concentration or initial frustration is involved, the child may still retreat. The immediate solution will need to involve some approach that eases the child into the process of attending long enough to do the task or solve the problem. At first this means, most probably, continuous positive feedback for things the child does do well and on which he spends some time and energy. Feedback should praise the sustained efforts perhaps even more than the outcome. So, if the child will not use blocks to add simple computations with sums less than 10 but she will play with cups and spoons in the sandbox, she may be encouraged first to put 2 cups of sand in the pile, then to watch the teacher put 1 more cup in the pile, and then to add up the number of cups. These same cups might be used as materials, initially, in computation procedures. At some point, however, such a learner will need to come to the awareness that some discomfort or challenge is inherent in any learning situation. That is, *all* learning involves confronting something new for which there is no immediate solution. The instructional goal is for the teacher to direct the child to the point where he associates initial problems or initial frustration with eventual success. This way the problem becomes a challenge, and its solution becomes a personal achievement for the learner. In fact, behavior modification programs suggest exactly the same thing. The recommended behavior modification continuum of reinforcement is to begin with a continuous positive reinforcement schedule. This has the effect of building up a history and, therefore, expectancy of success. If reinforcement stops at this point, however, the trained behavior will disappear very quickly. To sustain the behavior, the continuous reinforcement schedule will have to be followed by some kind of intermittent schedule. During intermittent reinforcement, not every correct response is rewarded. This way the child begins to associate unrewarded attempts with eventual success rather than with failure or intolerable discomfort. The teacher of preschool and early elementary school LD children is most likely to confront this kind of problem. For these children it is often their first experience in a highly demanding situation.

The kind of LD child who displays this pattern of unsustained attention has also been described as passive. Such a child simply does not actively or deeply think about, or process, what he is learning. If the meaning, or one of the meanings, of the experience is obvious to him, he acknowledges it and might remember it, if it is presented in a similar context next time. So he might learn how to carry in addition according to the standard algorithm:

$$\begin{array}{r} {}^{1}13 \\ + 29 \\ \hline 42 \end{array}$$

If he is presented with work sheets consisting of problems in exactly this format, he will most likely achieve a 100 percent correct solution. If, however, he is given a slightly different format, such as:

$$13 + 29 \text{ or } \begin{array}{r} 10 + 3 \\ + 20 + 9 \\ \hline \end{array}$$

he may not realize what is required. And if he cannot do this, he is unlikely to understand the implications of carrying for what they suggest about borrowing.

Deep processing, then, requires that the child go beyond the learning of correct performance. She must virtually (if subliminally) ask herself, "What does this mean to me? How does this fit into what I already know? What do I already know that helps me to make sense out of this new stuff?" Once she has gone through these procedures, she has effectively imposed her own meaning on the material. She has interpreted it in the context of what she can command and thus can command this new thing as well.

INTERROGATIVE STRATEGY

But what about the LD child who fails to do all this? An intervention that has been very effective is called the interrogative strategy (Borkowski & Cavanaugh, 1979). The goal is to provide the disordered learner with what he is unable to provide for himself. Since he does not interrogate himself in the manner just suggested, the teacher can do it for him. Consider the example of the LD adolescent who is being taught about double-entry bookkeeping or balancing a checkbook. To succeed, he must learn the concepts, if not the words, *credits* and *debits*. After an initial presentation and demonstration of what these are and how the system works, the teacher can begin an interrogative intervention. It might proceed as follows:

- In what way is the effect of a debit like subtraction?
- Why do you think credits are more like addition than subtraction?

Successive questions will depend on how the student answers these. Note that the questions *give* the learner all the information he needs. He is not required to discover the relationship between debits and subtraction, only to interpret it in his own context.

Although the passive learning problem described here is not a problem of attention to external cues, it is a problem of actively attending to the preexisting internal knowledge structure of the child. Because the disorder is so covert and only subtly manifested, it is one of which the teacher of the LD child should be especially wary.

Distractibility is another often-cited attentional problem of LD youngsters. It is the tendency to be drawn by first one thing and then another. The child who is distractible has no control over where his attention goes. He cannot block out or inhibit things that interfere with the task at hand. Viewed from a slightly different perspective, this kind of LD child cannot disregard aspects of a situation that are irrelevant or not central to what he is supposed to be learning. The problem for the child, then, is to be able to focus his attention selectively (Ross, 1976). Rather than trying to look at all aspects of a problem or a situation, he needs to decide what is critical or what is really relevant (Zeaman & House, 1979). Failure to focus attention selectively can result in an overload of information that is just too confusing. Even more problematic is the possibility of focusing on misleading or unimportant aspects of a problem that simply lead to wrong answers and faulty concepts. An example of the first case, the lack of focus resulting in overload, could involve a measurement problem of the kind:

> Mrs. Jones wants to carpet her entire living room floor. It is 18 feet by 20 feet.
> The carpet can be bought in square yards at $20.00 for each square yard.
> How much will Mrs. Jones need to pay?

Since this problem gives lots of information and implies the need to derive even more information during intermediate steps, the youngster will need to be able to focus his attention on each necessary step. He will need to recognize that he cannot do the whole problem at once, that some information in the problem is unnecessary during certain steps in the solution, and that he will need to ignore that information until it is useful. The second case, the problem of focusing on misleading or irrelevant aspects of the situation, might arise in problems that require the youngster to decide if he has enough, not enough, or too much information to solve a problem. Some of the problems in Project Math (Cawley, Fitzmaurice, Goodstein, Lepore, Sedlak, & Althaus, 1976) are designed to help learners recognize and avoid distractors.

In both cases, what the effective learner will need to do is scan the problem. She will need to look it over completely, noticing more if not all of what is involved. At this point she is ready to decide what is most critical for the first step, to focus on that, and to avoid systematically what is not central to that part of the solution. Instructional interventions to achieve this need to ensure that the learner peruses the entire situation first and that she does not dwell too long on too much information but, instead, decides on a reasonable focus and begins to pursue that. One way to encourage the child to scan the entire problem first is to present one piece of information at a time. In the previous measurement problem, each piece of information could be written on a separate index card or piece of paper:

> Mrs. Jones wants to carpet her entire living room. It is 18 feet × 20 feet.

> The carpet can be bought in square yards

at $20.00 for each square yard.

How much will Mrs. Jones need to pay?

By seeing one card displayed at a time, the child is able, in the absence of distractors, to attend to each separate item of information. She is also forced to wait before beginning to concentrate on any one aspect as most important or as first, second, or third. Next the learner may be encouraged to arrange the cards in the order in which they need to be considered. Then the task would be to do the computation implied by the information on each successive card until the final answer is derived.

There are times when the teacher may want to circumvent an LD child's attentional deficits. These include situations during which the teacher would like the child, not to learn how to attend, but to get the right answer as efficiently as possible. Consider the case of the child who has had some difficulty understanding place value and its implications for renaming. He can get neither the computational algorithm for renaming nor an understanding of what is actually being carried or borrowed. This child's attention could be directed to the different values of the different places by color coding. In the problem:

$$\begin{array}{r} 358 \\ + 679 \\ \hline \end{array}$$

the numbers in the ones column might be written in red, the tens column in blue, and the hundreds column in green. When 8 and 9 are combined to make 17, the 7 is written in red and the 1 is carried and recorded in blue. When the 1, 5, and 7 are combined to make 13, the 3 is written in blue, the 1 carried this time in green. This way, some attention is drawn to the fact that the two carried 1s are different. Exactly how they are different will require further instruction.

MEMORY

Attentional problems are not the only ones that LD children may suffer in learning of mathematics. Memory problems are cited at least as often as sources of LD problems. Since memory is not a simple, unitary process but rather a complex of component processes, memory problems can occur at any point within the system. The most widely accepted breakdown of the memory system is its division into two primary components: long-term memory and short-term, or working, memory. Long-term memory refers to the store of knowledge a learner has managed to acquire and to the network or idiosyncratic structure of that knowledge store. For example, suppose that two learners have committed the concept of place value to memory. Both, then, have similar knowledge. The structure of that knowledge or the things with which it is associated, however, can vary. In our example, one person may have learned place value in the context of money and making change. His concept, then, is bound up in this network of associations. The other person may have learned place value in a more abstract base-ten versus base-two system. This person has a different network of associations with the concept at hand.

Since the process of learning consists of fitting new information into the existing structure of knowledge already stored, it is critical that some harmony exist between a learner's knowledge structure and the to-be-learned material. At the long-term memory stage, then, the greatest potential impairment to learning is a misfit between the child's present knowledge structure and what is to be learned. For this reason mathematics programs for LD youngsters have stressed carefully sequenced programs that provide the learner with appropriate prerequisites and frames of reference. For the LD child who has not had the advantage of such a systematically designed longitudinal and cumulative curriculum, careful diagnosis is critical.

In this context diagnosis refers specifically to the identification of the knowledge structure of the learner. Reconsider the example of the LD child who has some practical knowledge of place value in the context of money and changemaking. He also can add and subtract without decimals. His carrying in addition is accurate, although apparently mechanical. He makes common borrowing errors in subtraction, such as always subtracting the smaller digit from the larger regardless of their positions and always subtracting a zero from the other digit, also regardless of position. Such a background suggests a knowledge structure that looks like this:

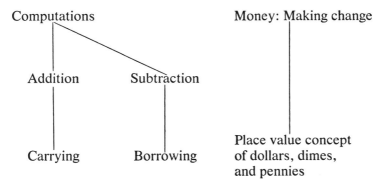

In this case the child's knowledge structure suggests a very specific route for instruction. Since he seems to have a beginning conceptualization of place value in the context of money but fails to demonstrate this same understanding in computational renaming, money provides a strong basis for instruction. The procedure, then, would be to use money computations to teach the role of place value in other computations. This may require instruction in decimals, which, although not in the traditional sequence, could certainly be done at least superficially. Or the decimal problem could easily be circumvented by dealing with hundreds of pennies, tens of pennies, and so forth. In any case the goal is to build a bridge within the existing network, thus maximizing the use of preexisting knowledge and making learning more efficient, meaningful, and permanent. The newly achieved network and its implications for future instruction may be depicted as in Figure 6-1.

With the exception of these considerations about the contents of the long-term memory store, it is generally accepted that disorders in learning seldom occur at this level of processing. Problems occur, rather, in the process of getting information to the point where it can be placed appropriately in the network. Information can be assigned to this long-term store only when the learner has been able to figure where it fits into the present structure. To do this, he must understand the new material well enough to see what role it plays in his larger organization of things. But all this takes time and some working over of the new information to be learned. This is the function of working memory and the source of a great many problems for LD youngsters.

It is during the working memory stage that new information is initially processed. Until this point incoming information is foreign. The learner has no immediate understanding of it as he would with old, familiar, already learned material. At first he has only a sensory impression of what he has just seen or heard. Now it is the learner's task to hang onto that initial impression and begin to make some sense out of it. Sense, however, consists of exactly what is missing at this processing stage. Sense would consist of either an obvious relationship within the aspects of the new, still foreign information or an obvious relationship between that information and the learner's knowledge structure.

The Importance of Meaning

In other words the information presented to a youngster will only be learned if it is meaningful in some way. That meaning might be made apparent in the materials used in instruction. An example is teaching equivalent weight measurement using a balance scale. The equation of 16

Figure 6-1 Individualized Approach to Instruction That Maximizes Previous Learning

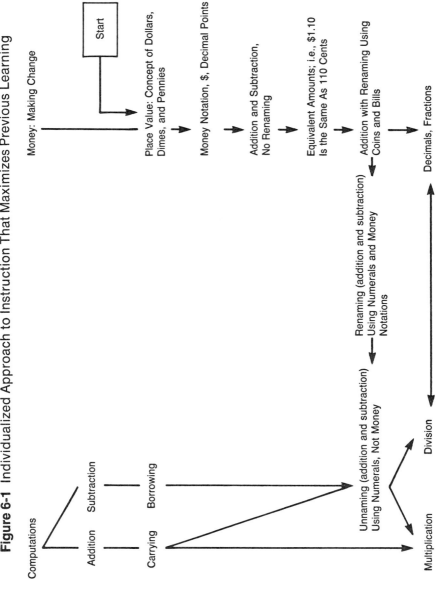

ounces with 1 pound can be shown directly by placing 16 1-ounce units on one side of the scale and one 1-pound unit on the other. This approach attempts to make the presentation display the basic relationship. Instruction may also place the emphasis within the context of the learner's background. In the preceding example, instruction may rely on previous experiences with equivalence and balancing. The teacher might ask the youngster to begin by describing things that he knows are equivalent but not exactly the same. Things that may be familiar to students are 2 small candy bars and 1 big one, ice cream and cookies and an ice cream sandwich, or more academic experiences, such as two 5s and one 10 or 12 inches and 1 foot. Instruction depends on the relationship of equivalence already existing for that youngster.

Working memory, then, involves the processing of not-yet-meaningful information until it can be stored in some sensible way. There are, however, limits to the amount of disconnected, unrelated information units that any individual can process. The average adult is thought to be able to handle 5 to 9 bits at a time. The early elementary school child is usually expected to be able to handle 3 or 4 units at a time. The greater the capacity for information, the greater the capability to learn more information, to learn more efficiently, and to be able to see the complexities among interrelationships. Capacity, however, depends on at least three critical factors: (1) developmental levels, (2) preexisting knowledge structure, and (3) disorders in processes that serve to increase actual capacity. Since the influence of developmental level is discussed in Chapter 4 in this text, no further discussion is required here. It is important to remember, however, that LD youngsters are described frequently as developmentally delayed in one or more areas of mathematics or any other content area. Developmental influences on capacity, then, are critical for the teacher of the LD youngster to consider.

Knowledge structure influences capacity in much the same way developmental level does. That is, the less naive the learner is about the aspect of math being taught, the more able he or she will be to cope with greater amounts of information at a given time. For example, assume that our student has been asked to learn and remember the following:

$$7 \quad 5 \quad 4 \quad 6 \quad 2$$

The learner who is naive about two-, three-, four-, and five-digit numerals will have five separate, disconnected numerals to remember. The demands on her capacity, then, are relatively high. The informed learner who already knows about five-digit numerals will be able to perceive this configuration as 75,462, will think of it as a single piece of information, and thus will have capacity to spare. Somewhere in between is the youngster who knows about two- and three-digit numerals and will group or chunk this information into two units: 75 and 462 or 754 and 62. This way, knowledge structure can influence the capacity of the learner directly. One kind of LD youngster, in fact the most common type, is said not to be *learning* disabled at all but has serious gaps in background that he needs to complete for further learning. For such a youngster, attention to his already existing knowledge structure and to providing the necessary background is critical. Suggestions for this have already been discussed.

Just as knowledge structure serves as a means to increase capacity, so do other processes. In the same way that knowledge structure compresses information by organizing it into larger units, working memory processes employ different organizational strategies, also with the goal of reducing or managing information load. What is critical about all the strategies discussed here is that they rely on organization to reduce the amounts of separate bits of information to be managed and to make the information more meaningful and, ultimately, more available to the long-term memory store. Strategies for organization become critical considerations whether the youngster is required to use memory or any other learning process.

Clustering

One kind of organizational strategy that has been used effectively with handicapped learners is called clustering, grouping, or sorting. The simplest case of grouping has already been suggested. Consider again the case in which we have asked a youngster to remember 75462. If our learner does not know place value yet, he will not be able to group the numbers in the efficient way already suggested. The teacher, however, can group the numbers for him by simply presenting them in the following way:

$$7\ 5 \qquad 4\ 6\ 2$$

This, in combination with rehearsal or repetition, will almost inevitably ensure retention in the working memory store. This is a logical approach for the memory of telephone numbers, but it is useful for almost nothing else. Since this list of numbers has no meaning, it cannot be understood. There are other forms of grouping, however, that are much more meaningful. At early developmental levels children are often asked, for example, to use attribute blocks or picture cards to group by category. Such activities include grouping first large shapes versus small ones:

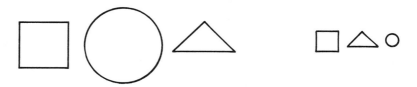

and then perhaps triangles versus circles:

Grouping and regrouping have obvious implications for place value as well. The teacher of the LD child will need to remember that such a learner is likely not to organize items this way without some prompting. So for this youngster, more frequent and more explicit grouping experiences should be provided. In the place value example, one important application is to demonstrate the idea of multiple groupings. The goal is for the child to understand that 284 can be grouped as:

2 hundreds	8 tens	4 ones
1 hundred	18 tens	4 ones
1 hundred	16 tens	24 ones
24 ones	1 hundred	16 tens

Mnemonic Devices

Another form of grouping that aids learning is the mnemonic device. Mnemonics link information in some convenient, easy-to-remember way. The computation of quadratic equations of the kind

$$(a + b)(c + d) =$$

is sometimes aided by the mnemonic device FOIL: multiply the *first* (F) of each multiple *(ac)*, then the outer (O) numerals *(ad)*, then the inner (I) *(bc)*, and then the last (L) *(bd)*. The solution looks like this:

$$ac + ad + bc + bd$$

Rhymes are sometimes used to help remember rules. Another approach is to formulate a sentence using the initial letters of sequences to remember. Mnemonic devices are most suitable when some arbitrary information has to be remembered.

The optimal instruction for LD youngsters, however, will avoid the need for superficial groupings whenever possible. Instead, students should be encouraged to organize information in some way that has real meaning for them. One technique used by some successful learners is imagery. An example follows of a task that can be facilitated if a child creates an image like the following:

> Mary is taller than Jane
> Jane is taller than Sue.

If the handicapped learner is given just this information, he is likely not to conclude automatically that there is an identifiable relationship between Mary and Sue and that he can know what it is. With the instruction to draw a picture of the three girls, however, the youngster is encouraged to integrate all the information into one single image. The example demonstrates how imagery can be used in situations that involve the principle of transitivity (for example, $A < B, B < C : A < C$). Although this is a valuable logical and mathematical principle, it is not the only case where imagery can improve the performance of an LD youngster. In any word problem, it makes sense to advise the learner with difficulty organizing information to create an image of the situation or draw a picture of it. This way he is compelled to set the various separate details into a connected, integrated theme. An example of a word problem that lends itself nicely to this kind of instruction is:

> Five boys wanted to have pizza for lunch. Two of them said they could eat a half pizza each. One said he would like two-thirds of a pizza. Another asked for one-fourth, and the last asked for one-third. How many pizzas will they need to order?

This approach has implications for measurement and geometry as well.

ORGANIZATIONAL DISORDER

What seems to underlie memory problems experienced by LD youngsters is a general disorder in organizing or managing information. Problems in organization, however, are not limited only to situations that require immediate processing or long-term memory. Piaget and other developmentalists have done much to demonstrate that learners have a basic set of organizational rules that allow them to understand their own individual experiences. Young children, according to developmental theory, have a more limited and more concrete set of rules for structuring experience than do older children. Whatever the set of rules a youngster has available, those are the ones she can and will use whenever she learns or reasons, whatever the context. It is important to know, then, which rules or procedures for processing information a child has. It is the teacher's goal to help the children apply their existing rules to as many situations as possible, as well as to build on existing rules to encourage more advanced, more complex forms of processing.

The set of rules Piaget has used as the model for reasoning in children has been drawn from the set of rules of formal logic. In math, logical rules for class reasoning have been shown to be the basis for the concept of number. Rules for forming classes and drawing inferences about classes of things, however, are just as relevant to any other kind of concept formation in math or in any other area. Classification is certainly relevant when the child learns about classes of shapes in geometry or when he learns about classes and subclasses in, for example, fractions or geometry. The LD child will be helped best by having the opportunity to apply the rule she already can command in one area to other areas as well. For example, the child who has applied class reasoning to the number concept can also apply it to the classification of rectangles and of triangles. She could be led to the realization that squares are subclasses of rectangles and that halves are subclasses of wholes.

Failure to apply logical rules for organizing information, however, is not the only difficulty LD learners are likely to have. They are just as likely to use loose-logical procedures for processing information that are either faulty or biased. Consider first the case of the youngster with some faulty mathematics rules. Faulty rules can roughly be classified in three types: (1) overzealous overgeneralization, (2) blind rule-following, and (3) inadequate exposure. These three categories are distinguished by the situations that are likely to cause them and, therefore, by the kinds of intervention implied by each.

Overzealous Overgeneralization

In the first case, overzealous overgeneralization, it is important to remember that this is a tendency all learners exhibit. It is especially obvious in young children as they begin to talk. Very few observers have failed to be impressed by the tendency of little children to call all four-legged animals "doggies" or "horsies." This is the earliest and perhaps best known case of extending a concept or a rule to more situations than are really appropriate. But adults do it, too, and they do it most frequently when they are just beginning to learn about some new thing (Cherkes-Julkowski, Guskin, Schwarzer, & Okolo, 1982). LD youngsters seem to persist in overgeneralizing to a degree not seen in these other cases. Take the LD child, for example, who has just recently learned how to add one-digit numbers. He can add these kinds of problems without difficulty. In fact his performance is excellent. He has learned his number facts with speed and accuracy. His responses are, in fact, automatic. Now he is given, for the first time, a problem of the sort:

$$\begin{array}{r} 23 \\ +\ 15 \\ \hline \end{array}$$

With the tremendous self-assurance that comes from a solid history of easy success, he proceeds to compute, saying, "3 plus 5 is 8; 8 plus 2 is 10, and 1 more is 11," and writes his answer neatly in the appropriate place. He may even tend to add all the digits automatically when confronted with subtraction or, if he should encounter them, multiplication signs. In some sense this is a positive tendency. The child is not put off by something new. He tries, even though he is not totally familiar with the situation. On the other hand, the LD child may not recognize that this is a different kind of problem. He may not have analyzed the details, the specific demands of this particular item. Instead, he assumes that his one rule will work in all cases. He does not realize that his answer cannot be accurate.

An appropriate intervention for such a problem is to help the child understand what the limits of his concept or rule are. In our example, we can go back to the kinds of problems the child can do—for example, 3 + 5. He should be asked to estimate answers. Since he already knows his facts so perfectly, however, he will not be likely to estimate. The teacher can try a couple of techniques to encourage estimation. One is to give two computations orally and ask the learner to answer immediately which he thinks would be more (or less). For example, the teacher may say, "Which is more—3 + 5 or 4 + 6?" Another approach is to provide three-number additions of the kind 4 + 3 + 2 and ask "about how much" it is. Once estimation is accomplished, the child can be asked to estimate answers to problems of the kind

$$\begin{array}{r} 12 \\ + 3 \\ \hline \end{array}$$

and then

$$\begin{array}{r} 12 \\ + 23 \\ \hline \end{array}$$

Some tricks about rounding off can be introduced. For this, the child should not be allowed to use paper and pencil. The child can be asked, if he had 12 candies and was given 10 more, how many he would have. He can be encouraged to say to himself "12 is 10 + 2; 10 and 10 is 20; 2 more is 2," and so forth. With all these experiences as background, the child can be re-presented with the paper-and-pencil task of computing two-digit numbers, no renaming.

Blind Rule-Following

Blind rule-following is not much different. It implies a more passive, less thoughtful, approach. The LD youngster who manifests this tendency may not be helped by the kind of intervention just described. He has not really understood the first rule well enough to begin to refine it. Instead he has been taught a procedure or rule in the absence of any real, internalized meaning. As a result, he has not been able to analyze why this particular approach is appropriate in this particular situation, nor can he infer for which other problems it might be appropriate and with which modifications. Take the case of borrowing in subtraction. The blind-rule-following child is likely to learn the procedure as taught. She is likely to use it accurately, although it is probably necessary to teach each subrule separately, such as borrowing from a zero and borrowing from multiple zeros, as well as other cases of multiple borrowing. However, she is not likely to generalize the rule spontaneously to borrowing in fractions problems such as:

$$\begin{array}{r} 4\tfrac{1}{3} \\ - 2\tfrac{1}{2} \\ \hline \end{array}$$

Nor is she likely to see the connection between borrowing as learned in basic subtraction with measurement problems of the kind:

2 feet and 5 inches
$$- \text{ 1 foot and 10 inches}$$

The teacher may also expect that after separate procedures are taught for each of these, the blind rule-follower probably will not later see the relationship between them, nor will she make unprogrammed generalizations. So, out of the school context, if she encounters a measurement problem involving weight and requiring borrowing, she may not recognize that she has a rule for doing this.

Any intervention designed for such a problem needs to include instruction that emphasizes the rule's basic meaning and wide applicability. Explicit statements of the rule provide only a rough beginning. Exercises that encourage the child to decide for which problem the rule is appropriate will promote attention to the rule rather than a procedure. In the borrowing example, the learner may be asked at Level 1 to check which ones call for the borrowing rule. A worksheet such as Exhibit 6-1 may be provided.

At Level 2 work sheets may include items that cannot be done at all, such as:

236
$$- \text{ 589}$$

And at Level 3 and higher levels, fraction and measurements examples can begin to be introduced.

Exhibit 6-1 Level 1: Work Sheet for Application of the Borrowing Rule

Name _____
Date _____

| 12 | | 12 | | 283 |
| − 10 | | + 9 | | − 19 |

| 305 | 31 | | 890 | | 802 |
| − 102 | − 20 | | − 32 | | − 89 |

| 113 | 600 | | 800 | | 235 |
| + 285 | − 30 | | − 39 | | − 112 |

Inadequate Exposure

The third kind of faulty rule is closely related to blind rule-following. Often an LD child will tend to focus on one aspect of a situation at the expense of the overall or general display, or she will focus on one aspect that is only incidental and not central to the lesson to be learned. Such a learner has had inadequate exposure to the lesson whether or not the lesson was well planned by the teacher. Aside from the suggestions made earlier about attention focusing, some general guidelines for planning instruction may be helpful. First, it is essential that the learner has the opportunity to experience the full concept in the full range of its examples as well as its counterexamples.

Consider the teacher who has designed a lesson about the basic concepts of sets. She introduced the concept of *all* previously, and now she is attempting to teach the concept *some*. She may draw a picture of a set on the board or a work sheet or make a display using cutouts or shapes. Such a presentation may look like this:

From this point the teacher may offer some examples:

"These are *some*."

"Here are *some,* also."

She may ask Johnny to draw a picture of *some*. He may provide a display like this:

Although these are all correct examples of *some,* this lesson would not necessarily provide adequate exposure to the concept. It would be perfectly valid for the learner to conclude that *some* equals two-ness. To avoid this kind of faulty rule formation to which LD youngsters, in particular, fall prey, it is helpful to include examples of the following kind as *some:*

It is also important to demonstrate that the following are *not some:*

PREFERENTIAL APPROACHES

In addition to faulty approaches to learning, there are also biased or preferential approaches. That is, some learners may "prefer" or have a mind set to add from left to right, or to use multiple additions for multiplication, or to draw pictures to solve problems. For LD children of this sort, it may be necessary to accept their bias and begin instruction within the context of their approach. The alternative is to ignore the child's tendency and to teach him the "proper" procedure or algorithm. This approach, which may be called "algorithmic bigotry," assumes that there is only one right way to do things. This is not necessarily true and is a particularly futile assumption when faced with an LD child who cannot adapt to someone else's way of doing things.

The LD child, for example, who has developed the habit of computing from left to right in addition and subtraction may be allowed to do so, but only in a way that is valid. One technique is to help him compute partial addends much the same way as it's done in multiplication. So 289 + 365 becomes:

$$
\begin{array}{r}
289 \\
+ \ 365 \\
\hline
500 \\
140 \\
+ \ \ 14 \\
\hline
654
\end{array}
$$

Eventually, if the teacher judges it important, the child can be brought to the traditional, right-to-left algorithm.

There are learning preferences that may be more inherent to the LD youngster. The teacher will have to be mindful of these and try to build instruction to appeal to them. One influence over preferred procedures for processing information that has already been discussed is the knowledge structure. There are also those children who prefer to process information verbally rather than spatially, or vice versa. There are those who are characterized as reflective or impulsive or as field dependent (context bound) versus field independent (able to abstract information from its context). These issues belong, however, to the domain of cognitive style and deserve mention here only as another influence over how and why LD children may have idiosyncratic ways of processing information.

Learning disabled youngsters, then, can have one or more of the processing disorders discussed in this chapter. Several ways of coping with various disorders have been suggested. None of these ideas is likely to work unless it is adapted to the particular, idiosyncratic needs of the individual learner. Effective instruction depends on the identification of the exact nature of the problem for any one child. This includes the child's individual history as well as his or her specific pattern of learning strengths and weaknesses. The challenge is to present an appropriate level of math instruction to learners in a way that considers their weaknesses and draws upon their strengths in learning.

REFERENCES

Borkowski, J., & Cavanaugh, J. (1979). Maintenance and generalization of skills and strategies by the retarded. In N. Ellis (Ed.), *Handbook of mental deficiency*. Hillsdale, NJ: Lawrence Erlbaum.

Cawley, J.F., Fitzmaurice, A.M., Goodstein, H.A., Lepore, A.V., Sedlak, R., & Althaus, V. (1976). *Project math*. Tulsa, OK: Educational Progress Corporation.

Cherkes-Julkowski, M.G., Guskin, S., Schwarzer, C., & Okolo, C. (1982). *Attitude formation: A case of loose-logic*. Paper presented at the Sixth Annual Congress of the International Association for the Scientific Study of Mental Deficiency, Toronto, Canada.

Miller, G.A., Galanter, E., & Pribram, K.H. (1960). *Plans and the structure of behavior*. New York: Holt, Rinehart & Winston.

Pribram, K. (1975). *Language of the brain*. Englewood Cliffs, NJ: Prentice-Hall.

Ross, A.O. (1976). *Psychological aspects of learning disabilities and reading disorders*. New York: McGraw-Hill.

Zeaman, D., & House, B. (1979). A review of attention theory. In N. Ellis (Ed.), *Handbook of mental deficiency* (pp. 63–120). Hillsdale, NJ: Lawrence Erlbaum.

Chapter 7

Thinking

John F. Cawley

Thinking is a phenomenon consisting of at least two global processes. One of these processes is the metacognitive act of pondering or deliberation and the setting aside of time to ponder or deliberate. Thinking is also a cognitive function during which many different cognitive acts may be used in varying combinations.

A major question is, "Do we in special education encourage the learning disabled to think, to ponder, and to use a variety of cognitive acts to examine or solve problems?"

Thinking, as the phenomenon is used in the present context, is more than noticing that a child is experiencing difficulty and then prodding the child with statements such as, "You can do it. Think about it. Think harder." Thinking is not encouraged by these types of statements. What is truly happening is that the child is being prodded to provide a correct response, and to do it quickly, because others are waiting or because time is running out.

That we all know what thinking is, is indeed a truism. Yet, as Bourne, Ekstrand, and Dominowski (1971) point out, thinking is one of those mysterious concepts that everyone understands and no one can explain.

Bourne and his colleagues provide an illustration of a mathematician proving a theorem. The mathematician's only observable behavior was a tendency to close the eyes, to cup the hands behind the head, and to make an occasional scribble on a paper. Though these behaviors may be part of the metacognitive process of deliberation, they are not evidence in themselves that cognitive acts are operating on stimuli. What seems to have happened is that our mathematician identified a problem, decided to work on it, organized the relevant information, developed alternatives, decided among them, and then tried them out. This mathematician had skill, possessed knowledge, selected cognitive alternatives, and then demonstrated a willingness to devote the time to the theorem and test his skill, knowledge, and cognitive capability against the problem. In all probability, the solutions will be presented to colleagues and its validity tested against other sources.

If learning disabled (LD) individuals are going to be *thinkers,* they also must have time to think. They must also possess knowledge, demonstrate skill, and experience a variety of activities involving cognitive acts. And they must not associate failure to solve the problem or to arrive at a singular satisfactory solution with inadequacy.

Four factors tend to limit the natural inclusion of thinking in mathematics programs for the learning disabled:

1. The pressure on the teacher or the system to help a child who is behind catch up. This situation leaves no time for thinking.
2. The relationships between stimulus selection (e.g., $2 + 4 =$) and response (i.e., 6) and the rate and associative manner by which these relationships are established can be limiting as well.
3. The practice of increasing response rates. Although high rates of response help maintain on-task behavior and habituate response accuracy, these very desirable achievements may be accomplished in a manner that does not develop meaning and understanding.
4. The instructional materials, which most frequently consist of paper–pencil formats, are drill and practice activities.

It takes time to think. The child who is pondering a choice between vanilla and chocolate ice cream has a problem and needs time to arrive at a solution—and to change his or her mind. In fact, the choice may be made more upon sensory influences than on cognitive influences.

Hildebrandt (1959) puts it nicely:

Seeds do not give evidence of producing shoots or sprouts in the first twenty-four hours after they have been planted. In the same way, one should not be too concerned if students do not respond the moment a new or difficult problem is posed. Problems require a period of time during which they can *germinate* in the subconscious or conscious mind. (p. 378–379).

The learning disabled individual, then, needs time.

Both the child and the school need to recognize that derivation of the correct solutions may require a number of attempts. If attempts reflect a systematic trial-and-error approach, obviously the individual is thinking. Amounts of prior knowledge and experiences will have an impact on the efficiency with which the individual solves a problem or provides a reasonable alternative to a problem.

It was noted in Chapter 1 that the learning disabled seemed to possess a variety of cognitive abilities but tend to be inefficient in their use (Swanson, 1982), or unable to utilize these abilities when necessary (Cermak, 1983), or require more time to master the knowledge and skills needed for thinking. Learning disabled children may be more impulsive than reflective and may not be able to take the time to think. They also seem more inclined to respond rather than taking the time to consider the appropriateness of their responses.

Examine the following:

> Mrs. Koch approached Rick and said, "Rick, how many ways can you represent the number 4?" Rick thought for a moment and replied, "Well, it depends. If you want me to use numerals, then I can write it many ways. I could write 96 minus 92, 95 minus 91, and I could continue on and on. If you want me to use objects or pictures, I could show 3 cats and 1 cat to represent 4 cats. I could show 3 dogs and 1 dog to represent 4 dogs. I could show 3 red chips and 1 blue chip to represent 4 chips. If I use numerals, I can arrange any combination of numerals to represent 4. Every time I do this, I use a different arrangement of the numerals. However, when I use materials such as chips or pictures, I can use the same arrangement (i.e., 3 + 1) but I use different items. So if you want to test my ideas about four-ness, you sort of have to let me know what you have in mind." Mrs. Koch moved away from Rick and went over to Beverly. "Beverly," said Mrs. Koch, "what would you rather have, one-half of something or one-quarter of something?" "Gee," replied Beverly, "I don't know. I'd have to know what the half and what the quarter are half or quarter of. If I could have a half of a dollar or a quarter of a tank of gas for my father's car, I would take the quarter."
>
> Mrs. Koch smiled and walked over to Kathleen and James. "Listen," said Mrs. Koch, "if you wanted to buy some fish and the fish came in two types of packages, one with 3 large fish to make a total of 6 pounds and the other with 9 smaller fish, to make a total of 6 pounds, which would you buy?" Kathleen looked up and said, "If I wanted to make a fish chowder, it probably wouldn't make any difference." "That's right" said James, "but if I was only going to eat some now and some later, I might buy the 9 individual fish so that I could freeze them."

"Good thinking," said Mrs. Koch. "Let's get the rest of the kids over here and talk about this for a few minutes."

Would the LD children you know respond as those in the illustrations? Would you as a teacher include similar experiences in their program?

Thinking, planning to include opportunities for thinking, and providing the opportunities and the time to think are as essential to mathematics proficiency for the learning disabled as is computational efficiency. The knowledge and skill involved in the operations of addition and multiplication should become the foundation for their use and application. They should not be ends in themselves.

No attempt is made to suggest an either–or choice between computation and thinking. Rather, the thrust is to argue for proportionate representation of both. These proportions may direct 90 percent of effort to computation and 10 percent to thinking during acquisition. Once mastery has been attained, the proportionate emphasis may be modified to 50–50 or some other combination. To illustrate:

Computation:
How much is 5 cents and 25 cents?
How much would you have if I gave you a nickel and a quarter?

Thinking:
What would you do if I said, "I will give you a nickel for every quarter you can stand on its edge"?
What would you do if I said, "I will give you a dollar for every quarter you can stand on its edge"?

In the nickel-to-quarter item (I did this on the first day of school each year) children are quick to stand a quarter on edge. Much to their dismay, they learn that "give you" means "I will exchange with you," as you take their quarters and give them nickels.

The same condition does not prevail in the quarter-to-dollar item (I never did this one) because the youngster could end up with either $.75 or $1.25.

Alley and Deshler (1979) indicate that efficient thinking and problem-solving strategies are necessities for the LD adolescent who faces the complex demands of school curricula. These same strategies are necessities for LD children of all ages. Thinking and problem-solving activities should be an integral component of the program throughout school.

Sharma (1984) has shown that the range of mathematics the learning disabled may encounter in the adult world far exceeds the monetary exchanges and related activities that Halpern (1983) feels should be stressed in the school program for the learning disabled. The implication of the

Sharma versus Halpern alternatives seems to be that the more we restrict curricular experiences, the more emphasis we need to place on thinking and learning to learn. If the school does not optimize the knowledge and skill repertoire of the learning disabled, it must provide the individual with the means to acquire needed skills and knowledge independently.

THINKING

This is a chapter about thinking and the inclusion of thinking activities in mathematics programs for the learning disabled. It is a given that knowledge and skill are prerequisites for effective thinking. It is recognized that thinking that is developed from a good base of knowledge and skill can lead to the acquisition of additional knowledge and skill.

Fundamental to the development of a perspective on thinking is the need to differentiate between the terms *concrete* and *abstract*. This is done most effectively by Ausubel and Robinson (1969), who stated:

> Concrete operational stages of cognitive development—that stage in which the child is capable, with the aid of concrete empirical props, of acquiring secondary abstractions and of understanding, using and meaningfully manipulating both secondary abstractions and the relations between them.

> Abstract operational stage of cognitive development—stage in which the individual is capable, without the aid of concrete empirical props, of acquiring secondary abstractions and of understanding, using, and meaningfully manipulating both secondary abstractions and the relations between them.

Notice that each definition encourages understanding, meaning, and relations. They differ primarily in the use of props or symbols. Both stages include opportunities for thinking and support the position that thinking activities can be developed with concrete aids or without them.

The remainder of this chapter is devoted to a presentation of selected perspectives on children's thinking and the development of a set of activities that imply different types or components of thinking for use in mathematics programs for the learning disabled.

PERSPECTIVES ON THINKING

Children's Thinking (Russell, 1956) is a comprehensive summary of research and teaching practices that include associative thinking, concept formation, and creative thinking. Russell feels that perception is vital to thinking. He cites the following as having important implications for mathematics.

Form—congruence, similarity, symmetry
Space—point, size, perspective
Time—speed, time–event relations; length such as day, week, year; measurement, clocks, calendars; sequences, today, tomorrow
Weight—size, sense, mass, density
Number—cardinality, sequencing, relations

Russell stresses the importance of the child's intuitive relations to number. In effect, children think about the concept of number even in situations where their responses may not be appropriate. In one illustration the child says, "I have three pencils" even though the child is holding a set of pencils that are both long and yellow, but not three in number. The teacher should not be concerned when the precardinal child says "three" when holding five. The child's use of three brings number into the language and the experience. What is important is that the child has distinguished one from many and has used a number term to demonstrate an awareness of number. The teacher of the learning disabled should examine the children's language for references to quantitative relationships and expressions. At some later point, after appropriate learning experiences, the teacher can examine these relationships for accuracy. Credit should be differentially given to both levels.

Associate thinking develops through experiences, some presented via directed instruction while others are part of one's natural experiences. Responses are specific and generally predictable. The relations and associations acquired by the child are essential to total growth. Knowing that $2 + 3 = 5$ and not 6 or some other number is an important bit of knowledge. It is important that the concept 2 and the concept 3 are understood and that their relationship to 5 is properly established. Brainard (1983) points out that excessive reliance upon recall to determine that the child knows $2 + 3 = 5$ has its limitations. The child may not recall 5 when given $2 + 3$ but may be capable of determining that 5 is the acceptable response. I have always advocated that LD children would be far better off if they were taught two or three combinations (e.g., 2×6, 3×4, 7×8) and then held accountable for learning others (Cawley, 1984). It makes little sense to force associations through memory activities such as drill and practice—better to learn the concepts via meanings and then habituate them via drill and practice.

Knowing that this ◯ can be called a circle or closed curve and that this ⊂⊃ and this ⬠ are also closed curves is an associative process. However, accepting the proposition that this ∿ and this ── are both curves (*curve* being defined as a set of points [May, 1967]) may not occur as readily.

Conceptualizations and rules enter when the child can accept ◯ , ⬡ , △ , and □ as closed curves (defined as a set of points that form a boundary).

Children associate *xxx* with 3 and *xxxx* with 4 through experience and direct instruction. An extension of these experiences leads to *xxx, yyy,* 222, and *xy2* as also being representative of 3. Other knowledge is required for the child to accept $2\overline{)6}$, $15 - 12 =$, $3\overline{)9}$, and the number of sides to be added to get the perimeter of △ as 3. These different illustrations were likely acquired through associative procedures and, for most LD children, they are likely to be viewed as independent items rather than representations of 3. Thus, it is necessary to move toward concept formation as a process that organizes and unifies.

CONCEPT FORMATION

Concept formation involves inclusion and exclusion. For example, a set of four dogs may be conceptualized as a set of 4 or a set of dogs, the latter developmentally preceding the former. Variations such as substitutions of number or category signal the interpretation being made by the child.

Concepts are formed on the basis of rules or attributes or combinations of both. In some instances concepts are formed by joining actions in which smaller sets are joined to form larger sets. In other instances concepts are formed by sorting actions in which larger sets are sorted into smaller sets. Successful concept formation can be influenced by learner variables, levels of complexity, familiarity, knowledge, and mediational influences such as cognitive style and memory.

Klausmeier, Ghatala, and Frayer (1974) list four levels of concept function:

- Concrete level is inferred when the individual cognizes an object that he has encountered on a prior occasion

- Identity level is inferred when the individual cognizes an object as the same one previously encountered when observed from a different perspective or sensed in a different modality
- Classificatory level is inferred when the individual treats at least two different instances of the same class as equivalent
- Formal level is inferred when the individual can give the name of the concept, can name its intrinsic or societally accepted defining attributes, can accurately designate instances as belonging to a set and can state the basis for their exclusion or inclusion in terms of defining attributes.

Discrimination of things on global or diffuse properties characterizes the concrete level, changes to discrimination of more specific and abstract properties at the identity and classificatory levels, and to discrimination and labeling of all defining attributes at the formal level (Klausmeier et al., 1974). These are important distinctions in mathematics for the learning disabled, for it may be the expected level of attainment that is too difficult, not the concept or its attributes. Conversely, an individual may demonstrate concept attainment at one level (e.g., identity level) and not at another (e.g., formal level). One could err by concluding that adequate performance at any lower level is sufficient to assure proficiency at a higher level. Further, a child could demonstrate formal level proficiency for one concept but not another.

The following are illustrative:

Concrete: recognizes ◯ as circle

▢ as square

Identity: recognizes ▢ as square

◇ as square

Classificatory: recognizes ▢ as square

▢ as square

Formal: symbolizes following as squares ▢ ▫ ▢ ◇

Cueing can be introduced by preparing each match-to-sample tasks as follows:

See this. Find one just like it here.

▢ ▱ ▢ ▭ ◿

See this.   Find one just like it here.

See this.   Find three like it here.

Extending the use of geometric figures to the concept of area, we find the following:

All have areas that are determined by the same rule. The student who learns this rule (i.e., $L \times W = $ area) encounters quite a different problem (Wertheimer, 1959) in determining the area of

and obviously quite another with

and still another with

The aforementioned is not to suggest that all LD youth will successfully attain all the concepts at all the levels across the content areas. It is to say, however, that some will master all and all will master some.

The efforts of Wertheimer are particularly noteworthy and relevant to the learning disabled. To begin with, there is the perceptual difficulty associated with the learning disabled (Glennon & Cruickshank, 1981) and the discrimination required between the rectangle, parallelogram, and trapezoid. Assurance that proper discrimination is taking place precedes cognitive-knowledge-based activities. Sorting, match-to-sample, and two-choice visual discrimination models with congruent and similar stimuli may be used. There is the cognitive act requiring that different approaches be taken to determine the area of these "perceptually similar" but conceptually different figures.

The one thing Wertheimer did was take the needed time. His chapter on the area of a parallelogram is some 65 pages in length and contains numerous steps and substeps.

In developing such an approach to thinking, there is the need for both expository and guided techniques with the learning disabled. The teacher can introduce specific vocabulary (e.g., perimeter, square) and can work with the individual to develop meaning. *Perimeter* can be defined as distance around. *Square,* however, needs a bit more elaboration because *square* has to be conceptualized both as a figure with four sides equal and as a unit within a unit—that is, the unit we use to describe the units that comprise *area*. Distinctions between *perimeter* and *square* must be clearly understood. As these distinctions become clear, the relationship between the perimeter of the square and the area of the square can be developed. When these relationships are fully cognized, the rectangle can be introduced. The individual can be encouraged to explore the relationships between square and rectangle, as shown below.

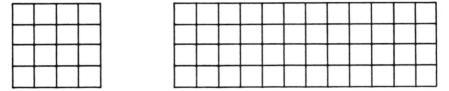

This will provide an opportunity to develop the distinction between $A = S^2$ for the square and $A = L \times W$ for the rectangle. Observe the learner, and look for systematic and logical approaches to the problems. Employ manipulatives, and allow the child to place chips to fill in the areas as shown in the following:

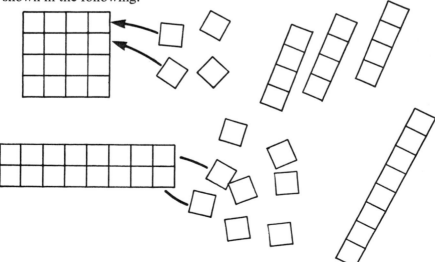

Since the individual is quite likely to understand multiplication before an introduction to the formula for the area of a square, activities can be developed to describe the area of a square as an array. The same is true for the area of a rectangle. Thus, the number of square units in a square region is comparable to the number of units in an array of the same magnitude. This transition via arrays will enable the LD youngster to build upon something that is known (i.e., the concept of arrays) and to apply this knowledge to a specific concept, namely *area*. The youngster can be led to discover the meaning of S^2 as it relates to a square region and the meaning of $L \times W$ as it relates to a rectangular region. This awareness should alert the individual to think about the need to examine different alternatives relative to the computation of the area of the parallelogram when it is introduced. In effect, a measure of cognitive status will be obtained when the parallelogram is introduced. Should the individual arbitrarily select S^2 or $L \times W$ and hold firmly to either of these, he or she would be overgeneralizing and our goal to encourage thinking would not be obtained. Note, we are not as interested in the parallelogram, the square, or the rectangle as we are in concept formation and thinking.

Perceptually the individual must notice the differences between the parallelogram and the rectangle.

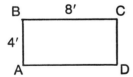 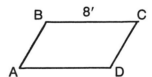

They may see the distances between *AD* and *BC* as being the same or different in each of the figures. These can be determined by formal or informal measurement (e.g., a piece of string) techniques. What is more confusing for the learning disabled is the *AB* and *CD* relationships in each figure. The fact is that the rules and relationships of perimeter and area that were established in the rectangle no longer apply. We need to assist the learner to discover the relationship between *AB* and *CD* in each figure. Ultimately, the learner must realize that *AB* and *CD* in the parallelogram are comparable to the hypotenuse in a triangle. The preferred way to make this known is to measure—initially with nonstandard units such as a piece of string and then, if desired, in standard units with a ruler. The important principle is the notion of differences, not the actual differences.

Construct a rectangle comprised of chips made of triangular pieces.

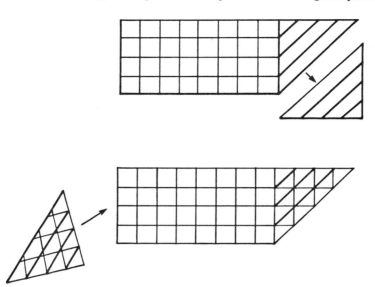

Move the chips, and change the rectangle to a parallelogram. Use many combinations, and have the learners construct many combinations. Ask the learner to show or tell if the total area changes as a result of these movements. Construct parallelograms of the same materials, and convert these back to rectangles. Again, highlight changes or lack of changes in area. What the learner must cognize is that the area itself is invariant. What is needed are different approaches to compute.

Continue to develop concepts of area, highlighting the different arithmetical arrangements among square, rectangle, and parallelogram. Young LD children can observe the teacher rearranging regions. They can construct many diverse regions using the same number of chips. They need not compute. They should become familiar with the invariance of area as the shapes of the regions change.

If desired, continue with triangles, trapezoids, and other figures even using some for which there are no standard terms. Do not, however, approach these in a rote manner for the purpose of getting to computation. Use them conceptually to highlight the similarities and differences in the figures and, where appropriate, in the methods used to compute their characteristics. There may be five or six years difference in age between the youngster who can construct the models and compute the number of squares and the one who understands area and can compute to determine it.

Young LD children can play with and specify many conceptual characteristics of mathematics stimuli. Numerous opportunities should be given to enable them to do so. Given the chance to start young and have regular and systematic opportunities across the age span, LD children will be more sophisticated and practical in both their understanding and applications of mathematics. This will enable them to interact with the symbolic representations of the field, and formal levels of concept formation can be attained.

PRODUCTIVE THINKING

Much of the history of productive thinking is traced to the work of J.P. Guilford (1967). It was Guilford who set forth a major treatise stressing the great diversity in structure of the intellect. And it was Guilford who established a foundation on which the psychologist and the educator could permutate thinking into endless areas of study and application.

Torrance (1965, 1974) stimulated research in the area of productive thinking because he developed instruments to assess different components of productive thinking and laid the foundation for many to develop instructional approaches (e.g., Renzulli & Callahan, 1973).

Interestingly, whereas the field of mental retardation shows a sporadic, but lengthy commitment to inquiry relative to productive thinking, the field of learning disabilities has failed to demonstrate any comparable commitment. By contrast, educators of the gifted have become involved in nearly every facet of research and programming relative to productive thinking. A major question remains unanswered—namely, "If productive thinking is a valid way of examining the developmental characteristics of gifted children, why is it not also a valid field of inquiry among the learning disabled?" It is hoped that the illustrations in this section will lead to further advances in basic and applied research. It may be that the learning disabled manifest considerable latent talent in this domain. What may be limiting to them is not the absence of productive thinking capabilities but, rather, an inability to overcome the effects of mediational deficiencies. It may be, as Reid and Hresko (1981) point out, that the learning disabled lack an efficient and effective control system to edit and direct behavior. These authors point out that individuals learn not only by acting and experiencing the consequences of their action; they also learn by:

- observing and imitating;
- watching demonstrations, listening to explanations, and participating in discussions;

- being cognizant of the need to be active in the learning process; and
- being involved in activities that affect behaviors over the long term.

All the above are representations of the considerations included in the model of productive thinking. The model provides for the integration of directed instruction, contrasts between logical and exact responses and the inclusion of judgment, values, and opinions in a quantitative setting. For purposes of this chapter, attention is directed only to the following facets of productive thinking.

- Convergent thinking or reproduction involves tasks that elicit one single best or appropriate response.
- Divergent thinking or production seeks tasks that encourage variety, differences, and rearrangement of responses.
- Evaluative thinking or production involves judgment, opinion, and values. Evaluative thinking plays a major role in critical thinking and appraisal.

Meeker (1969) makes the point that convergent production is "rigorous thinking." The process involves more than just recall. It may involve problem solving that requires many steps and the analysis and synthesis of considerable information and data. I have a similar view of all three processes. Accordingly, it seems that one must differentiate the knowledge and process requirements when undertaking productive thinking appraisal or instruction.

ILLUSTRATIONS OF PRODUCTIVE THINKING ACTIVITIES

Convergent Thinking

Task 1
See this representation of three:

Find another in the following:

Task 2
See this representation of three: 2 + 1

Find another in the following: | 1 + 2 | 2 + 3 | 2 + 0 |

Each of the preceding required the understanding and application of a principle or rule. In Task 1 the individual had the opportunity to respond with the same number, a greater number, or a smaller number. The cognitively directed child would be guided by number and would select the three squares. The perceptually guided youngster may not analyze for number and may pick the greater number, 4, because the representation is in the form of circles. In Task 2, the commutative property is displayed. It is important that the teacher determine whether the choice is made on the basis of the commutative property—a cognitive choice—or on a basis of there being a 1, a + sign, and a 2—a perceptually directed choice.

Task 3
   Read the problem and give the answer.
   A girl has 3 grapes.
   The girl bought 2 more grapes.
   How many grapes does the girl have now?
Task 4
   Read the problem and give the answer.
   A girl has 3 grapes.
   The girl sold 2 grapes.
   How many grapes does the girl have now?

Each of the preceding requires an understanding of the action denoted by *bought* and *sold*. The two sets of information are exactly the same except as noted by the differences in the two verbs. Each question is worded in a neutral manner and, in a sense, is useless as an aid in this situation. This is quite a different occurrence from that described by Schoenfield (1982) in noting that 97 percent of the word problems in one elementary textbook series could be solved by the key-word method. Convergent production tasks can be developed to integrate other cognitive functions. Meeker's point relative to these tasks being more than recall is readily demonstrated.

Divergent Thinking

Task 5
   See this representation of three:
   Take these materials and make as many
   different representations of three as you can.
Task 6
   See this representation of three:
   Use this set of numbers and make as many
   representations of three as you can.

2 + 1

2, 0, 1, 6

The divergent production in each instance leads to a greater generalization of threeness. Threeness is learned as a concept, not as a single paired associate.

Task 7
  Read the problem. Complete the task as directed.
    A girl has 3 grapes.
    The girl _____ 2 grapes.
    The girl now has 5 grapes.
  Write in as many words as you can to make the outcome true.
Task 8
  Read the problem. Complete the task as directed.
    A girl has 3 grapes.
    The girl _____ 2 grapes.
    The girl now has 1 grape.
  Write in as many words as you can to make the outcome true.

Tasks 7 and 8 involve verbal production. Performance can be judged by fluency, the number of responses; by flexibility, the number of different responses; and by originality, the number of unique responses. Performance is measured by the number and diversity of actions expressed by the children to make each outcome valid. Given that language deficiencies are continually associated with the learning disabled, activities such as these provide opportunities for both language and quantitative needs to be given attention.

Evaluative Thinking

Task 9
  See this representation of three:
  Which of these is a better representation of three?

Task 10
  See this representation of three: $2 + 1$
  Which of these is a better representation of three?

111	$1 + 2$	$15 - 12$

Three factors are included in Task 9. Three is represented sequentially, spatially, and perceptually. In Task 10, three is represented by one three times, by the commutative representation of the standard, and by 15 −

12. All three are situationally the best. For example, 15 − 12 could be the best if one bought 12¢ worth of candy and is awaiting change from 15¢. The development of situations, positions, and alternatives to establish the basis of one's choice is the key factor in this activity. No single choice is the only choice, and each must be seen in its own perspective.

Task 11
Read the problem and complete the task as directed.
The girl had 3 fruits.
She bought 2 pears
        peas
        potatoes
She now has 5 fruits.
Mark the word that shows the better choice and that also makes the outcome true.
Task 12
Read the problem and complete the task as directed.
A girl has 3 fruits.   apples
She sold 2   pears
              peas
              potatoes
She now has 1 fruit.
Mark the word that shows the better choice and that also makes the outcome true.

Tasks 11 and 12 involve conceptualization in that apples and pears have to be identified as elements in the set of fruit. Exclusion or negation is also involved in that peas and potatoes are not part of the set of fruit. Judgment enters when one decides that one fruit is preferred over the other. There is no "better choice" except in the opinion of the individual making the choice or in the specific situation the individual uses to validate the choice. Children should be made aware of the role of judgment and opinion and the influence of quantitative and nonquantitative information in making choices and decisions. Simple activities such as those illustrated are easily incorporated into the program. More sophisticated levels of stimuli can be incorporated into the program for older children. As illustrated previously (Cawley, 1984), evaluative thinking activities can be developed to elicit values and emotions. For example, what if you were asked to explain the feelings in each of the following:

Lola was very happy that she had 3 trout.
Angela was very unhappy that she had 3 trout.

Lola was happy that she had 3 trout.
Angela was very happy that she had 2 salmon.

Lola was unhappy that she had 3 trout.
Angela was unhappy that she had 2 trout.

In the first contrast, Lola was happy and Angela was unhappy, yet each had the same number of trout. Any number of explanations can be elicited from the children to explain the feelings of happiness or unhappiness. In the second situation both the number of fish and the type of fish are different. Here we see the potential for other types of values, tastes, and opinions to enter the discussion. In the third situation, both have the same feeling even though the number of trout differ. Possibly, neither likes trout.

Commercial materials (e.g., Renzulli & Callahan, 1973) offer many opportunities to combine productive thinking with mathematics (see Exhibit 7-1). There does not seem to be any limit on the number of activities that can be incorporated into programs for the learning disabled. Convergent thinking activities must be in the majority, for they provide direction and closure. They do not, however, have to be rooted in recall and rote memory. Convergent thinking activities are directed toward the one or best response, and this can be attained in many ways. Evaluative questions should be used sparingly. They have an element of ambiguity about them, and there are times when children do not have sufficient sophistication or knowledge to understand or tolerate this ambiguity.

TEACHING FOR THINKING

One of the more extensively illustrated sources of thinking activities is *Teaching for Thinking: Theory and Applications* (Raths, Wasserman, Jonas, & Rothstein, 1967). The focus of this resource is a variety of thinking operations and thinking-related activities that are applicable at both the elementary and secondary levels. The authors took an interesting position on thinking and the impact of selected thinking and mediating behaviors on thinking. For example, they indicate that teachers feel many impulsive children "jump the gun" or begin to respond before the question. In effect, the process of thinking is not activated, because the child did not initiate the initial metacognitive act of pondering. Raths et al. (1967) indicate that if these children had more opportunities for thinking, their tendency toward impulsivity would be diminished.

Raths and colleagues also point out that the lack of concentration and attention are both behaviors of concern to teachers. Teachers tell children to concentrate (i.e., ponder) and to think (i.e., the cognitive act), but they fail to differentiate between these phenomena. In effect, teacher monitoring and self-monitoring of attention may not be as effective an approach as is the development of classroom activities requiring thinking operations. This is a most enticing position given the considerable emphasis in special

Exhibit 7-1 Sample of Commercially Available Material

NAME _____ DATE _____

12 FIGURE FAMILIES (A)
 STUDY THE FIGURES BELOW AND GROUP THEM TOGETHER ACCORD-
 ING TO CHARACTERISTICS THEY HAVE IN COMMON. SEE HOW MANY
 GROUPS YOU CAN DISCOVER. YOU CAN USE EACH FIGURE AS MANY
 TIMES AS YOU WISH. SOME EXAMPLES ARE GIVEN BELOW.

$$0 \quad 2 \quad \mathrm{II} \quad \mathrm{I} \quad \bullet$$

$$= \quad \mathrm{M} \quad \sqrt{} \quad ? \quad \text{two}$$

$$\mathrm{S} \quad \mathrm{C} \quad 5 \quad \mathrm{A} \quad \$$$

COMMON CHARACTERISTICS   FIGURES

_____   _____

_____   _____

_____   _____

_____   _____

_____   _____

Source: Reprinted from *New directions in creativity Mark 3* by J. Renzulli & C. Callahan with permission of Harper
& Row Publishers, Inc., ©1973.

education on self-monitoring, cognitive behavior modification, and other strategies designed to help the individual maintain the proper behavioral orientation toward a task.

Teaching for Thinking identifies many thinking operations and provides illustrations for the use of these operations in all subject areas at both the elementary and secondary levels. Table 7-1 contains a listing of some of these operations. Along with the listing is an illustration of the operation using money for the elementary levels and fractions for the secondary levels. Any content may be used.

Table 7-1 Examples of Components of Teaching for Thinking

Operations	Elementary	Secondary
Comparing Identification of similarities and differences among objects, pictures, and symbols in terms of absolute value, temporal qualities, and so forth.	Here is a nickel, a dime, and a quarter. Tell me the ways in which they are alike or different.	Here are some numbers. Tell me ways in which they are the same or different. 20% .50 ¼ 50% .75 ½
Summarizing The narrowing down or delineating of a large amount of information or data.	The class wanted to buy some candy. You checked the price at eight stores. Every store had a different price. What would you tell the class? (Lowest one or two.)	Three stores were having sales on jackets. One store offered 25% discount, another offered ¼ off, and the third had a discount of .25. What would you tell your friends (best buy after you checked original prices and computed).
Classifying The bringing together or sorting of things into groups according to some qualities or rules.	Here are some coins. Group them together so that those that go together are in the same set.	Here are some numbers. Write them in groups so that those that go best together are in the same group. .50 ¼ 20% ½ .25 15% 50% ⅛
Interpreting Explaining the meanings of information or data to self or others.	Three stores were selling the same candy. At one store the candy cost 25¢ for one piece. At another store the candy cost 20¢ for one piece. At another store the candy cost 30¢ for two pieces. Tell the class what this means.	Three stores were selling the same jackets. At one store it cost $40, at another $42, and at another $38. Tell the class what this means.

Table 7-1 continued

Operations	Elementary	Secondary
Criticizing Making judgments or findings, making evaluations.	A person paid 25¢ for one candy. Another person got two of the same candies for 30¢. What do you think about what the first person did?	Two people wanted to buy the same jacket. The newspaper ad showed the jacket cost $38 at one store and $42 at the other. They each went to different stores. Why do you think this happened?
Looking for Assumptions Examining the basis or substance of something that is taken for granted.	A person paid 25¢ for five candies at one store. What do you think each candy cost? Why?	A jacket was for sale at one store for $42. The same jacket was for sale in another store. What do you think it will cost at the second store? Why?
Imaginings Forming ideas about that which is not present or which has not been experienced directly.	You go into a store to buy candy. You have two quarters, one dime, and two nickels. The candy costs 80¢. You mother is outside in the automobile. Tell me what you would do in this situation.	You want to buy a jacket at a store near your home. The jacket costs $42. You only have $40. The same jacket costs $39 at a store four miles away. Tell me what you would do in this situation.
Hypothesizing The making of a statement or prediction about a possible outcome or solution.	A person bought some candy for 25¢ at one store. The person went to another store. What do you think the person will pay at the second store?	A person bought a jacket at 20% discount. The same jacket was for sale in another store. What do you think it would cost in the second store?
Decision Making Coming to a conclusion or an action relative to information and data that may or may not be contaminated by values.	One store sells three candies for 25¢. A second store sells the same candies for 10¢ each. The stores are next to each other. What would you do?	A jacket costs $38 and is for sale at 20% off. Another store has the same jacket at a cost of $42 and it's for sale at 25% off. What would you do?

SUMMARY

This chapter was formulated to stimulate concern for thinking and the role of thinking activities in math programs for the learning disabled. An effort was made to confine the illustrations to a few content areas so that one may observe the variety of thinking operations that can be used on any topic. Some children may respond better on one thinking operation than on another. All children may not respond in the same way to every operation. Accordingly, the teacher should be prepared to introduce thinking operations of many types into the math activities. Also, if specific plans are made to conduct thinking lessons, math may be an interesting topic on which to conduct the lesson.

Thinking is a more comprehensive topic than the present chapter could cover in entirety. It is hoped, therefore, that the reader will pursue other theories and approaches to thinking and integrate them into the program for LD children.

REFERENCES

Alley, G., & Deshler, D. (1979). *Teaching the learning disabled adolescent: Strategies and methods.* Denver: Love Publishing.

Ausubel, D.D., & Robinson, F.G. (1969). *School learning: An introduction to educational psychology.* New York: Holt, Rinehart & Winston.

Bourne, L.E., Ekstrand, B.R., & Dominowski, R.L. (1971). *The psychology of thinking.* Englewood Cliffs, NJ: Prentice-Hall.

Brainerd, C. (1983). Young children's mental arithmetic errors: A working memory analysis. *Child Development, 54,* 812–830.

Cawley, J.F. (1984). Selection, adaptation and development of curricula and instructional materials. In J.F. Cawley (Ed.), *Developmental teaching of mathematics for the learning disabled* (pp. 227–252). Rockville, MD: Aspen Systems.

Cermak, L. (1983). Information processing deficits in children with learning disabilities. *Journal of Learning Disabilities, 16,* 599–605.

Glennon, V., & Cruickshank, W.M. (1981). Teaching mathematics to children and youth with perceptual and cognitive processing deficits. In V. Glennon (Ed.), *The mathematical education of exceptional children and youth* (pp. 50–94). Reston, VA: The National Council of Teachers of Mathematics.

Guilford, J.P. (1967). *The nature of human intelligence.* New York: McGraw-Hill.

Halpern, N. (1981). Mathematics for the learning disabled. *Journal of Learning Disabilities, 14,* 505–506.

Hildebrandt, E.H.C. (1959). *Mathematical modes of thought in the growth of mathematical ideas, grades K-12* (Twenty-fourth Yearbook). Washington, DC: The National Council of Teachers of Mathematics.

Klausmeier, H.J., Ghatala, E.D., & Frayer, D.A. (1974). *Conceptual learning and development: A cognitive view.* New York: Academic Press.

May, L. (1967). String and paper teach simple geometry. *Grade Teacher, 84,* 110–112.

Meeker, M.N. (1969). *The structure of intellect: Its interpretations and uses.* Columbus, OH: Charles E. Merrill.

Raths, L., Wasserman, S., Jonas, & Rothstein, A. (1967). *Teaching for thinking: Theory and applications.* Columbus, OH: Charles E. Merrill.

Reid, D.K., & Hresko, W.P. (1981). *A cognitive approach to learning disabilities.* New York: McGraw-Hill.

Renzulli, J., & Callahan, C. (1973). *New directions in creativity. Mark 3.* New York: Harper & Row.

Russell, D.H. (1956). *Children's thinking.* Boston: Ginn.

Schoenfield, A.H. (1982). Some thoughts on problem solving research and mathematics education. In F. Lester & J. Garofolo (Eds.), *Mathematical problem solving: Issues in research* (pp. 25–35). Philadelphia: The Franklin Institute Press.

Sharma, M. (1984). Mathematics in the real world. In J. Cawley (Ed.), *Developmental teachings of mathematics for the learning disabled* (pp. 207–226). Rockville, MD: Aspen Systems.

Swanson, H.L. (1982). A multidirectional model for assessing learning disabled students' intelligence: An information processing framework. *Learning Disability Quarterly, 5,* 312–326.

Torrance, E.P. (1965). *Constructive behavior: Stress, personality and mental health.* Belmont, CA: Wadsworth.

Torrance, E.P. (1974). *The Torrance Test of Creative Thinking: Norms-technical manual.* Bensenville, IL: Scholastic Testing Services.

Wertheimer, M. (1959). *Productive thinking.* New York: Harper & Brothers.

Chapter 8

Solving Story Problems: Implications of Research for Teaching the Learning Disabled

Jeannette E. Fleischner
Michael O'Loughlin

One of the major goals of education is to facilitate the development of problem-solving skills. Everyday acts require application of problem-solving skills. As we attempt to understand the problems confronting us, to sort through the information we have, to determine the additional information we need, and to formulate a plan of action, we are engaged in the process of problem solving. Throughout our lives, problems such as how to decide whether we can afford to purchase a car, or to take a vacation, confront us. Kilpatrick (1925) suggested that skill in application of problem-solving skills can be equated with quality of life, in that those of us who are adept at problem solving, and can apply the principles of problem solving to everyday life, may make better decisions about common problems. Polya (1945) asserted that mastery of problem-solving skills leads to independent thinking, which is surely one of the goals of education in our society.

While problem-solving skills are taught in all parts of the school curriculum, formal methods for teaching those skills are most often associated with the mathematics curriculum. Consistent with our understanding of cognitive development, the skills taught and the opportunities for practicing application of those skills change throughout the school years. During elementary school, students learn problem-solving skills through the medium of "word problems" or "story problems." In secondary school, the skills learned through this medium are formalized, and students are taught to symbolize problem solving through the abstract statements of algebra and through the proofs of geometry. During these latter years of schooling,

---

Much of the preparation of this chapter was supported by the Research Institute for the Study of Learning Disabilities, Teachers College, Columbia University, under a contract (300-77-0491) with the Office of Special Education, through Title VI-G of Public Law 91-230.

the opportunities continue for application of problem-solving skills in word problems. Who among us has not considered the situation of two trains moving toward each other at a speed of 35 miles per hour, and who has not attempted to determine the point at which their disastrous encounter would occur?

The point to be drawn from this illustration is that "story problems" are created to provide practice in the application of problem-solving skills or to evaluate the extent to which these skills have been developed. Story problems are problems that require the student to apply mathematical knowledge (Davis & McKillip, 1980). Story problems may be presented orally or in writing, and they may be simple or complex. It is widely accepted now that automaticity in the basic facts is a prerequisite for success at solving story problems and that proficiency in solving problems is related to IQ, to reading comprehension, and to overall measures of quantitative ability (Suydam, 1980). Considerable progress has been made in describing the problem-solving process, and this is discussed in a following section. For success, it is expected that students must be able to relate to the context of the problem, capable of analyzing the key factors, and able to select and apply the mathematical operations that are needed to solve the problem. It is these skills that must be taught in the domain of the mathematics curriculum. A key question that confronts teachers of learning disabled (LD) students is how best to teach these skills to pupils who are known to have difficulty in abstracting information, in approaching tasks in a planful manner, and in transferring skills from one context to another. As Cawley (1983) has said, word problems may constitute a medium through which these skills, taught singly, can serve as integrative opportunities, through which students with learning disabilities can learn to select and apply strategies necessary for coping with all problems.

The present chapter reviews what is now known about the processes of problem solving and suggests an approach to teaching problem-solving skills to LD students that may improve not only their performance on measures of mathematical achievement but their ability to apply these skills to everyday situations as well.

WHAT AFFECTS PROBLEM SOLVING?

Task Variables

The nature and influence of problem complexity have been described from many different perspectives. Bana and Nelson (1977) have suggested that difficulty in problem solving arises because students have trouble processing story problem content that is nonmathematical, while Davis and McKillip (1980) suggest that problems can be made easier by using smaller numbers for required computations, as well as less elaborate stories. Thus, there is no clear understanding of exactly what elements influence the ease with which particular problems can be solved. Among the factors that have been shown to be associated with ease of solution of story problems, the following seem the most critical.

Language of the Problem

Barnett, Sowder, and Vos (1980) suggest that the language in which the problem is couched contributes to the complexity of the solution. They cite studies by Earp (1970) and Henny (1971) that have identified certain language factors as contributing to problem difficulty. The density of the language in the problem, the lack of contextual clues, the lack of continuity among ideas, and the way in which numerals are interspersed in the prose influence the ease with which story problems are solved. While some have argued that "readability" of the problem is a prime consideration, the preponderance of evidence suggests that readability is not as big a deterrent to problem solving as is commonly believed (Lester, 1980; Suydam, 1980). In fact, Suydam (1980) suggests that when techniques of multiple factor analysis have been applied, no factors have been identified that account for a major portion of problem complexity. Carpenter (1980) suggests that success at problem solving is a function of the information-processing demands of the task and, therefore, requires proficiency in both linguistic and mathematical aspects of the task.

Soviet researchers who study mathematical problem solving have taken a somewhat different view than have U.S. researchers. For instance, as early as 1969, Yaroschuk conducted experiments in which children were asked to solve both story problems and numerical problems. Based on his data, Yaroschuk concluded that the children were more successful at solving story problems and simple problems. The higher level of abstraction required for complex and numerical problems created a lower level of success for the children. Yaroschuk also observed that in numerical problems, the mathematical structure is clear but the subject is unfamiliar, whereas the converse is true in story problems. This observation suggests that when children are processing story problems, they may well understand the subject matter but are likely to have difficulty relating it to mathematical operations. It is consistent with Ginsburg's (1977) notion that even very young children are able to solve story problems that they can consider, although they may not have at their disposal the means to state their solutions mathematically. For example, consider this instance:

"How many objects are on the table?"

In addressing this problem, a child can act directly upon the objects by counting. In a more typical story problem, it has been asserted that the complexity of the solution is increased by the number of steps the child must take to reach it (Shchedrovitskii & Yakobson, 1975). It may be that a problem increases in complexity as its object content and the need for counting decline. Numerical problems in textbooks may be difficult for children because the problems have no relationship to real objects and because all the numbers are present, requiring no counting by the children. In processing a complex problem, it may be that children must first visualize the problem and then construct a mental model of the situation before devising a plan for solving it.

However, the actual complexity of the problem does have some influence on whether its solution is achieved. Shchedrovitskii and Yakobson (1975) point out that children who have no difficulty solving this problem:

A boy had 7 pencils. He lost 2. How many did he have left?

often cannot solve this one:

A cat had some black kittens and 2 gray ones. Altogether there were 5. How many black ones were there?

They hold the view that the child's increasing difficulty is caused by the increasing complexity of the problems. As the problems grow more complex, the child no longer can make parallel models of the aggregates; instead, he or she must have a deep understanding of the conditions of the problem so as to establish the order in which to begin counting the various numbers in the problem. Thus, Shchedrovitskii and Yakobson conclude that problem complexity is a function of problem structure.

Perhaps the person who has contributed most to our evidence on the question of problem complexity is Kuzmitskaya (1975). He required children to reproduce problems orally, and an analysis of their responses led him to conclude that accurate reproduction of a problem requires both comprehension and interpretation of the relations existing in the problem. From this, Kuzmitskaya developed the hypothesis that problem complexity is related to its structure. He classified problems with direct, observable relations as simple problems and problems with indirect relations as complex problems. To test whether the structure of the problem or the number of relations in the problem was the primary contributor to complexity, he gave four problems to his subjects. The problems used were simple story problems in addition and subtraction, and each was either high or low in complexity or number of elements. Using a mentally retarded population, Kuzmitskaya found that more than twice as many students were successful with the simple problems, indicating that the difficulty of a problem depended largely on the character of the relations present in the problem.

While the most important variable in determining the difficulty of the content of a problem seems to be the nature of the relations in it, some investigators have found that the vocabulary of a story problem is important, too. For instance, Barnett et al. (1980) warned teachers that there is a specialized vocabulary in mathematics that students must learn. Bogolyubov (1972) wrote that each story problem consists of vocabulary words and operation words. The operation words are formal mathematical terms for which no substitution is possible. Without a precise understanding of the meaning of these terms, no solution is possible. Vocabulary words might seem to be readily substituted, but Bogolyubov quotes many examples that indicate the importance of using words that are both appropriate to the context and meaningful to the child. His studies show that when meaningfulness or appropriateness is varied, problem solution becomes difficult, if not impossible. He points out, too, that particular care should be taken in differentiating closely related or visually or auditorily similar words.

Computational Requirements of the Problem

Another important structural variable associated with ease or difficulty of solving story problems is the difficulty and complexity of the computations required to achieve solution. When Loftus and Suppes (1972) explored the factors related to the probability that a student would get correct or incorrect solutions to story problems, they found that the number of different arithmetic operations needed to achieve solution was very important. Others have also found that computational skills are related to ultimate success in problem solving (Jerman, 1973; Knifong & Holton, 1976; Vanderlinde, 1964). While computational skills obviously are necessary to solve story problems, and it has been shown that problems with complex computational requirements are more difficult that those requiring simple computation, the major factor contributing to difficulty seems to be the clarity of the relationships stated in the problem.

Subject Variables

General Abilities and Aptitudes

As Suydam (1980) pointed out, it is not necessarily advantageous to delineate the characteristics of good problem solvers since, ultimately, we have to deal with the general population of problem solvers. This is particularly true for those who work with students with learning disabilities, for many of the correlates of good problem solving appear to be relatively immutable factors and often are cited as areas of weakness in LD students. However, it is possible that an enumeration of the characteristics of good problem solvers may highlight appropriate objectives toward which we can attempt to direct instructional efforts.

Kruteskii (1976) analyzed the solution process of many mathematically expert problem solvers and concluded that the most important problem-solving abilities were the abilities to generalize, to switch methods easily, to skip some steps, and to recall the general features of the problem, rather than superfluous details. From a review of contemporary literature, Suydam (1980) identified the characteristics of good problem solvers. She wrote that it is reasonable to expect good problem solvers to have high IQ scores and reasoning ability, high reading comprehension scores, and high scores in quantitative and spatial abilities. Lester (1980) agrees with the characteristics identified by Suydam but adds that a positive attitude and appropriate cognitive style are important, too. By appropriate cognitive style, Lester means a high level of field independence.

Vaidya and Chansky (1980) take this argument further, stating that mathematical achievement is strongly correlated with cognitive style, but also that the optimal situation for developing problem-solving skills is one that ensures a matching of teacher and pupil cognitive styles. The influence of cognitive style is strongly questioned by Fennema and Behr (1980), however, who say that the aptitudes that are relevant to mathematical problem solving are of two types. While they agree that cognitive aptitudes (i.e., IQ score, verbal and numerical ability, reasoning ability, spatial visualization ability) are important, they argue that affective aptitudes are equally important. The notion of "affective aptitudes" refers to the positive relationship that exists between attitude and achievement, the child's level of achievement motivation, and the possibility of sex differences. Fennema and Behr suspect that sex differences are related to the confidence or anxiety level of the student.

In dealing with the difficulties of children who are weak at story problem solving, the dichotomy described by Fennema and Behr must not be forgotten. If, as described earlier, the solution of complex problems depends on the perception of relations among parts, as well as certain reading and mathematical skills, it is clear that the child's level of cognitive aptitudes will affect the outcome. Perhaps even more potent, though, will be the effect of affective aptitudes. If a child is beginning to fail, or has already experienced persistent failure, account must be taken of his or her level of achievement motivation and the quality of the attitudes he or she exhibits. This notion is of utmost importance when teaching problem-solving skills to LD students, for they may display some characteristics of "learned helplessness." If this is so, they may require substantially more encouragement to attempt problem solution and more reinforcement of their efforts than do other students.

The Effect of Learning Disabilities on Problem Solving

All the cognitive characteristics of LD students that Cawley delineates in Chapter 1 may exert an influence on their ability to solve story problems. Because the term *learning disabilities* seems only to provide a rubric for considering the diverse symptomatology of several different syndromes, it is difficult to generalize about the effect of learning disabilities on the ability to solve story problems. As Torgesen (1977) wrote, the heterogeneity of the group classified as learning disabled makes understanding the effects of a learning disability difficult at best.

Certain inferences can be drawn, however. Problem solving seems to require complex cognitive processing abilities. By definition, LD students have a "disorder in one or more of the basic psychological processes." (Federal Register, August 23, 1977). While it was assumed for many years that "basic psychological processes" referred to such constructs as perception and perceptual-motor integration, it is now generally acknowledged that a disturbance in *cognitive* processes, such as thinking, conceptualizing, abstracting, reasoning, and evaluating, is an underlying cause of learning disabilities (Hall, 1980). This shift in emphasis has led to investigation of the effects of variations in internal processing mechanisms during acquisition, manipulation, and retrieval of information (Nuzum, 1983). As Reid and Hresko (1981) have put it, this effort to understand learning disabilities as an information-processing disorder is in its embryonic stages. Farnham-Diggory (1976) points out that students with learning disabilities can be characterized by their difficulty in acquiring or using information or skills that are essential to problem solving.

Others have identified students with learning disabilities as "passive learners" who do not call on behaviors within their repertoire when they are confronted with a learning task (Kauffman & Hallahan, 1979; Markman, 1977; Torgesen, 1977). Students with learning disabilities may not adopt a planned or organized approach to a problem-solving task (Torgesen & Kail, 1980) and may not invoke the strategic behaviors within their capacity when asked to solve a problem. Flavell (1976) points out, however, that failure to use appropriate strategic behavior seems to be a contributing factor to difficulty in solving problems in the entire population. It remains to be seen whether this apparent deficiency is more pronounced in the group identified as learning disabled than in the general population.

Process Variables

The notion of process variables relates to how one organizes the approach to problem solution. While there are broad interindividual differences in approaches to problem solution, it is possible to describe in general terms the processes that are involved, including the nature and sequence of strategies that seem to be associated with good problem solving.

Problem-Solving Strategies

Ginsburg (1976) suggests that the child's knowledge of arithmetic be described in terms of three cognitive systems that may operate concurrently as the child solves a problem. The first system is described as *natural,* because it is prenumerical and develops outside of school. The *informal* system also develops prior to schooling, but it involves the use of counting strategies, which the child has picked up incidentally. The techniques used by the child to deal with symbolic arithmetic are generally taught in school, and these are termed the *formal* system. We are concerned here with the behavior of the child who has already encountered the formal system, although it is clear that the child's earliest exposure to quantitative reasoning comes in response to the need to solve "real" story problems. Consider the following situation:

> Sally enters the house and asks Mother if she and her friends may have milk and cookies. Mother says, "Yes, but how much do you need? How many kids are playing here?" Sally must:
> 1. count her friends (Josey, Tom, and Megan)
> 2. remember to add herself
> 3. assign a number to this total
> 4. accurately report this number to Mother to know how many cups of milk are needed
>
> Mother then says, "Each child may have two cookies. Please get them from the cookie jar." Sally must:

1. remember the total number of children
2. count twice that number, or use some other strategy for doubling the set of cookies that would represent one cookie for each child
3. accurately count the total number of cookies.

Only if these steps are taken can Sally solve the problem of how to get milk and cookies for herself and her friends. It is apparent that young children solve these everyday problems with relative success and without the benefit of the formal instruction in arithmetic computation that is offered them in school. Sally has solved her problem through applying an informal system of counting strategies but would be hard pressed to solve the same problem as expeditiously if 53 friends were waiting in the yard for milk and cookies!

By the end of the primary grades, we expect children to be able to solve problems that are more complex and require the use of *formal* procedures. Therefore, we provide instruction in standard algorithms for the solution of mathematical problems. Ginsburg (1976) says that, typically, the teacher gives instruction on a new algorithm, and the child is then expected to master it and apply it. Ginsburg points out that although the child may "learn the algorithm," this does not imply understanding. Suydam and Dessart (1976) support the view that, to be effective, algorithms should be taught rationally (i.e., with explanation). All children seem to "invent" algorithms for solving problems, whether computational or story problems. These "invented procedures" may work well in some cases; even when the final answer is incorrect, the approach often can be demonstrated to be rational from the child's perspective. Children use unique but intuitively rational approaches in solving problems. Our task in teaching LD children is to help them discard "invented procedures" in favor of standard algorithms and learn to select and apply these algorithms appropriately.

There is a good deal of evidence that children's mistaken procedures in solving problems rarely are random: instead, the errors appear to be rule governed and systematic (Ginsburg, 1976; Radatz, 1979; Shchedrovitskii & Yakobson, 1975). A general conclusion of these researchers is that children arrive at an incorrect solution, not because they do not understand the problem, but because they select an inappropriate but (to the child) intuitively acceptable algorithm by which to solve it. It seems that children often understand the requirements of a problem and can state a correct procedure for solving it informally, but they cannot select and employ the correct, formal mathematical operation from those they have learned. Shchedrovitskii and Yakobson suggest that this may occur because the child's understanding relates to his or her own, intuitive problem-solving methods (cf. Ginsburg's "invented procedures") and not to the socially fixed mathematical methods used by adults. Sally, in the instance cited earlier, is unable to use a formula such as the following:

Let $M = K + 1$
and
let $C = 2(K + 1)$
where M equals milk, C equals cookies, K equals other kids, and 1 equals self

Like Ginsburg, Shchedrovitskii and Yakobson (1975) emphasize the developmental aspects of problem solving. They say that a child's strategy is very much a function of how he or she assimilates formal algorithms into the personal solution system. The logical outcome of this, they point out, is that we should be attentive to the appropriate presentation of algorithms to children, as these techniques are apt to become an enduring part of their scheme.

Mikhalskii (1975) looks at another aspect of the student's strategy. He believes that a preliminary analysis of the conditions of the problem is essential to success. Mikhalskii says that the conditions of the problem consist of:

- the requirement or question of the problem
- the data given in the problem
- the relationships within the given data

Analysis of these conditions leads to comprehension and thus enables the student to select the appropriate arithmetic operations to solve the problem. In effect, according to Mikhalskii, this approach causes the problem solver to break a complex problem into its component parts. To test the importance of preliminary analysis, Mikhalskii compared the effectiveness of analysis, synthesis, and solution by analogy as problem-solving strategies. To his surprise, Mikhalskii discovered that analysis was not a differentially more effective technique than either of the others. It is clear, both from Mikhalskii's work and from the studies of Kuzmitskaya (1975), that training in analysis improves oral reproduction of problems. This skill alone appears to have little bearing on the ability to solve problems. Mikhalskii discovered some interesting things about the strategies children employ in problem analysis. In describing the solution orally, the most common method employed by children was the synthetic method. The students first carried out the calculation, and only then addressed themselves to the question posed in the problem. When he attempted to focus their attention on the question, the children usually stated the question without referring to the conditions of the problem. Furthermore, young children tended to perseverate, or repeat the solutions from an earlier problem in a stereotyped manner. Older children were able to solve sub-parts of the problem without understanding the overall question. Mikhal-skii concludes that considerable time should be devoted to techniques that help the child analyze the problem question and break up its subparts. This view is supported widely in the literature (Bogolyubov, 1972; Schoen & Oehmke, 1980).

Knowledge Required to Solve Story Problems

Riley, Greeno, and Heller (1983) provide a theoretical model of the knowledge required to solve story problems that is consistent with our best understanding, based on computer simulations and research in the actual performance of children and adults. Three main kinds of knowledge are needed during problem solving:

a) schemata for understanding semantic relationships within the problem
b) schemata for representing the actions involved in solving the problem
c) strategic knowledge which will permit the development of an effective and efficient plan for solving the problem [p. 165].

In this description, "schemata" refers to the general notion of under-standing specific references in the story problem, as well as the ability to expand these references, to access information that pertains to these references but is not explicitly contained in the story problem. For instance, it is understood in the preceding example that action was required of two persons for Sally to get milk and cookies: her mother and herself. This was not explicit in the problem statement but would be understood by an adept problem solver.

In a more general sense, according to Newell and Simon (1972), problem solving consists of three steps:

1. recognition that a problem exists or has been posed
2. creation of a plan for solving it
3. use of appropriate heuristics

Other cognitive psychologists have expanded this notion to include such things as analysis of the conditions of the problem, searching for information embedded in the problem, manipulation of the information, and knowing how to proceed to achieve the solution.

From summarizing the literature on problem-solving strategies, two main themes emerge. First, attention must be given to breaking up the problem question to focus the child's attention on the conditions of the problem. Once this has been achieved, the unique strategies each child employs must be considered. If, as has been suggested, these strategies are intuitively rational but cannot lead to correct solution, the basis of the child's strategic choices must be examined before remedial instruction can begin.

TEACHING STUDENTS WITH LEARNING DISABILITIES TO SOLVE STORY PROBLEMS

It is clear that students with learning disabilities rank poorly in most measures of story problem solving. The Arithmetic Task Force of the Research Institute for the Study of Learning Disabilities conducted wide-scale surveys of computational and problem-solving skills of students with learning disabilities and found that these students were consistently below the performance levels of nonhandicapped peers. Even when reading and computational skills are appropriate for grade level, there appears to be a substantial subset of LD students who are unable to apply these skills to the task of solving story problems (Nuzum, 1983). In this section, we consider how to teach problem-solving skills to LD students and then look at what to teach. In considering what to teach, an instructional sequence is described that accounts for both procedural and task-specific knowledge.

A Method of Teaching

Evidence for the type of teaching that is most highly correlated with student achievement has come from a variety of sources. Carroll (1963) pointed out that student achievement is highly related to the opportunity to learn or academic engaged time. This implies that the longer a teacher spends in actual teaching activities, as opposed to managerial tasks or behavioral or procedural interventions, the higher student achievement will be. Recent studies have supported this view (Gettinger & White, 1980; Rosenshine & Berliner, 1978). Kounin (1970) identified a number of teacher managing behaviors that were highly correlated with pupil achievement. Kounin stated that teachers who were alert, who created smooth transitions between activities, and who monitored seat work carefully had higher achieving pupils. These observations have been corroborated by a number of other researchers (Anderson, Evertson, & Brophy, 1978; Brophy & Evertson, 1976; Good & Grouws, 1979). In a review of teacher behavior studies, Brophy (1979) says that teacher talk in the form of demonstration or explanation is highly correlated with students' achievement. If all these separate views are combined with the widely recognized "direct teaching" principles of being precise in stipulating objectives for student learning, presenting material in small units, providing drill and practice until mastery has been achieved, and then arranging for periodic review, a picture of what is known as the "direct teacher" emerges.

Some recent, large field studies have provided compelling evidence that this type of teacher produces greater student achievement. Bennett (1976) clearly demonstrated the greater effectiveness of formal teachers than informal ones. Solomon and Kendall (1979) showed that teacher directiveness was the factor most strongly associated with pupil achievement.

When considering how best to teach students to solve story problems, it is reasonable to state that direct teaching is likely to be more effective than less structured methods in improving the solution skills of LD students. It remains, then, to be considered what must be taught to effect the necessary improvement.

Suggestions for Teaching Problem-Solving Skills

If we are to improve the problem-solving skills of LD students, certain conditions must be met. It is generally agreed that the problems we pose must be apprehended by the students who are asked to solve them; the problem statements ought to deal with material that is familiar to the students and of interest to them. The complexity of the problem statements ought to correspond to the general level of language proficiency of the students who will solve them, but should not be simplified to the point of eliminating the relational aspects of the problem.

Cawley (1970) proposed that matrix programming provides a reliable and efficient means of developing problems appropriate to the student's abilities and needs. To use this method of developing story problems, the teacher must first consider the dimensions of the problems that will be varied according to students' needs. For instance, a matrix might include variables such as (adapted from Cawley, Fitzmaurice, Shaw, Kahn, & Bates, 1979):

- *Sentence Structure*   Simple sentence
                            Simple sentence with prepositional
                              phrase
- *Computational Complexity* Single digit × single digit
                            Two digit × single digit, no regrouping
                            Two digit × two digit, regrouping
- *Reading Level*   Fourth–Fifth grade level

When such a matrix has been created, a pool of problems is analyzed according to its dimensions; the problems are numbered and will serve as an easy source of problem sets that are appropriate for particular students. For example, consider these problems, which differ only in computational complexity:

> Jill had 10 glasses of lemonade. She spilled 3 glasses and sold 3 glasses. How many glasses of lemonade are gone?
> Jill had 124 glasses of lemonade. She spilled 25 glasses and sold 39 glasses. How many glasses of lemonade are gone?

The reading level of the problems is the same, and solution requires the same arithmetic operation. Both problems contain extraneous information. However, the first requires computation of a simple basic fact (3 + 3), whereas the second requires addition with regrouping.

Another consideration in deciding what to teach LD students about problem solving derives from the skills they appear not to have. Careful analysis of their problem-solving behaviors can reveal the areas of poor performance. Any effort to improve performance in solving story problems must take account of all the tasks involved. Nuzum (1983) devised an instructional sequence that seems useful as a basis for teaching problem-solving skills to LD students. Fleischner and Garnett (1983) summarized Nuzum's study.

This instructional plan was based on current understanding of the information-processing demands of problem solving and on the kind of task analysis often suggested by cognitive psychologists. Nuzum concluded that three categories of knowledge must be mastered if students are to succeed in solving story problems.

The first, *procedural knowledge,* involves awareness of the problem state and the ability to devise, execute, and monitor a cognitive plan to solve the problem. This type of knowledge frequently is considered to involve metacognitive skills. The second type of knowledge is *information provided by the problem* and requires that the student be able to abstract information given in the problem statement and identify the information required to reach solution. The third type is *task-specific knowledge*, such as selecting the correct computational operation or knowing when a two-step procedure must be employed. Exhibit 8-1 summarizes the types of knowledge included in the instructional plan.

Nuzum relied on direct instruction, and certain tenets of cognitive behavior modification were employed. For instance, students were taught to talk themselves through the process, first by speaking out loud, then by "speaking silently," to help themselves internalize the steps they had to consider when faced with a problem. They were taught that they should have a plan and what the steps in a good plan were. They were taught to state clearly the information provided in the problem and to restate the question asked. Finally, the students were taught task-specific information as was necessary. For example, several students lacked skill in determining when a two-step computational procedure was required. Exhibit 8-2 shows how students were taught to question themselves about a specific problem in a way that is consistent with the model presented in Exhibit 8-1.

Fleischner and Garnett (1983) report that this instructional plan has been validated in experiments based on a single subject design (Nuzum, 1983) and, with minor modification (e.g., to test the effect of using calculators as well as the instructional plan), on a group design (Marzola, in preparation). The LD students who mastered the material contained in this instructional sequence showed significant posttreatment gains in problem-solving performance.

SUMMARY AND CONCLUSIONS

The purpose of this chapter was to discuss current understanding of how story problems are solved, to review some of the information available

---

Exhibit 8-1 Model of Knowledge and Processes Involved in Solving
Story Problems

1. *Procedural Knowledge*
    Recognize problem state
    Recognize role in determining the solution process
    Plan solution process
2. *Information Needed from the problem*
3. *Task Specific Knowledge*
    Strategic or procedural steps
    Hypothesis about solution process
    Solution operation
4. *Verify Answer*

Exhibit 8-2 Instructional Model and Related Self-Questioning Strategies

There are 103 students in the fourth grade. There are 38 students in Mrs. Smith's class, and there are 35 students in Mrs. Jones's class. How many students are there in the two classes?	
Recognize Problem State	There is a problem that has a question, and I can try to answer the question.
Recognize role in determining the solution process	To answer the question, I must pay attention to what I am doing. I must evaluate my work.
Plan solution process	I have an overall plan that I should follow. Read Reread Think Solve Check
Information needed	
from the problem	Wanted Given Unnecessary Two steps
task-specific	Operations Calculation
transformed task-specific	Combining - addition
strategic or procedural	Think of a related problem Draw a diagram or chart Think of the action sequence part–part–whole
Hypothesis	Untested solution
Solution	Equation
Verification	Label Does the "answer" answer the question? Recheck calculations

about the factors related to being a good problem solver, and to suggest how the problem-solving skills of LD students may be improved. We have seen that it is unlikely that LD students will be naturally good at solving story problems, for many of the cognitive deficiencies associated with the LD syndrome are required for proficiency in solving problems. There is evidence that teachers can assist LD students in learning to solve story problems. It is suggested that a direct teaching style be employed and that specific objectives for student learning be set based on observed skill deficits. By employing matrix programming, the teacher can create a pool of story problems that vary according to the dimensions that affect problem difficulty, such as reading level, relationships stated within the problem, and computational demands of the problem. Finally, we have seen that a number of important skills required to solve problems can be taught directly, in an integrated instructional plan that takes account of the demands of procedural knowledge, task-specific knowledge, and the requirement that certain information must be abstracted from the problem itself.

REFERENCES

Anderson, L., Evertson, C., & Brophy, J.E. (1978). *The first-grade reading study group: Technical report of experimental effects and process–outcome relationships* (Report No. 4070). Austin: University of Texas, Research and Development Center for Teacher Education.

Bana, J.P., & Nelson, L.D. (1977). Some effects of distractions in nonverbal mathematical problem solving. *Alberta Journal of Educational Research, 23,* 268–279.

Barnett, J.C., Sowder, L., & Vos, K.E. (1980). Textbook problems: Supplementing and understanding them. In S. Krulik (Ed.), *Problem solving in school mathematics.* Reston, VA: National Council of Teachers of Mathematics.

Bennett, N. (1976). *Teaching styles and pupil progress.* London: Open Books Publishing.

Bogolyubov, A.N. (1972). Work with words in the solution of arithmetic problems in elementary school. In J. Kilpatrick & I. Wirszup (Eds.), *Soviet studies in the psychology of learning and teaching mathematics, 6.* Chicago: University of Chicago Press.

Brophy, J.E. (1979). Teacher behavior and its effects. *Journal of Educational Psychology, 71,* 733–750.

Brophy, J.E., & Evertson, C. (1976). *Learning from teaching: A developmental perspective.* Boston: Allyn & Bacon.

Carpenter, T.P. (1980). Research in cognitive development. In R.J. Shumway (Ed.), *Research in mathematics education.* Reston, VA: National Council of Teachers of Mathematics.

Carroll, J.P. (1963). A model of school learning. *Teachers College Record, 6,* 723–733.

Cawley, J.F. (1970). Teaching arithmetic to mentally handicapped children. *Focus on Exceptional Children, 2*(4).

Cawley, J.F., Fitzmaurice, A.H., Shaw, R., Kahn, H., & Bates, H. (1979). Math word problems and suggestions for LD students. *Learning Disabilities Quarterly, 2,* 25–41.

Cawley, J.F. (1983). *Developmental teaching of mathematics for the learning disabled.* Rockville, MD: Aspen Systems.

Davis, E.J., & McKillip, W.D. (1980). Improving story-problem solving in elementary school mathematics. In S. Krulik (Ed.), *Problem solving in school mathematics.* Reston, VA: National Council of Teachers of Mathematics.

Earp, N.W. (1970). Procedures for teaching reading in mathematics. *Arithmetic Teacher, 17,* 575–579.

Farnham-Diggory, S. (1976). Toward a theory of instructional growth. In D. Klahr (Ed.), *Cognition and instruction.* Hillsdale, NJ: Lawrence Erlbaum.

Federal Register (August 23, 1977) *Part B, Education of the Handicapped Act 42,* 42473.

180 COGNITIVE STRATEGIES AND MATHEMATICS

Fennema, E., & Behr, M.J. (1980). Individual differences and the learning of mathematics. In R.J. Shumway (Ed.), *Research in mathematics education*. Reston, VA: National Council of Teachers of Mathematics.

Flavell, J.H. (1976). Metacognitive aspects of problem solving. In L.B. Resnick (Ed.), *The nature of intelligence*. Hillsdale, NJ: Lawrence Erlbaum.

Fleischner, J.E., & Garnett, K. (1983). Arithmetic difficulties among learning disabled children: Background and current directions. *Learning Disabilities, 2*, 9, whole issue.

Gettinger, M., & White, M.A. (1980). Which is the stronger correlate of school learning? Time to learn or measured intelligence. *Journal of Educational Psychology, 72*, 338–344.

Ginsburg, H. (1976). Learning difficulties in children's arithmetic: A clinical cognitive approach. In A.R. Osborne (Ed.), *Models for learning mathematics*. Columbus, OH: ERIC.

Ginsburg, H. (1977). *Children's arithmetic: The learning process*. New York: VanNostrand.

Good, T.L., & Grouws, D.A. (1979). The Missouri mathematics effectiveness project: An experimental study in fourth-grade classrooms. *Journal of Educational Psychology, 71*, 355–362.

Hall, R.J. (1980). Cognitive behavior modification and information-processing skill: Of exceptional children. *Exceptional Education Quarterly, 1*, 9–15.

Henny, M. (1971). Improving mathematics verbal problem-solving ability through reading instruction. *Arithmetic Teachers, 18*(4), 223–229.

Jerman, N. (1973). Individualized instruction in problem solving in elementary school mathematics. *Journal for Research in Mathematics Education, 4*, 6–14.

Kauffman, J.M., & Hallahan, D.P. (1979). Learning disability and hyperactivity (with comments on minimal brain dysfunction). In B.B. Lahey & A. Kazdin (Eds.), *Advances in clinical child psychology, 2*. New York: Plenum.

Kilpatrick, W.H. (1925). *Foundations of method: Informal talks on teaching*. New York: MacMillan.

Knifong, J.D., & Holton, B.D. (1976). An analysis of children's written solutions to word problems. *Journal for Research in Mathematics Education, 7*, 106–112.

Kounin, J. (1970). *Discipline and group management in classrooms*. New York: Rinehart & Winston.

Kruteskii, V.A. (1976). The psychology of mathematical abilities in school-children: In J. Kilpatrick & I. Wirszup (Eds.), *Soviet studies in the psychology of learning and teaching mathematics, 2*. Chicago: University of Chicago Press.

Kuzmitskaya, M.I. (1975). Basic difficulties encountered by auxiliary school students in solving arithmetic problems. In S. Clarkson (Ed.), *Soviet studies in the psychology of learning and teaching of mathematics, 9*. Chicago: University of Chicago Press.

Lester, P.K. (1980). Research on mathematical problem solving. In R.J. Shumway (Ed.), *Research in mathematics education*. Reston, VA: National Council of Teachers of Mathematics.

Loftus, B.B., Suppes, P. (1972). Structural variables that determine problem solving difficulty in computer assisted instruction. *Journal of Educational Psychology, 63*, 531–542.

Markman, B.M. (1977). Realizing that you don't understand: A preliminary investigation. *Child Development, 48*, 986–992.

Marzola, E. (1985). *An arithmetic problem solving model employing cognitive behavior modification, mastery learning, and calculator use in a resource room setting*. Unpublished doctoral dissertation, Teachers College, Columbia University, New York .

Mikhalskii, K.A. (1975). The solution of complex arithmetic problems in auxiliary school. In S.P. Clarkson (Ed.), *Soviet studies in the psychology of learning and teaching mathematics, 9*. Chicago: University of Chicago Press.

Newell, A., & Simon, H.A. (1972). *Human problem solving.* Englewood Cliffs, NJ: Prentice-Hall.

Nuzum, M. (1983). *The effects of an instructional model based on the information processing paradigm on the arithmetic problem-solving performance of four learning disabled students.* Unpublished doctoral dissertation, Teachers College, Columbia University, New York.

Polya, G. (1945). *How to solve it.* Princeton, NJ: Princeton University Press.

Radatz, H. (1979). Error analysis in mathematics education. *Journal for Research in Mathematics Education, 10*(3), 163–172.

Reid, D.K., & Hresko, W.P. (1981). *A cognitive approach to learning disabilities.* New York: McGraw-Hill.

Riley, M.S., Greeno, J.G., & Heller, J.I. (1983). Development of problem solving ability in arithmetic. In H. Ginsberg (Ed.), *The development of mathematical thinking.* New York: Academic Press.

Rosenshine, B., & Berliner, D. (1978). Academic engaged time. *British Journal of Teacher Education, 4,* 3–16.

Schoen, H.L., & Oehmke, T. (1980). A new approach to the measurement of problem-solving skills. In S. Krulik (Ed.), *Problem solving in school mathematics.* Reston, VA: National Council of Teachers of Mathematics.

Shchedrovitskii, G.P., & Yakobson, S.G. (1975). An analysis of the process of solving simple arithmetic problems. In J.W. Wilson (Ed.), *Soviet studies in the psychology of learning and teaching mathematics, 13.* Chicago: University of Chicago Press.

Solomon, D., & Kendall, J. (1979). *Children in the classroom: An investigation of person-environment interaction.* New York: Praeger.

Suydam, M.N. (1980). Untangling clues from research in problem solving. In S. Krulik (Ed.), *Problem solving in school mathematics.* Reston, VA: National Council of Teachers of Mathematics.

Torgesen, J. (1977). The role of nonspecific factors in the task performance of learning disabled children: A theoretical assessment. *Journal of Learning Disabilities, 10,* 27–34.

Torgesen, J., & Kail, R.V. (1980). Memory processes in exceptional children. In B.K. Keogh (Ed.), *Advances in special education, 1.* Greenwich, CT: JAI press.

Vaidya, S., & Chansky, N. (1980). Cognitive development and cognitive style as factors in mathematics achievement. *Journal of Educational Psychology, 72*(3), 326–331.

Vanderlinde, L.F. (1964). Does the study of quantitative vocabulary improve problem solving? *Elementary School Journal, 65,* 143–152.

Yaroschuk, V.L. (1969). A psychological analysis of the processes involved in solving model arithmetic problems. In J. Kilpatrick & I. Wirszup (Eds.), *Soviet studies in the psychology of learning and teaching mathematics, 3.* Chicago: University of Chicago Press.

Chapter 9

Questions for and by the Learning Disabled Student

Dan G. Bachor

INTRODUCTION

Questions have been demonstrated to have a direct influence on student achievement (Andre, 1979; Redfield & Rousseau, 1980); however, for any set of students, that influence may not always be consistent or even positive (Dillion, 1981). Similar questions asked of different students may result in widely divergent answers. Sometimes these answers are humorous, sometimes embarrassing. The purpose of this chapter is to examine the how, what, why, and when of question–answer exchanges in order to suggest some general guidelines, which, in turn, may have a positive influence on the achievement of students who have learning problems in mathematics.

Questioning procedures are used extensively in both assessment and instructional procedures for mathematics in special education. For example, questions are used in structured interviews to help identify the logic students use to solve problems (Baroody, Ginsburg, & Wakman, 1983; Brownell, 1928; Liedtke, 1982). In addition, questions form an important part of word problems to probe comprehension of both textual and pictorial information (Cawley, Fitzmaurice, Shaw, Kahn, & Bates, 1979). In the pages that follow three aspects of questions are explored. First, the development of appropriate oral questioning techniques and the preparation of written questions are examined. Second, suggestions are offered as to how to respond orally to either written or oral answers. Finally, the use of questions as a monitoring device for students who are experiencing learning problems in mathematics is discussed.

In exploring these three aspects of questions, two main sources of information will be used. The research literature on questioning generally and questioning for specific subject matters is one source of information. In particular, the literature on reading and reading comprehension is referenced because of the close connection between learning problems in reading and learning problems in mathematics (e.g., Bartel, 1984). This connection is especially obvious when the area of concern is performance on word problems. In addition, the importance of reading in mathematics is apparent when students cannot read instructions, or other task-relevant information, or both. As a result, they are unable to complete their mathematics assignments. The second source of information for this chapter is personal clinical experience garnered from working with children and young adolescents at the Learning Assistance Center (LAC) at the University of Victoria (see Bachor [1983] for a description). Approximately 50 percent of the clients seen at the LAC in any given year are referred for mathematics.

TEACHER-DIRECTED QUESTIONS

A Brief Overview

Oral Questioning

Traditionally, teachers have adjusted the way they question depending upon who they are instructing. In the case of handicapped learners, teachers have been criticized for asking predominantly factual questions (e.g., Cawley, Goodstein, & Burrow, 1972; Herman, 1967). In contradistinction, Brophy (1979) points out that differing teacher behaviors result in maximum performance for students of "high ability" as compared to those of "low ability." For the low-achieving group, rephrasing questions, being warm and encouraging, giving hints, and allowing more time to respond were some of the factors that resulted in maximum performance. These same techniques did not appear necessary with the high-achieving group. Instead, it was important to move at a quick pace, to have high expectations, and occasionally to criticize inferior work. The criticized techniques of asking factual questions and prompting answers, then, appear productive for specific purposes and specific learners.

Written Questions

A different set of concerns arise when the form of the question is written. Each one may need to be addressed when questions are designed for students with learning problems in mathematics, depending on the nature of the question being asked. Variations in such factors as syntax (Larson, Parker, & Trenholme, 1978), reading level (Cawley et al., 1979), and mathematical vocabulary (Sharma, 1981) all influence the probability of a question being answered correctly. In addition, the presence of misleading information (Case, 1978a, 1978b) can affect students' answers.

ISSUES IN DESIGNING QUESTIONS

Each of the concerns for oral questions or written questions may need to be considered in question design, and each is detailed later in this chapter. One other consideration is important in designing questions for children and young adolescents with learning problems in mathematics: the type of question. Factors relating to the type of question will be constant regardless of whether it is presented orally or in written form. Before examining what might influence whether a question or a questioning procedure is well received, the issue of levels or types of questions is examined.

Types or Levels of Questions

The use of questions, whether oral or written, has been thought of as allowing students to demonstrate that they have attained a certain competency or disposition. The typical procedure is for a teacher to ask or write a question at some level of difficulty, according to a hierarchy or taxonomy; this has the result, one hopes, of a student answering it at the same level of complexity (Bloom, Engelhart, Hill, Furst, & Krathwohl, 1956; Sitko & Slemon, 1978).

When a teacher asks different types of questions, each one may require, for any particular student, different thinking skills. In some cases an individual must remember information; in other cases, information or rules are to be applied to new situations. Thus, when different types of questions are suggested as being necessary, a kind of levels-of-question is implied. This is not, however, what is typically meant by levels-of-question. Each type of question is classified further as either high or low level. Implied, too, is the assumption that high-level questions are more desirable or result in better answers, or even better thinkers (e.g., Cawley et al., 1972; Sitko & Slemon, 1982).

The suggestion of a second-order set of levels is somewhat worrisome. It is suggestive of the possibility that not only the type of question but levels, too, fall into discrete categories. An example may illustrate that types of questions or students' answers may not fall into discrete categories. Take the simple case of a teacher asking a young child, while he or she looks at a set of figures, "What color is an apple?" From the teacher's viewpoint, this question is one asking for recall. The child being questioned should have to remember only that an apple is red or green or yellow. For the majority of students this question will involve only recall. The teacher, in this case, will be correct in believing that a recall question has been asked.

For other students, much more than recall will be required to arrive at an appropriate response. For some students, the first response will be another question, "What kind of apple is it?" Their knowledge base is such that they will need to know more in order to answer the initial question. For those students, the question requires the classification of information, with the result that they can answer only by requesting more information. Still other students face different issues. They may not know what an apple is or may not know what *color* means as they have only recently been integrated from an English-as-a-second-language class into a regular class placement. Still other students may be able to recall a relevant answer but may not know how to state it or write it appropriately. Although the teacher intends to ask a particular kind of question, it may not be the same type that some students are attempting to answer.

Dillion (1982) examined this issue of the answer being different from the question when he studied the question–answer exchanges of normally achieving high school students. He found that these students answered approximately one-half of the questions asked with an answer of a different type from the question the teacher asked. This phenomenon of question–answer mismatch is observed at the LAC, too. In completing word problems, for example, children try to make the question more difficult than it is. They may tell elaborate stories about a person or character in the problem, thereby complicating the problem to be solved. Or, when trying to solve a multiplication problem, they will simplify the solution strategy they use to answer; for example, "I can't multiply so I'll add up the numbers." Thus, it seems that both normally achieving high school students and children with learning problems in mathematics attempt to answer at least some questions with different types of answers or with strategies different from what was called for in the original problem.

Even this degree of mismatch is a challenge to the notion that question and answer type will correspond. Add the further complication of another set of levels (high and low), and the case becomes even more muddled. Andre (1979) attempts to clarify the issue of levels by describing what the two levels, low and high, require of students. Low-level questions are defined as those requiring the student to recognize or recall information. In low-level questioning, for example, the teacher may ask a student to state the first ten cardinal numbers. High-level questions are assumed to require the student to transform the information given in some way. For example, the student answering may have to tie together logically concepts that have been presented as separate entities by the teacher, such as applying the rules for adding fractions and whole numbers to adding mixed numbers. Some students with learning problems in mathematics do not apply what they have learned earlier; for them, each topic is new material. Any resultant written or oral questions, therefore, may not result in students transforming information. Rather, they may be attempting to recall what they consider task-relevant information.

In summary, at least for students with learning problems or learning disabilities, it does not seem reasonable to assume that questions result in answers that match the type of question asked. Rather, in thinking of how to question students with learning difficulties in mathematics, it is more reasonable to make only the following two assumptions. First, the written or asked question has a differential impact on the obtained answer. Different questions do contribute to better, more carefully formulated answers. In addition, in some cases, appropriately worded questions permit students to answer when before they could express only uncertainty. The specific type of question, however, may need to be adjusted to take learner background into account. Second, as a corollary to the first point, no question can guarantee that any learning disabled (LD) student will be able to or will even want to respond to a question, in either written or oral form. The answer, or lack of same, may need to be clarified or elaborated. Such follow-up, even for normally achieving students, may be more important than the original question to students' achievement (Crawford, Brophy, Evertson, & Coulter, 1977; Stallings, 1976).

Examples of Questioning Taxonomies

Two examples are used to illustrate types of teacher questioning techniques. In each case, questions are construed as either relating to the text to be read, the answer to be given, or both. In short, questions are not seen as isolated units intended to result in corresponding types of answers. Rather, they are dependent on the situation, where and how the information is given (text, test, discussion, and so on), and on the learner's knowledge base (Goelman, 1982; Raphael, 1982).

The first sample taxonomy is one developed by Pearson and Johnson (1978) to address the issue of reading comprehension. Questions are examined in terms of the degree to which the answer is found in the presented information.

Raphael and her coworker (Raphael, 1982; Raphael & Pearson, 1982) argue that two things are accomplished by selecting a questioning taxonomy such as the one proposed by Pearson and Johnson. First, the number of categories are reduced so the question–answer relationship is simplified.

Second, the categories indicate the nature of the reader's response and the question requirement at the same time. Three categories of question are suggested in this taxonomy: (a) text-explicit, (b) text-implicit, and (c) script-implicit.

Text-explicit questions are ones in which information is found in a ready-to-be-used format in the text. The following is an example of a text-explicit word problem:

> John had four apples.
> He got four more apples.
> How many apples does John have altogether?

In this problem only the information "four apples," "four more apples," and "is how many apples" needs to be taken from the text to obtain an answer. It is stated explicitly in the problem.

In text-implicit questions, the information is found in the text as well. The information, however, is more obscure or requires the student to integrate information or both. The following example illustrates this type of question.

> John had four apples and two oranges.
> He ate one apple and one orange.
> Both apples and oranges are fruit.
> How many pieces of fruit does John have left after he has finished eating?

In script-implicit questions, the requirements are different. The information required to answer the question is not located in the text but is assumed to be part of the student's knowledge about the topic in question. The following is an example of such a question:

> John had four apples and three oranges.
> Susan had six pears and five chocolates.
> They ate one piece of fruit each.
> How many pieces of fruit do the children have now?

In this case the student must depend on his or her own knowledge to determine how to solve the problem. Neither the operations (the question does not specify that both addition and subtraction are to be performed) nor the numbers to be used in the calculations (the question of which data to use is confounded by the problem of having to classify what is fruit and what is not fruit) can be determined by reading the information given. The student must bring to bear his or her own knowledge, information not given in the problem, making it script-implicit.

The second example of a questioning taxonomy is the one proposed by Sitko and his colleagues (Bachor, 1981; Bachor, Sitko, & Slemon, 1980; Sitko, Bachor, Slemon, & Turner, 1980; Sitko, Slemon, & Bachor, 1983; Slemon, Bachor, Sitko, & Turner, 1980). In their taxonomy, questions are placed into the context of a simple decision-making model (see Figure 9-1) in which questioning is only one strategy available to the teacher. If the teacher decides to question, he or she selects from one of four types of questions. As is the case with the Pearson–Johnson taxonomy, only a small number of types of questions are to be learned. Such a taxonomy has two main advantages. It is easily remembered; as a result, the likelihood of anyone asking a specific type of question increases. Second, students with learning problems in mathematics may be encouraged to learn such a taxonomy. Students referred to the LAC ask better questions as a result of learning this taxonomy. While the contribution to improvement in achievement cannot be separated from other parts of the intervention in mathematics, students are better able to clarify what they want to know.

In Table 9-1, the four types of questions are defined, and examples are given for each one. The purpose of asking discrimination questions is to make sure the student can identify and differentiate between concrete stimuli. This can range from discriminating between numbers to discriminating between geometric shapes. When asking relating concepts questions, the teacher's purpose is to ensure that the student, for example, can compare the cardinal and ordinal number systems. Or the question may require an explanation of the concept *fraction,* given a pictorial example. In this case, note that the learner does not recall the information but rather explains, contrasts, or compares known information. In recall, information is retrieved from memory. This type of question can range from requiring a student to complete 25 single-digit addition problems to remembering a theorem. Finally, problem solving requires that information be applied in places other than the original instructional task.

In deciding to ask a question, it must be remembered that there is no inherent benefit in asking any one type over another one (Brophy, 1979). The choice of the question (or even the taxonomy) is a function of what the teacher is trying to find out. In addition, as was pointed out earlier, the answer to a question may be of a type different from the original question. For example, a teacher asks a problem-solving question, but the asked student has read the answer elsewhere. For him or her, the question is no longer one requiring problem solving. Similarly, if a recall question is asked and the student cannot remember the answer, it is no longer a recall question. When this latter mismatch occurs, the student with learning problems in mathematics is at a disadvantage. Allowing for discrep-

Figure 9-1 A Decision-Making Model for Questioning and
Interpretation Strategies

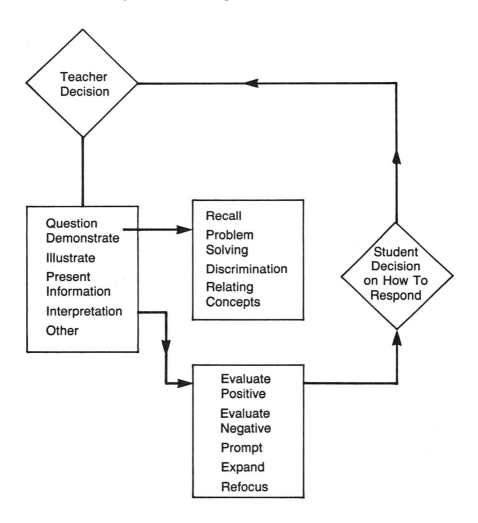

Source: Adapted from "A questioning and feedback system for developing comprehension skills" by M. Sitko, A. Slemon, & D. Bachor in *Special Education in Canada,* vol. 57, no. 2, with permission of the Council for Exceptional Children. © 1983.

Table 9-1 Categories in the Teacher Pupil Request System: TPRS
(Sitko, Bachor, Slemon, & Turner, 1980)

Category	Definition
Discrimination	A distinction must be made between two or more concrete, objective stimuli. For example, "Is this number (showing a 2) different than or the same as this one? (showing a 5)"
Relating concepts	The meaning of a concept must be explained or compared and/or contrasted with other concepts. For example, "How are adding and multiplying alike?"
Problem solving	Previously learned rules, principles or information are applied in arriving at solutions. For example, "Can you prove that the opposite angles of a diamond are equal?"
Recall	Single or multiple bits of information must be retrieved from memory. For example, "What do you call the number on the bottom in a subtraction question?"

ancies between question and answer may help to explain why seemingly obvious questions are answered slowly, if at all, by some students. Thus, in the decision-making model presented in Figure 9-1, it can be seen that questions are not intended to stand alone. Rather, they are part of a question–answer dyad or a question–answer–interpretation triad. The assumption inherent in the suggestion that the majority of answers need to be followed up is that it cannot be assumed students with special needs know how or why they have reached a given conclusion (Feuerstein, 1979). Specific suggestions for the interpretation of answers, whether the original question was written or oral, are given later in this chapter.

QUESTIONS: LOOKING BEYOND THE TYPE OF QUESTION ASKED

While questioning may facilitate learning for students with learning problems in mathematics, it may not, too. For example, questions may be poorly worded, which may result in confusion either in not being able to read the question or in not being able to discuss it. In addition, the teacher may request an answer before the student is prepared to give it. Another possibility is that the student may not have the necessary skills to answer the question as asked. In general there are two clusters of factors that are not related to the type of question but need to be kept in mind when asking questions. The first relates to the question, the way the teacher asks it or writes it. The second factor concerns the student with learning problems in mathematics, the way he or she construes or reads the question.

Teacher-Question Related Factors

Oral Questions

Well-formulated questions, may, on occasion, unwittingly sabotage the efforts of the student with learning problems in mathematics to answer correctly. Poorly timed questions (or other instructional moves) may result in the LD student believing that the teacher presence is necessary before he or she is able to arrive at a correct answer.

Too rapid a questioning pattern may frustrate the LD student and result in a high frequency of incomplete or yes and no answers. Banton (1978) reports that some teachers asked 35 questions in five minutes, an average of 7 questions per minute. In a similar study, Rowe (1978) noted a question per minute rate of 10 to 12. Rowe observed that while the teacher is working hard, the student is not. The observed students increased their breathing rates and their sighing rates as the frequency of questions increased.

If the purpose of the questions asked by the teachers Banton and Rowe observed was to obtain elaborate answers, their questioning pattern was ineffective. The reaction of the children reported by Rowe (1978) supports this conclusion. There are, however, appropriate times for rapid questioning patterns with students with learning problems in mathematics. At the LAC, high-speed questions have proved effective when used in gamelike drill routines where the purpose was to help the student give automatic responses to previously practiced material, such as in the case of over-learning addition facts. Samuels (1981) makes the same point in studying reading. He suggests that decoding automaticity is necessary before text comprehension will occur.

The issue of timing of questions has been examined from a different perspective by Dillion (1983). He reports that the amount of time necessary to answer a question varies as a function of the question asked. Simply put, Dillion's findings may be interpreted to mean that the more difficult the question for the learner, the more time it takes to provide a complete answer.

An issue related to the timing and length of answer is the amount of time is takes to formulate an answer to a question. Rowe (1973) refers to this as wait time. More specifically, wait time refers to the amount of time the teacher waits before calling for an answer and, secondly, the length of time paused before commenting on the answer or asking another question.

Given some of the clinical and research evidence reported earlier in this chapter, it would seem logical that the amount of wait time needed for students with learning problems in mathematics would be, at least in some cases, longer than that required for normally achieving students. For example, MacGinitie (1983) reports that one student who had reading problems took at least 15 to 20 seconds to formulate an answer. He observed that this student was still answering the previous question when a new one was being asked of him. Yet Rowe (1973) reports that the top five students in various groups observed "received nearly 2 seconds to answer while the bottom five received slightly less than 1 second (0.9 seconds) to respond [p. 250]." Whether these lower achieving students had learning problems in mathematics or not, a shorter wait time for students who may need more time to think of an answer would seem to be counterproductive.

In a teacher in-service training session, Rowe (1973) recommended an increase in wait time. When teachers used longer wait times, they noted, among other things, three outcomes: (a) contributions by presumed slower students increased, (b) length of answers increased, and (c) answers were supported and stated with more confidence. In a later article, Rowe (1978) recommended a wait time of 3 to 5 seconds. Based on observations completed at the LAC, wait time for students with learning problems in mathematics is a function of perceived problem difficulty. In some cases, wait time may need to be as long as 10 to 30 seconds.

There are times when questions are asked for which an answer is not expected. Dillion (1981) points out that such questions are inappropriate at any time. There are times, however, when teachers use questions as a discipline technique; for example "What do you think you are doing over there?" The teacher selecting this technique may be surprised and upset to find the LD or other special needs student answering such questions. Rhetorical questions or leading questions are two types that may be added to Dillion's implied list of questions to be avoided, at least for students with learning problems.

The timing of the question in relation to the instruction provided or a request to read information is the last issue to be considered. If a question is asked before presenting information or material, the result is that the learning (language) disabled student is able to remember information better (Goelman, 1982). The information remembered, however, may not relate to the question asked; rather, it may relate to the general recall of listened-to or read material. LD students may lack the specific question-answering skills necessary to be able to locate the specific information required to answer the question. Questions asked before, then, act as a general signal to "look more carefully" for LD students, with the result of an increase in non-question-specific recall. Since most researchers (e.g., Durkin, 1981) report that questions asked before instruction improve the answers for those specific questions, teachers need to be alert for a general increase in the amount remembered as opposed to more precise answers. For LD students, this general improvement in remembering should be encouraged while providing more practice and training in finding question-relevant information. Questions asked after instruction tend to aid the student in recalling two kinds of information: (a) information specific to questions and (b) other information that is not queried specifically. For LD students, carefully worded questions after instruction also act as prompts to find information for which they might not otherwise search (Bachor, 1981).

Written Questions

When the teacher is designing written questions for mathematics, a new series of considerations emerge over and above the type of question. To the extent that resource room, or other special education, or regular classroom teachers use written questions as a source for discussion, the preceding considerations for oral questions apply. Often, however, the expectation is that the student with learning problems in mathematics will read and answer questions in a textbook.

An important consideration in evaluating the appropriateness of written questions will be factors associated with reading. For example, Bartel (1984) suggests that in completing assessments for learning problems in mathematics, reading problems were one of the four major contributors to student difficulties. More specifically, Larson, Parker, and Trenholme (1978) demonstrated that varying syntax had an influence on the probability of any student solving a problem correctly. Easy syntax (e.g., Bill had two apples. He got one more apple. How many did he have altogether?) was solved with less difficulty then moderate or complex syntax (e.g., When Bill went to the store he bought two apples, then he bought one more; how many did he have now?). Sharma (1981) adds that knowledge of mathematical vocabulary will also influence whether or not a student arrives at a correct answer.

One student seen at the Learning Assistance Center is a good example of the importance of reading. If left on his own to complete his assignments in mathematics, Michael would spend approximately 10 percent of his time on task. During this time he may have completed one question, which may or may not have been answered correctly. In one observation, which took place over the period of one hour, Michael managed only to scrape and recolor his pencil. The final result was a colorful, striped pencil and no mathematics completed. When an Individual Educational Program was put in place and instructions were read to him or taped for him, his time spent working increased to 80 to 90 percent on task. In addition, he was accomplishing nearly the same amount of work as his peers, with the same number of correct answers.

Other considerations arise when word problems are designed. For example, Case (1978a, 1978b) has demonstrated that students who can successfully answer questions or problems will fail them when irrelevant or misleading information is introduced. Children arriving at the LAC display this pattern of performance and invent strategies in the attempt to solve these types of problems. For example, they read each problem, then answer by adding together all numbers in the question. Such children do learn correct strategies if both the inappropriate strategies (Bachor, 1979) and the problems are broken down (Case, 1978b; Cawley, Fitzmaurice, Shaw, Kahn, & Bates, 1978).

Cawley, Fitzmaurice, Shaw, Kahn, and Bates (1979) propose a grid system that allows anyone designing word problems to take into consideration the foregoing concerns. In using this system to design word problems at the LAC, however, one practical problem has emerged. It is very difficult to generate word problems for children in grades three or four who have the reading skills of a grade one student. This practical problem, usually, is overcome as a student's vocabulary increases.

Learner-Related Factors

Bachor, Sitko, and Slemon (1980) note that there are three factors specific to learners that influence their ability to answer questions: (a) whether the students want to answer, (b) the amount and kind of experience they bring to the question, and (c) their ability to process information and to apply rules and strategies.

LD students may not want to answer a question or may be unable to answer because, for example, they are afraid or anxious. These students tend to make negative self-attributions and cease work easily. They have been referred to as being "learned helpless" (Dweck, 1975; Dweck & Repucci, 1973; Dweck & Wortman, 1982). A large part of learned helplessness may turn out to be a student's anxiety. In a recently completed study, Summers (1984) found that 50 percent of the variance of learned helpnessness was accounted for by anxiety.

The frequent expression of anxiety is quite common among students referred to the LAC for mathematics. Often they perceive mathematics as a series of discrete tasks for which there is no logical pattern. The following generalized examples are summaries of the behavior patterns of children and adolescents who have been observed at the LAC over the past four years. Such students may refuse to give any answer, either spoken or written, of which they are not absolutely certain. Others may refuse to cooperate in order to obtain teacher attention. Back in the regular classroom, they may adopt the role of class clown or try to make themselves as invisible as possible. While such behavior is not always related to uncertainty or lack of confidence, it often is.

A second factor relates to the amount of experience brought to the question. There are two aspects of experience with questions: practice answering generally and practice answering specific types of questions. Students with learning problems in mathematics (or reading) become better able to answer questions as they obtain more practice. The more questions answered, the more confidence they have in answering and the more willing they are to answer.

Practice alone, however, is not enough. If students with learning problems or learning disabilities answer only a restricted range of questions, they may not be able to answer other types.

> As an example, consider the case where the only questions a student had ever been asked required him or her to restate or recall what the teacher has said. [After several recall questions were asked, a different type of question, for example, relating concepts, is asked. Given this new question, the student might respond] when asked to compare an apple and an orange: "An apple is round, an orange is round; an apple is red, an orange is orange." (Bachor, Sitko, & Slemon, 1980, p. 103)

In this case, the probability of answering correctly was reduced because the well-practiced answering routine of recalling information interfered with the process of comparing. The LD student, or other student with learning problems in mathematics, requires practice answering a variety of questions, so he or she is more likely to know how to, as in the preceding example, draw a comparison between an apple and an orange.

Jasmine, a grade six student, is a good example of the effects of affective factors and of practice answering specific questions. When Jasmine first arrived at the LAC, she believed she could not do mathematics and answered even the easiest questions randomly, saying such things as "6 + 6 = 72." Incorrect random answers and other similar tactics were Jasmine's way of saying "I can't" or "I won't" or both. After practice completing several different types of mathematics problems, along with some considerable emotional support, Jasmine started to believe she could succeed in mathematics. The next step involved practice with different types of questions in mathematics. After four weeks of instruction, Jasmine could solve fractions, the reason for her referral, and—just as importantly—she believed she could succeed in learning other areas in mathematics. On the last day at the LAC, Jasmine brought in a graphic illustration of her change in feelings (see Figure 9-2) about mathematics.

The last learner-related factor is a student's ability to process information and to apply rules (Case, 1978b). LD students, on occasion, will try to simplify questions to make them easier for themselves; for example, "I can't multiply, so I'll add." They may have learned to use rules or strategies to answer questions that only work part of the time. For example, young children are observed to use the strategy of adding from left to right. This particular way of solving addition is a natural extension from reading and will work as long as regrouping is not necessary. In other cases, LD students will omit information or add information to the question so they may obtain an answer. They may try to answer by relating incidents that only indirectly, and then only if the teacher uses imagination, apply to the question to be answered. Or the LD student may apply a rule blindly, such as in the following example:

Consider Edward, one of Holt's fifth graders who has learned a rule for counting. Edward was given 15 10-cm. rods and 1 4-cm.

Figure 9-2: Jasmine's Changes in Attitude

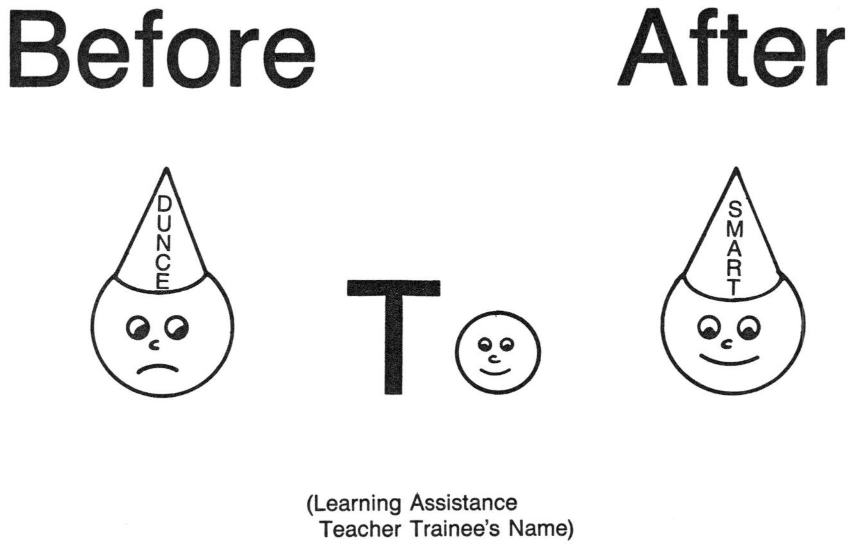

Before   After

(Learning Assistance
Teacher Trainee's Name)

rod and asked how many single units he would need to make that many. (The answer is 154.) First, he lined up the 10-cm. rods and put the 4-cm. rod on the end. Then, he began to count the rows, reciting 10, 20 . . . [Thus, he reached 100. Next, he counted by hundreds to 600, following 600 by 604.] . . . his solution. Asked to try again, [he counted in a slightly different way but used the same rule to arrive at 109. Intervention was tried . . . a simplification of the problem] . . . Now, Edward could answer with no hesitation. The two sections were pushed together in front of him and Edward was asked the original question. He proceeded through the original routine and again came up with 604 [Brown, 1978, pp. 106–107].

Therefore, the teacher working with the LD student faces the complication that the question-answering routines brought by the learner to the immediate situation may be irrelevant, inappropriate, or incorrect.

INTERPRETATION OF ANSWERS

To ensure that LD students perform to the best of their abilities, follow-up is necessary. Asking carefully constructed questions is insufficient. Crawford et al. (1977) report that a large portion of the achievement of a grade four classroom (approximately 20 percent of the variance of the class scores on the Metropolitian Achievement Test) was due to teacher follow-up of instruction or discussion. Such teacher reaction to student answers, following the decision-making model presented in Figure 9-1, will be referred to as interpretation. Brophy (1979) suggests that interpretation is necessary for maximum achievement of low-ability students to occur. Stallings (1976) reports that linking questions and interpretation resulted in improved achievement. It is recommended, to the extent possible, that questions be matched to instructional goals or objectives. As already suggested, questions, which have been derived from objectives, usually need to be followed up with appropriate interpretation of LD students' answers.

As with questions, there are a variety of interpretations possible and some cautions necessary to maximize their effectiveness for LD students. One taxonomy that may be used for interpretation is outlined next.

Types of Interpretation and the Use of Them

Interpretations may range from response confirmation ("That's correct") or response appraisal ("The first part of the calculations is correct;

however, you made a mistake when you added in this piece of information'') to response modification (''You told me that we subtract the top number from the bottom number, but what do we call these top and bottom numbers?''). Five types of interpretation are given in Table 9-2. As with the four types of questions, the number has been kept small so that teachers will be able to master them quickly and use them effectively.

Of the five suggested, there are two main groupings of types of interpretation: indirect influences and direct influences. Evaluate positive and evaluate negative are employed mainly to affect learner self-confidence. They only indirectly affect answers by increasing or decreasing the probability of occurrence of a response. Expand, refocus, and prompt are used to influence an answer directly. They are employed when you want a learner to say more, to refine an answer, or to change an answer.

Observations of LD students at the LAC suggest that they require more evaluate positive (praise) than do normally achieving students. Brophy (1981) points out, however, that much of this praise is given inappropriately and results in ''embarrassment, discouragement and other undesirable outcomes'' (p. 13). Praise must be contingent, specific, and credible; that is, LD students must understand what they are being praised for, be clear on why they are being praised, and believe they deserve that praise.

Table 9-2 Categories in Interpretation of Pupil Answers: IPA
(Slemon, Bachor, Sitko, & Turner, 1980)

Category	Definition
Evaluate positive	A positive judgment of a response is given. For example, "Yes, that is the correct way to solve word problems that contain extra information; well done!"
Evaluate negative	A negative appraisal of response is given. For example, "The problem is that you can't compare the area of a triangle and a rectangle by using the same formula."
Prompt	A hint, cue or clue is given. For example, "Before you can subtract here $(13 - 8)$, you must regroup. Does that reminder help?"
Expand	An expansion, or explanation is requested. "Could you show me (using base 10 blocks) how you take away 4 from 7?"
Refocus	Attention is drawn either to a particular point in a question or answer or to a different viewpoint that must be developed. For example, "Yes, that is how you regroup whole numbers when adding, but I asked you how you convert two unlike fractions to a common denominator."

For a long time teachers believed they should avoid negative evaluation (criticizing) with LD or other special needs students or, for that matter, anyone at all. While extra care must be employed in criticizing, letting LD students know they have made a mistake may be very helpful. If pointing out an error is followed by carefully selected interpretation that results in appropriate responses, the LD student may learn that failure is not bad and need not be feared. As with praise, criticism must be specific, credible, and contingent (Brophy, 1981). In addition, as stated earlier, evaluate negative must be followed up. For example, the appropriate way of answering should be prompted or the student redirected, so that he or she is pointed in a positive direction.

Fish and White (1978–1979) report that the preceding two types of interpretation (evaluate positive and evaluate negative) are only effective when students are working to the best of their ability and they receive information as to the precise nature of their performance. The accuracy of answers is not likely to improve when praise and criticism are used by themselves. While a prompt, expand, or refocus may be used alone, each should be accompanied by meaningful praise, at least until fear of failure has been reduced, if the patterns of students at the LAC are typical.

One final factor must be remembered in interpreting the answers of LD students. Many of our signals to each other are nonverbal. LD students tend to be poor readers of such signals and may misinterpret nonverbal behavior. Extra care, then, must be taken to ensure that interpretations of LD students' answers are, in addition to the preceding, specific in voice, tone, and nonverbal signals.

SELF-DIRECTED QUESTIONS

In reported observations of classrooms where students are achieving well, one key component has been singled out. These students are academically engaged; that is, a large proportion of their available time is time on task (Rosenshine, 1979; Stevens & Rosenshine, 1981). In short, students are doing what they are supposed to be doing when they are supposed to be doing it. Their teachers maintain an academic focus; they spend more time ensuring that students are working on instructional materials. Homework is assigned, and students are held responsible for its completion. Students are expected to demonstrate their knowledge.

In considering academic engagement, however, the focus is not as much on what the student is doing for him- or herself as it is on what the teacher is doing to encourage learning. The emphasis is on what the teacher does to help the student with academic skills. Such a conceptualization of achievement downplays the learner's role in study. The kinds of phenomena discussed in the section on "Learner-Related Factors" illustrate the importance of what the student does. For present purposes, only one component of the learners' contribution to the instructional cycle will be isolated: the ability to monitor the effectiveness of their own work habits.

Several of the students seen at the LAC referred to earlier in this chapter did not monitor what they did or how well they did it—Michael is one example—when they first arrived. Self-monitoring seems to be a skill that is lacking in LD students (Torgesen, 1979). Perhaps *lacking* is too strong a word to describe self-monitoring in this case. LD students, at least those seen at the LAC, do attempt to organize and make some sense of their school-related world; however, their efforts may not be directed to what teachers would like them to be. Or the students may not be as efficient as others when they are working. Again the examples mentioned earlier bear repeating. Michael and his pencil and Jasmine and her random answer patterns are two cases of poor work habits. In this sense, the LD student is analogous to the very young child who reads a book upside down. Both the toddler and the LD student may lack the cognitive awareness or the self-monitoring skills necessary to complete some mathematics tasks successfully.

Brown (1975, 1978) has suggested that such self-monitoring or cognitive awareness be called metacognition. Metacognition refers, then, to our own awareness of whether we are performing effectively. For example, a spelling error may not be noticed, even after careful editing, if the writer's attention is focused on what is being said rather than on how well it is said. The error may not be noticed until some interruption occurs, or until some time has passed and the writer is less text-bound. Such a lack of error awareness reflects poor metacognitive skills. LD students referred for writing to the LAC typically do not self-monitor in a positive sense of the word. To compound the problem, they have difficulty thinking of what to say and how to say it. Often they never reach the point where they want to read and correct their manuscript for technical adequacy. These same students struggle when they are asked to write, for example, mathematics word problems as suggested by Liedtke (1984).

An example from reading comprehension illustrates how effective self-monitoring takes place. Anderson (1980) suggests that good readers are not even aware that they are using metacognitive skills until failure takes place. That is, in reading text, good readers self-monitor or check for understanding continually; however, they may be unaware of such monitoring until they fail to comprehend some aspect of a passage. Failure to comprehend acts as a signal to reread or to do something else, such as take a break, so that successful comprehension will be the end result. For

LD students, such a signal of "I don't understand" may not trigger any form of self-help. Equally probable are actions such as stopping work completely or knocking their books on the floor. The action, or lack of it, taken may vary as a function of the age and gender of the student and the circumstances surrounding the perception or realization of failure.

In both the writing and reading examples just given, then, the LD student may have been monitoring his or her work routines. The resulting action, however, was either ineffective or inappropriate. When failure occurs, often the observed action is not to redo or recheck, but to react. LD students may, for example, find themselves in trouble because they answered when an answer was not expected. Or they persist in conversation when they should stop. In mathematics period, such students continue to use, for example, a counting technique to solve addition problems; although resulting in the correct answers, the technique may consume 10 to 15 minutes per problem. This lack of or "lagging cognitive awareness of task demands may express itself insidiously. Such children may appear to themselves and their teachers to be working diligently (and indeed may be), but yet not be progressing" (Loper, 1980, p. 2). Teaching LD children and young adolescents to monitor both work completed and the accuracy of that work may be an effective method of providing the beginning steps to a higher proportion of engaged time.

Self-monitoring strategies have been demonstrated to be useful in reducing academic failure for LD students. Schumaker, Deshler, Alley, Warner, and Denton (1982) demonstrated that adolescents could use strategies to obtain information. Chi (1981), working with younger children, pointed out that content-specific categorization improved when children were encouraged to use knowledge-based information rather than perceptual similarities. Gerber (1982) found that self-monitoring affected spelling accuracy. Loper, Hallahan, and Ianna (1982) report that self-monitoring focused LD students' attention better.

Questions seem to provide yet another means of self-monitoring. In a series of studies, Wong (1979, 1980) has demonstrated that questions influence reading comprehension. Specifically, Wong (1979) found that the use of questions facilitated main idea retention for LD students. In her 1980 study, Wong found that the recall of implied information (script-implicit) improved to the extent that the performance of the LD group equaled that of the control group. Wong and Jones (1982), too, found that self-questioning was important—this time in making LD students aware of textual units.

In learning to self-question, two distinct phases appear necessary. During the first phase, students need to learn to move away from old habits, to begin reflecting before acting. Secondly, LD students need to learn to generalize their new routines. The specific procedures that follow were developed for use at the LAC and have been tested only with individual students. In trying this two-step technique, teachers should proceed with caution since no formal studies have been conducted to evaluate the effectiveness of the procedures that follow.

Beginning Steps

When an LD student is beginning to learn to ask self-questions about personal work habits, some extra teacher support may be necessary. Reassurance, if it is necessary, may best be provided when students learn new algorithms, extend previously learned or new algorithms, attempt a difficult task, or stretch their content knowledge. The result of any of these may be emotional turmoil. For example, Susan became upset when she was unable to complete her mathematics assignment. She had been very carefully following a list of self-monitoring questions, which she had memorized; however, a few of the mathematics problems were ones she had not faced. Her reaction was to retreat back to an old habit of refusing to work. After some time and considerable emotional support, she was able to start work again; however the limitations of self-questioning were brought home.

Initially, then, encouraging students to learn to self-question requires several teacher precautions. First, task difficulty should be carefully monitored, if not controlled directly. The example given in the last paragraph illustrates the results of student overextension. Second, it is useful to model self-questioning in situations where the advantages of following this procedure are immediately evident. Third, either oral rehearsal while working or following a written checklist is necessary until the routine is overlearned.

Teaching for Transfer

Not much is known about how to teach LD students to transfer from setting to setting. The debate continues as to whether to provide similar conditions for learning or to provide strategies as a way of effecting transfer. In a recently completed study, Freeze (1984) reports that providing strategies, such as teaching rules for mathematics questions, was the more effective technique for four LD students in grade four.

Two other considerations may be useful as well. First, the content difficulty level may be increased. There are two assumptions in making this change: (a) the self-monitoring techniques are held constant and (b) the content is familiar. Gradually, the content may be adjusted so that the student is applying self-checking techniques as necessary. The second step is to encourage students to apply self-monitoring skills to problems where the problem structure is less straightforward. They may be encouraged, for example, to try word problems with extraneous information or problems that are script-implicit.

A Final Caution

It was suggested earlier in this chapter that questioning does not always facilitate learning. The goal in self-questioning is for the student to use it only when necessary. To accomplish this goal, continuous use of self-questioning (or any other self-monitoring technique) must be eliminated, as such techniques are a hinderance in some instances. Self-questioning will not be effective when the task has time constraints or when the goal is to achieve automaticity of skill. Thus, as LD students become more confident in applying self-questioning strategies, they should be encouraged to forgo any overt cues or prompts they have adopted in learning these techniques.

CONCLUSION

Three different types of suggestions have been offered to help LD students be more effective learners. The first suggestions were related to question asking, the second ones to responding to answers, and the third set to using questions to self-monitor.

Questions do have an influence on a student's achievement; however, at any one time that effect may be positive, neutral, or negative. To increase the probability that this effect will be positive, questions should be designed to take into account the type of question asked or written, the way the question is presented, and the history of the learner. Further, questions appear to have a more positive influence when they are thought of as being linked to the text or dependent on the learner, or as question–answer or question-answer-interpretation relationships.

REFERENCES

Alley, G., & Deshler, D. (1979). *Teaching the learning disabled adolescent strategies and methods*. Denver, CO: Love Publishing.

Anderson, T.H. (1980). Study strategies and adjunct aids. In R.J. Spiro, B.B. Bruce, & W.F. Brewer (Eds.), *Theoretical issues in reading comprehension* (pp. 484–502). Hillsdale, NJ: Lawrence Erlbaum.

Andre, T. (1979). Does answering higher-level questions while reading facilitate productive learning? *Review of Educational Research, 49,* 280–318.

Bachor, D.G. (1979). Using work samples as diagnostic information. *Learning Disabilities Quarterly, 2,* 45–52.

Bachor, D.G. (1981, April). *Responding to questions to continue classroom participation.* Paper presented at the 59th Annual Conference of the Council for Exceptional Children, New York.

Bachor, D.G. (1983). Personnel preparation for learning assistance teachers: School based instruction. *Special Education in Canada, 57*(2), 29–32.

Bachor, D.G., Sitko, M., & Slemon, A. (1980). Information processing demands of questions on the student with special needs. In G.M. Kysela (Ed.), *The exceptional child in Canadian education* (7th Yearbook of The Canadian Society for Studies in Education, pp. 100–108).

Banton, L. (1978). Broadening the scope of classroom questions. *Educational Digest, 43,* 36–28.

Baroody, A.J., Ginsburg, H.P., & Wakman, B. (1983). Children's use of mathematical structure. *Journal for Research in Mathematics Education, 14,* 156–168.

Bartel, N. (1984). Problems in mathematics achievement. In D.D. Hammill, N.R. Bartel, & G.O. Bunch (Eds.), *Teaching children with learning and behavior problems* (Canadian ed., pp. 199–246). Toronto: Allyn and Bacon.

Bloom, B.S., Engelhart, M.D., Hill, W.H., Furst, E.J., & Krathwohl, D.R. (1956). *Taxonomy of educational objectives: The classification of educational goals. Handbook 1. Cognitive domain.* New York: McKay.

Brophy, J.E. (1979). Teacher behavior and its effects. *Journal of Educational Psychology, 71,* 733–750.

Brophy, J.E. (1981). Teacher praise: A functional analysis. *Review of Educational Research, 51,* 5–32.

Brown, A.L. (1975). The development of memory: Knowing, knowing about knowing and knowing how to know. In H.W. Reese (Ed.), *Advances in child development and behavior* (Vol. 10, pp. 103–152). New York: Academic Press.

Brown, A.L. (1978). Knowing when, where, and how to remember: A problem of metacognition. In R. Glaser (Ed.), *Advances in instructional psychology.* (pp. 77–165). Hillsdale, NJ: Lawrence Erlbaum.

Brownell, W.A. (1928). *The development of children's number ideas in the primary grades.* (University of Chicago Supplementary Educational Monographs, No. 35). Chicago: University of Chicago.

Case, R. (1978a). A developmentally based theory and technology of instruction. *Review of Educational Research, 48,* 439–463.

Case, R. (1978b). Piaget and beyond: Towards a developmentally based theory and technology of instruction. In R. Glaser (Ed.), *Advances in instructional psychology* (Vol. 1, pp. 167–228). Hillsdale, NJ: Lawrence Erlbaum.

Cawley, J.F., Fitzmaurice, A.M., Shaw, R.A., Kahn, H., & Bates, H. (1979). Math word problems: Suggestions for LD students. *Learning Disabilities Quarterly, 2*(2), 25–41.

Cawley, J.E., Goodstein, H.A., & Burrow, W.H. (1972). *The slow learner and the reading problem.* Springfield, IL: Charles C. Thomas.

Chi, M. (1981). Representing knowledge and metaknowledge: implications for interpreting memory research. In F. Weinert & R. Kluwe (Eds.). *Learning by thinking*. West Germany: Kuhlhammer.

Crawford, J., Brophy, J.E., Evertson, C.M., & Coulter, C.L. (1977). Classroom dyadic interaction: Factor structure of process variables and achievement correlates. *Journal of Educational Psychology, 69,* 761–772.

Dillion, J.T. (1981). To question and not to question during discussion: II. Non-questioning techniques. *Journal of Teacher Education, 32*(6), 15–20.

Dillion, J.T. (1982). Cognitive correspondence between question/statement and response. *American Educational Research Journal, 19,* 540–551.

Dillion, J.T. (1983). Cognitive complexity and duration of classroom speech. *Instructional Science, 12,* 59–66.

Durkin, D. (1981). What is the value of the new interest in reading comprehension? *Language Arts, 58,* 23–43.

Dweck, C.S. (1975). The role of expectations and attributions in the alleviation of learned helplessness. *Journal of Personality and Social Psychology, 31,* 674–685.

Dweck, C.S., & Repucci, N.D. (1973). Learned helplessness and reinforcement responsibility in children. *Journal of Personality and Social Psychology, 25,* 109–116.

Dweck, C.S., & Wortman, C.B. (1982). Learned helplessness, anxiety, and achievement motivation: Neglected parallels in cognitive, affective, and coping responses. In H.W. Krohne & L. Laux (Eds.), *Achievement, stress, and anxiety* (pp. 73–125). Washington, DC: Hemisphere.

Feuerstein, R. (1979). *The dynamic assessment of retarded performers: The learning potential assessment device, theory, instruments, and techniques*. Baltimore: University Park Press.

Fish, M.C., & White, M.A. (1978–1979). The effects of verbal reinforcement, interest and "usable performance feedback" upon task performance. *Journal of Experimental Education, 47,* 144–148.

Freeze, D.R. (1984). *A comparison of cognitive and behavioral programs to promote the transfer of learning across educational settings for four learning disabled children*. Unpublished master's thesis, University of Victoria, Victoria, British Columbia.

Gerber, M.M. (1982, April). *Effects of self-monitoring on spelling performance of learning-disabled and normally-achieving students*. Paper presented at the American Educational Research Association Conference, New York.

Goelman, H. (1982). Selective attention in language comprehension: Children's processing of expository and narrative discourse. *Discourse Processes, 5,* 53–72.

Goelman, H. (1983, October). *Question answering in normal and language disabled children: An exploratory study*. Paper presented at the International Conference on Learning Disabilities, San Francisco.

Hall, R.J. (1980). Cognitive behavior modification and information processing skills in exceptional children. *Exceptional Education Quarterly, 1,* 9–15.

Herman, W.L. (1967). An analysis of the activities and verbal behavior of selected fifth-grade social studies classes. *Journal of Education Research, 60,* 339–345.

Larson, S.C., Parker, R., & Trenholme, B. (1978). The effects of syntactic complexity upon arithmetic performance. *Learning Disability Quarterly, 1,* 80–85.

Liedtke, W. (1982). Learning difficulties: Helping young children with mathematics—subtraction. *Arithmetic Teacher, 30*(4), 21–23.

Liedtke, W. (1984). Learning difficulties: Dealing with problem solving in mathematics. *Special Education in Canada, 58*(3), 82–85.

Loper, A.B. (1980). Metacognitive development: Implications for cognitive training. *Exceptional Education Quarterly, 1,* 1–8.

Loper, A.B., Hallahan, D.P., & Ianna, S.O. (1982). Meta-attention in learning-disabled and normal students. *Learning Disability Quarterly, 5,* 29–36.

MacGinitie, W. (1983, October). *Vocabulary and comprehension discrepancies.* Paper presented at the International Conference on Learning Disabilities, San Francisco.

Pearson, P.D., & Johnson, D.D. (1978). *Teaching reading comprehension.* New York: Holt, Rinehart & Winston.

Raphael, T. (1982). *Improving question-answering performance through instruction* (Reading Education Rep. No. 32). Champaign, IL: Center for the Study of Reading, Bolt, Baranek and Newman.

Raphael, T., & Pearson, P.D. (1982). *The effect of meta-cognitive training on children's question-answering behavior* (Tech. Rep. No. 238). Champaign, IL: Center for the Study of Reading, Bolt, Baranek and Newman.

Redfield, D.L., & Rousseau, E.W. (1981). A meta-analysis of experimental research on teacher questioning behavior. *Review of Educational Research, 51,* 237–245.

Rosenshine, B.V. (1979). Content, time and direct instruction. In P.L. Peterson & H.J. Walberg (Eds.), *Research on teaching: Concepts, findings and implications* (pp. 28–56). Berkeley, CA: McCutchan.

Rowe, M.B. (1973). *Teaching science as continuous inquiry* (Chap. 8). New York: McGraw-Hill.

Rowe, M.B. (1978). Wait, wait, wait . . . *School, Science, and Mathematics, 78,* 207–216.

Samuels, S.J. (1981). Some essentials of decoding. *Exceptional Education Quarterly, 2*(1), 11–25.

Sanders, N. (1966). *Classroom questions: What kinds?* New York: Harper & Row.

Schumaker, J.B., Deshler, D.D., Alley, G.R., Warner, M.M., & Denton, P.H. (1982). Multipass: A learning strategy for improving reading comprehension. *Learning Disability Quarterly, 5,* 295–304.

Sharma, M.C. (1981). Using word problems to aid language and reading comprehension. *Topics in Learning and Learning Disabilities, 1*(3), 61–71.

Sitko, M., & Slemon, A.G. (1982). Developing teachers' questioning skills: The efficacy of delayed feedback. *Canadian Journal of Education, 7,* 109–121.

Sitko, M.C., Bachor, D.G., & Slemon, A.G. (1980, July). *A critical review of teacher questioning techniques: Implications for research and teacher training.* Unpublished manuscript, University of Western Ontario, London, Ontario.

Sitko, M.C., Bachor, D.G., Slemon, A.G., & Turner, L.A. (1980). *Teacher pupil request system.* London, Ontario: University of Western Ontario, Faculty of Education.

Sitko, M.C., & Slemon, A.G. (1978). *The development and evaluation of a training package for inservice teachers on hierarchical questioning strategies for teaching children with learning disabilities* (Final Report to the Ministry of Education). London, Ontario: University of Western Ontario, Faculty of Education.

Sitko, M., Slemon, A., & Bachor, D. (1983). A questioning and feedback system for developing comprehension skills. *Special Education in Canada, 57*(2), 19–32.

Slemon, A.G., Bachor, D.G., Sitko, M.C., & Turner, L.A. (1980). *Interpretation of pupil answers.* London, Ontario: University of Western Ontario, Faculty of Education.

Stallings, J.A. (1976). How instructional processes relate to child outcomes in a national study of follow through. *Journal of Teacher Education, 27*, 43–47.

Stevens, R., & Rosenshine, B. (1981). Advances in research on teaching. *Exceptional Education Quarterly, 2*(1), 1–9.

Summers, G.C. (1984), *Learned helplessness, test anxiety, and learning disabilities: An assessment with intermediate-age children.* Unpublished master's thesis, University of Victoria, Victoria, British Columbia.

Torgesen, J.K. (1979). Factors related to poor performance on memory tasks in reading disabled children. *Learning Disability Quarterly, 2*, 17–23.

Wong, B.Y.L. (1979). Increasing retention of main ideas through questioning strategies. *Learning Disability Quarterly, 2*(2), 42–48.

Wong, B.Y.L. (1980). Activating the inactive learner: Use of questions/prompts to enhance comprehension and retention of implied information in learning disabled children. *Learning Disability Quarterly, 3*(1), 29–37.

Wong, B.Y.L., & Jones, W. (1982). Increasing metacomprehension in learning disabled and normally achieving students through self-questioning. *Learning Disability Quarterly, 5*, 228–240.

Chapter 10

Classroom Implications

Anne M. Fitzmaurice Hayes

Ideally, curriculum should be purposefully based on a body of content and a set of learning principles. A curriculum designed for children with special needs should also reflect an attempt to provide for those needs. Mathematics curricula can be no exceptions to these observations.

The preceding chapters of this volume are replete with descriptions of the cognitive characteristics of learning disabled (LD) students and the effects of such characteristics on learning mathematics. These traits include problems in developing effective memorization strategies, including rehearsal techniques, difficulties in the areas of written and spoken language, the inability to attend to tasks for appropriate amounts of time, and so on. In mathematics such problems can present themselves as the inability to read or to produce written symbols, whether numerals or signs of operation, pronounced difficulty in remembering the basic number combinations, ineffective attempts to remember a sequence of steps for an algorithm, or the inadequate interpretation of a set of information necessary to solve a problem, especially when the medium through which the information is expressed is the spoken or written word.

Kosc (1981) specified four factors affecting mathematical ability:

> (1) psychological factors such as cognitive style and intellectual attributes; (2) educational effects of appropriate and inappropriate instructional practices and curriculum patterns; (3) personality factors that influence learning styles and performance capabilities; and (4) the individual neuropsychological pattern or developmental status [p. 19].

Clearly, a chapter entitled "Classroom Implications" should have as its focus the second of these factors. The writer must admit to a bias in favor of the beneficial impact that good instruction—that based on sound learning principles—can have on the learning of mathematics, even by those students who appear to bring inherent obstacles to such learning.

Certainly, the development of an entire mathematics curriculum designed to represent both a comprehensive theory of learning and learning disabilities (should either set of knowledge exist) is beyond the scope of this chapter. On the other hand, principles of learning and the reduction of the influence of impediments to learning can and should be translated into classroom practice. This chapter is devoted to suggestions for instructional activities representing accepted theories of learning, with a view to their use in circumventing some of the problems LD students bring to the attainment of skills and concepts in mathematics.

Greenwood and Anderson (1983) provided a framework for the organization of such suggestions when they recommended the following guidelines for mathematics instruction:

- the provision of an environment that stimulates communication between instructor and student;
- the requiring of a demonstration of conceptual understanding before skills are emphasized;
- a definition of computational proficiency in terms of both speed and accuracy;
- a focus on students' ability to observe patterns and relationships;
- the explicit appreciation of novel ways of approaching problems and skills; and
- the promotion of self-diagnosis, self-evaluation, and self-awareness procedures for all students [p. 49].

When followed, each guideline can reduce the impact of learning disabilities on learning mathematics.

DEVELOPING AN ATMOSPHERE OF COMMUNICATION

Benefits

As a form of language, mathematics is a form of communication. Our emphasis here, however, is on helping students communicate their knowledge and understanding of mathematics through the spoken word. Encouraging students to communicate orally with the mathematics instructor can provide many benefits.

Such communication can serve as a diagnostic aid. Sam, a third grader, was asked to work out loud during his solution to an exercise like the one shown in Figure 10-1. Accustomed to such requests, he began confidently, going across the top row. "Three and two—that's thirty two. I write it here." He pointed to the box in the upper right-hand corner.

His procedure seemed to indicate a misunderstanding about place value and the addition of two-digit numbers. Further probing, however, revealed that even though Sam knew that the directions called for the operation of addition, the absence of the symbol + led him to believe that he was to do something different. What that might be, he had no idea, but Sam was convinced that he "couldn't add unless there was a plus sign." Because the classroom environment encouraged students to express their notions of what they were doing, Sam's problems came to light.

The interview technique is a time-honored strategy for diagnosis. As LD students progress through school, they sometimes invent their own methods for computation. Occasionally, these algorithms defy analysis if the analysis must be based on written work only. When students are asked to explain their procedures, they often reveal the aberrant behaviors, and the instructor can design appropriate remedial experiences.

Communication from instructor to learner and from learner to instructor can serve yet another function amenable to the learning process—rehearsal. Some LD students seem to lack appropriate strategies for rehearsal. By encouraging students to rephrase mathematics content, to list steps in a process, to provide examples of a concept, or the like, the instructor can provide cues for such rehearsal. Since the rehearsal of inappropriate behaviors should be avoided, the instructor must provide much assistance at the beginning of such a process. Gradually, however, the number of cues provided can become fewer, as the learner assumes more and more responsibility for providing his or her own cues.

Figure 10-1 An Exercise in Addition of Two-Place Numbers

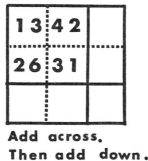

Add across.
Then add down.

Oral communication can help students to integrate new knowledge with old. Such integration helps to avoid a piecemeal approach to the learning of mathematics. Of course the instructor in the course of a presentation must of necessity tie new concepts to those already attained. Equally important, however, is an approach that encourages students to do some linking by themselves, and to share those insights with others. This process enables the LD student to assume a more active role in the learning process.

Finally, there is evidence to support the contention that requiring low-achieving students to vocalize their approaches to problem-solving activities, and to listen to the vocalizations of others (both proficient and nonproficient problem solvers), serves to improve skills in problem solving (Whimbey, 1977, 1979). Such vocalization must take place regularly and should occur within a structured program of problem-solving activities.

Teaching with an Emphasis on Oral Communication

Communication techniques can be developed formally and informally during mathematics instruction. Cawley's Interactive Unit (1984) provides for four instructor/learner combinations that require oral responses on the part of the learner; manipulate/state, display/state, state/state, and write/state. Through skillful use, these combinations can be effective in helping an LD child develop facility in expressing his or her understanding of mathematics content. The following lessons illustrate how these combinations might work across different mathematics topics.

Topic: Parallel lines
Interaction: Manipulate/state
Using suitable materials, the instructor makes several models of parallel line segments, as illustrated in Figure 10-2.

The instructor asks the student to describe what has been done. The instructor, if necessary, provides cues until the student describes the instructor's behavior as that of laying out the material so that, within each model, the distance between the represented line segments was everywhere the same. If the student uses the word *parallel* before giving the correct description, the instructor continues prodding—for example, "What does parallel mean? Can you describe it?"

Interaction: Display/state
The instructor shows the learner models of parallel line segments. The instructor asks the student to tell what the pairs of lines have in common. If necessary, the instructor provides cues, as before.

Figure 10-2 Models of Parallel Lines

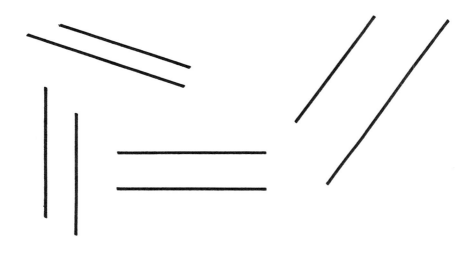

Interaction: State/state

The instructor states the definition of parallel lines, using whatever definition the student's mathematics program provides, and then asks the student to tell what the definition means. The instructor next asks the student to repeat the definition, at first with the instructor, and then alone. When the student can repeat the definition alone and unaided, the instructor asks the student to provide examples of models of parallel lines. The student is encouraged to provide as many examples as time allows.

Interaction: Write/state

The instructor shows the student the word *parallel* written on one card and the definition of parallel written on another card. The learner is asked to read the word and the definition aloud. The instructor removes the card containing the word *parallel* and asks the student to read the definition aloud and to provide the word. The instructor removes the definition, shows the student the word *parallel,* and asks the student to recite the definition. If the student falters, the written definition is provided as a support and the request repeated. Finally, the instructor asks the student to tell what the definition means in her or his own words, and to provide examples from everyday life and from other mathematics content (e.g., geometric shapes).

These activities, when carried out as described, provide specifically for the following needs that LD students may demonstrate:

- *The need to assume a more active role in the learning process.* In the manipulate/state and display/state combinations, the learner is required to develop the definition of parallel, aided only by appropriate questions from the instructor. Such a procedure is consistent with the requirement for building solid concepts, and its frequent use can create within the student an attitude of searching for meaning in the mathematics content presented.

- *The need for rehearsal.* The concept of parallel lines is a relatively easy one for most students to comprehend. The implications of parallelism, however, are many, and the formal definition finds many applications in geometry. Both the state/state and the write/state combinations, as described, provide much opportunity for the rehearsal and, ideally, the memorization of the definition. The acquisition of such material in a meaningful context serves to develop in the learning disabled the awareness that mathematics is an area of content under her or his control, rather than a subject the knowledge of which is largely a hit-or-miss matter. This latter approach becomes more and more characteristic of LD students as they progress through school.

- *The need to relate mathematics content to other contexts.* The request that the student name instances of parallel lines from everyday life is designed not only to check on the student's understanding and identification of parallelism, but also to help the student become aware of the role parallelism plays in building, design, organization, and so forth. The student who is proficient at this kind of linking might be further challenged to discuss with the teacher a world in which parallelism was outlawed. What would some of the consequences be? How would life as we know it be changed? Such a discussion offers much possibility for growth in the area of divergent production.

The next set of activities examines more instructional techniques effective in meeting some of the cognitive needs of LD students. At the same time, they provide suggestions on how role reversal can enhance the rehearsal process.

Topic: Measuring length with a ruler
Interaction: Manipulate/state

While the student watches, the instructor slowly and carefully demonstrates the procedure for measuring the length of a pencil with a ruler. The instructor then repeats the demonstration, this time asking the student to describe orally, in his or her own words, the action taking place, prompting the student to attend to salient points, if necessary. This process is repeated as many times as deemed necessary.

Interaction: Display/state

The instructor displays, one at a time, a set of illustrations depicting a sequence of steps used to measure the length of an item with a ruler. As each illustration is presented, the child is asked to describe orally, in his or her own words, the action taking place in the picture. As before, the instructor prompts where necessary.

Interaction: Write/state

The teacher gives the child a set of written directions for measuring the length of an item. The student reads the directions aloud, and then explains the process in his or her own words. If necessary, each step is presented singly.

Interaction: State/manipulate

For this lesson, student and teacher exchange roles. The teacher asks the student to give directions as the teacher measures the length of an item. The teacher follows the student's directions exactly and accepts corrections as they are given.

As before, the student's oral responses in the preceding lessons provide verbal rehearsal of a sequence of steps to be followed when measuring length. The exchange of roles in the last activity can serve as a self-monitoring technique for the child. The teacher's behavior provides instant feedback on the correctness of the direction given. The child's behavior consequent to watching the instructor perform in response to an incorrect direction can offer the instructor some diagnostic information. The child who recognizes the teacher's error and rephrases the direction is of much less concern than the child who fails to perceive the error at all.

The provision of an environment that stimulates communication and, in particular, oral communication between instructor and student, as just described, can encourage LD students to elaborate on the material presented, to connect newly learned material with that previously understood, and hence to retain better the new material.

In general, LD students do not demonstrate effective problem-solving strategies, at least not when problems are presented in the course of mathematics instruction. Whimbey (1979) described a program found to be effective for teaching analytical reasoning to educationally disadvantaged students. The simplicity of the program recommends it for consideration by teachers of LD students, who exhibit many of the same characteristics found in Whimbey's group of adolescents.

The program is ten weeks in duration. A major component of the format is the vocalization of the mental processes used to solve the problems presented. This vocalization takes place between students and instructors or between students working in pairs and alternating roles as vocalizer and listener. The listener's role is one of attending to the problem-solving strategies of the vocalizer and correcting errors when they occur. Students in Whimbey's program also read transcribed protocols of good problem solvers working on similar problems. For LD students with limited reading skills, these protocols could be recorded on cassette tapes and played for the learners.

The problems chosen for the instructional program are quite simple in nature, initially requiring very little in the way of arithmetic skills. A sample problem is the following: "If three days before tomorrow is Thursday, what is four days after yesterday [Whimbey, 1979, p. 311]?" The reader is reminded that the problem exists not for the purpose of quickly arriving at the answer but for providing students with an opportunity to develop skills in analyzing given information in sequence and using the results of the analysis to arrive at a solution.

The reader attempting to solve the problem will note that the context and information lend themselves to visual organization, or diagramming. Students in the program receive help in building the diagram and in vocalizing their way to a solution of the problem. After one type of such days of the week problems are considered, other, similar forms are presented. In every case vocalization appears to be effective in helping students sort out and organize the information given.

It seems reasonable to claim, then, that the structuring of situations that demand that the child use language orally to communicate mathematics content should be a regular part of lesson planning. The meaningless repetition of a learned script is to be avoided, however. Such a concern brings us to the next recommendation of Greenwood and Anderson (1983): the requiring of a demonstration of conceptual understanding before skills are emphasized.

BUILDING AN UNDERSTANDING OF MATHEMATICS

Benefits

Van Engen (1953) pointed out that the student who claims, "I know what you mean but I don't understand it," can be making a great deal of sense. Students can, quite often, attach meaning to a set of directions, without understanding the why behind the procedure. Unfortunately, for many LD students, the focus has centered for too long on "how" to perform an operation, rather than on "why" the how works.

Ausubel (1968) noted that "Meaningful learning presupposes . . . that the learner manifest . . . a disposition to relate the new material nonarbitrarily and substantively to his cognitive structure [p. 38]." Among the reasons for learners not manifesting such a disposition, Ausubel listed the following:

- teacher expectation. That is, the child has learned that any response which deviates from the parroting of the material presented meets with disapproval.
- a generally high level of anxiety.
- chronic failure experience in a given subject.
- excessive pressure to produce "right answers" [p. 38].

Many teachers of LD children, concerned with mathematics instruction, will recognize one or more of the preceding traits as becoming more and more characteristic of LD students as they make their way through school. How does an instructor teach mathematics so that conceptual understanding takes place? Here we define "conceptual understanding" as knowing the reasons for the "how" in mathematics—that is, an understanding that makes unnecessary the claim: "I know what you mean, but I don't understand it."

Developing Understanding

Understanding the "why" behind the "how" requires the learning of concepts and rules. Gagne (1970) defined concept learning as "putting things into a class and responding to the class as a whole [p. 172]." In concert with other theorists, Gagne recognized both concrete concepts and abstract concepts. At a higher level, because of its dependence on previously formed concepts, Gagne (1970) placed rule learning: "an internal state of the individual which governs his behavior . . . . A rule, then, is an inferred capability that enables the individual to respond to a class of stimulus situations with a class of performances, the latter being predictably related to the former by a class of relations [p. 191]." More simply stated, a rule is formed from concepts and a recognized necessary relationship between or among them. This relationship governs responses to situations in which the concepts are operative together. Learning mathematics requires the attainment of a limitless number of concepts and rules.

As noted before, Ausubel (1968) made explicit the requirement that a learner desire to relate new material to that already present in the learner's repertoire of knowledge if meaningful learning is to result. Gagne (1970) listed among the conditions for concept learning to take place the following:

- the presence in the learner of previous knowledge on which the new concept is to build. For example, before a child can develop a concept of *even number,* the concepts of numerosity, pairing, etc. must be present
- the use of verbal instructions (for more efficient human learning)
- the pairing of the verbal label with instances of the concept
- the requiring of the learner to provide the verbal label when new instances of the concept are presented
- the verification of the learning by asking for identification of several additional examples of the concept. [pp. 200–202]

Klausmeier and Ripple (1971) spelled out these steps in greater detail. We have used their list in Table 10-1, along with our own examples from mathematics, to illustrate an approach to concept building.

Rule Learning

The topics chosen for the examples of activities designed for building concepts lead us to the consideration of rules and instruction ordered to meaningful rule development. Although representable with pictures and objects, perpendicular is more properly viewed as an abstract concept. Likewise, one-half and the class of rational numbers of which one-half is a member are not concrete concepts. Their definitions actually provide an example of one type of rule, according to Gagne (1970).

Mathematics as a discipline is a system of rules. The reader may recall his or her introduction to the study of geometry, when the structure represented in Figure 10-7 might have been explained. The reader may also recall that each time a new theorem was shown to be true, by way of the rules of logic, that new theorem could in turn be used to demonstrate the truth of another proposition and, in that way, chains of propositions were linked together to form the body of content called geometry.

To a certain degree, children acquire a body of content in much the same way, according to Gagne. Rules are chains of concepts, and a primary prerequisite for learning rules is a knowledge of the concepts in the chain.

Table 10-1 Steps in Concept Building

Instructional Guide	Concept	Concept
	Perpendicular	One-half
1. Emphasize the attributes of the concept.	Display several examples of perpendicularity, as shown in Figure 10-3. In each case emphasize by pointing or shading the "square" corners. The examples should consist of both pictures and three-dimensional objects.	Display several examples of one-half, including models like those in Figure 10-5. The models should consist of both pictures and three-dimensional objects.
2. Establish the correct terminology for concepts, attributes, and instances.	Point out that each item on display shows what perpendicular means. Display written word.	Point out that each item on display shows what one-half means. Display ½, words *one-half*.
3. Indicate the nature of the concepts to be learned.	Tell students that during the lesson they will learn the meaning of the word *perpendicular*.	Tell students that during the lesson they will learn the meaning of one-half.
4. Provide for proper sequencing of instances of concepts.	Point out each item in the display, telling students that the item represents an example of perpendicular. Also point out some examples of nonperpendicularity (Figure 10-4).	Point out each item in the display, telling students that the item represents an example of one-half. Also point out some examples that do not illustrate one-half (Figure 10-6).
5. Encourage and guide student discovery.	Ask the students to name the characteristic that the examples in Figure 10-3 have in common, that is not characteristic of the examples given in Figure 10-4. Guide students to form an appropriate definition of perpendicular.	Ask the students to tell how all the examples shown in Figure 10-5 are alike. This same property is missing in the examples in Figure 10-6. Guide students to a formulation of the definition of one-half.
6. Provide for use of the concept.	Ask students to label (either orally or in writing) examples of perpendicular line segments or surfaces found in the classroom.	Display some examples of one-half mixed in with examples of other rational numbers and whole numbers. Ask students to label the exam-

Table 10-1 continued

Instructional Guide	Concept	Concept
		ples of one-half. Ask each student to draw an example of one-half different from any on display.
7. Encourage independent evaluation of the attained concept.	Encourage each child to answer these questions for himself or herself: Do I know what perpendicular means? Can I give examples of perpendicular? Could I explain to someone else the meaning of perpendicular?	Encourage each child to answer these questions for himself or herself: Do I know what one-half means? Can I give examples of one-half from my surroundings? Could I explain to someone else the meaning of one-half?

Source: Data in the first column are reprinted from *Learning and human abilities* by H. Klausmeier & R. Ripple, pp. 422–423, with permission of Harper & Row Publishers, Inc., ©1971.

In addition to this knowledge, and presupposing its existence, Gagne listed the following conditions for rule learning:

- a statement by the instructor of the general nature of what the student is to be able to do when the learning task has been completed
- the recall of the concepts to be joined or elaborated upon
- the provision of verbal cues leading the student to formulate the new rule
- a request that the student demonstrate his or her knowledge of the new rule
- a request that the learner state the rule aloud or in writing

The reader will note the similarities between the steps just listed and the sequence illustrated for the topics perpendicular and one-half. Common to both sets of procedures are the requirements that the learner come to the task with the necessary prerequisite concepts and/or rules, and that instances of the new concept or rule be presented. Two cautions must be attended to when the student is learning disabled.

The first of these is the possible need for many instances of the rule or concept to be presented before the defining attributes or concept chains are recognized and verbalized correctly. Textbooks may not always provide the necessary number of examples. In this area computer-assisted

Figure 10-3 Models of Perpendicular Lines

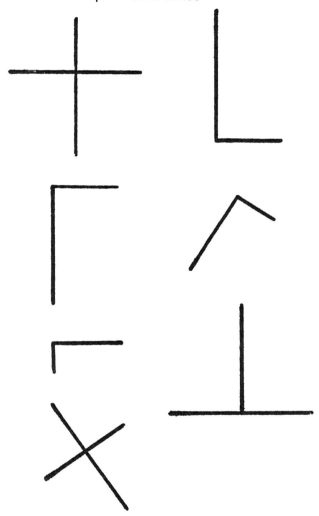

instruction can be quite beneficial. Properly programmed, software packages have the potential for providing many varied instances of a concept or rule, thus providing the LD child with the opportunity to formulate the rule or concept.

The second caution concerns the failure of some LD students to generalize rules that have been learned. The LD student in the regular math-

Figure 10-4 Examples of Not Perpendicular

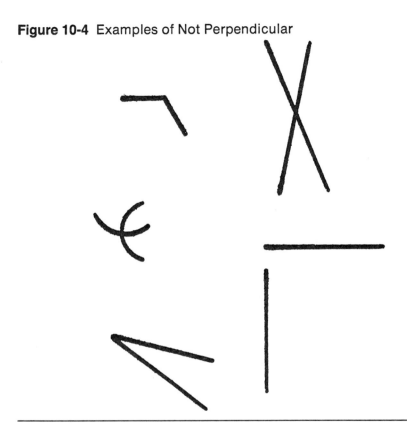

ematics classroom can be often heard to complain, "But you didn't teach us how to do that," *that* being an example that differs only slightly from the type that were explicitly taught. Blankenship and Baumgartner (1982) distinguished between students who "can't" generalize and students who "can but won't" generalize (p. 161). In their study of the ability of LD students to generalize from instructed to noninstructed types of subtraction examples, the investigators found that each member of the group of nine students, all of whom performed similarly during the collection of baseline data, fell into one of three categories. One group of students were able to learn the skills and apply the skills to examples of different types. For a second group of students, initial failure to generalize was remedied when reinforcement was provided specifically for such generalization behavior. The members of the third group, however, did not improve in generalization behaviors, even when reinforcement was provided. For the latter group, Blankenship and Baumgartner recommended instruction

Figure 10-5 Models of One-Half

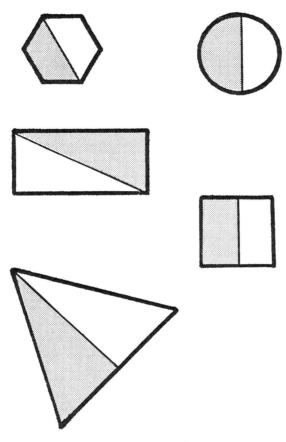

designed to make explicit similarities between instructed and noninstructed tasks. The teacher of mathematics must be aware of the difficulty of generalization characteristic of some students and must provide explicit instruction when necessary.

This instruction should be designed, whenever possible, to lead the students to see similarities among problems or examples independently. Initially, the teacher may have to go through a set of exercises with the students, pointing out the application of the learned skill in each case. After some practice in acknowledging similarities that have been pointed out to them, students should be challenged to find the similarities on their

Figure 10-6 Examples of Not One-Half

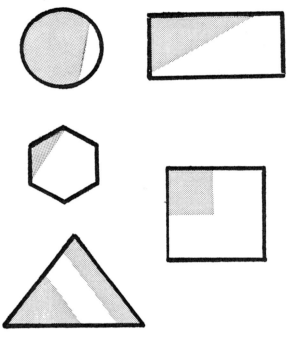

own. After much guidance, generalization may begin to occur spontaneously.

The rules in any subject area, particularly in mathematics, form a hierarchy. Good instruction is based upon such a hierarchy and leads the student up through the hierarchy one step at a time. Unfortunately, the hierarchy is not always linear, nor does a single upward line represent the path. Anyone who has attempted to perform a task analysis for any but the simplest of desired behaviors will readily admit the truth of the preceding statement. However, rules are more easily and certainly retained when the approach to them has included the verification that prerequisite concepts and rules are in place.

Once prerequisite concepts and the resulting rules are in place, skills can be emphasized so that certain behaviors can be performed with facility and speed. These skills include, but are not limited to, computation. Hence we are led to consider the next guideline in Greenwood and Anerson's list: a definition of computational proficiency in terms of both speed and accuracy.

Figure 10-7 Structure of Geometry

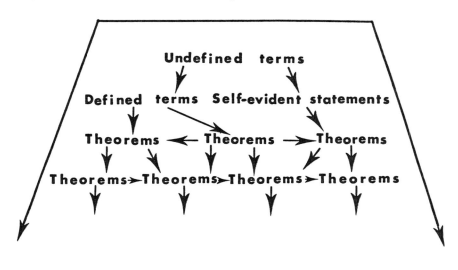

COMPUTATIONAL PROFICIENCY

Perhaps because so much emphasis is placed on computational proficiency in the elementary and secondary school setting, the computational deficits of LD children have received much attention. From a curriculum standpoint, one must approach the topic of computational proficiency with the answers to three questions in hand:

1. What levels of computational proficiency are desirable?
2. What levels of mastery are desirable?
3. What prerequisite skills and abilities does the attainment of the desired level of mastery of a given level of proficiency require?

Assuming that the answers to those questions are available, and that they represent reasonable objectives for an LD child, the question faced by the classroom teacher is, "What are the learning experiences most conducive to the attainment of computational proficiency?"

What are the problems manifested by LD children who are deficient in computation skills? Levy's analysis (1979) of the terminology that has been developed to label these obstacles gives some idea of the multitude of possible answers to this question. Levy reported 37 terms used to describe problems LD children may bring to arithmetic calculations. Many of these difficulties seem related to memory and the recall of appropriate responses (verbal or graphic) to stimuli of a mathematical nature.

Such difficulties are well documented in the educational literature. The ability to retain facts and skills and to retrieve such information from memory is crucial in mathematics. Not only must such retention and retrieval be operative, but speed and efficiency must also mark these components of memory.

Sternberg and Wagner (1982) described the LD person as one who "again and again must devote attention to tasks and task components that others have long ago mastered. Processing resources that in others have been freed and used to master new tasks are in the disabled person devoted to tasks that others have already mastered [p. 2]." The secondary school teacher of basic algebra will readily recognize the student who questions every step in the solution of a linear equation, long after the process has become all but automatic to other students. For such a student, even the clearest explanation of the factoring method of solution of quadratic equations can have little meaning, for he or she becomes mired in confusion resulting from falling behind because of the need to supply every step of a process overly familiar to other students.

Likewise, the elementary school student who is dependent on charts or finger counting for answers to most of the basic combinations of addition and multiplication can at best regard only with wonderment and awe a demonstration of the multiplication algorithm. The child who is still struggling with a subtraction algorithm cannot help but be overwhelmed by the demands of a division algorithm based on subtraction skills.

One is tempted to say that in each case the child should not be receiving instruction in the more advanced skill, but LD children are frequently faced with such instruction. As one young lady remarked, "I always felt that I was at least three years behind where my teacher was in mathematics."

This theoretical issue of automaticity has received attention here because, in practice, it does seem to influence the experiences of LD children in mathematics. Fleischner, Garnett, and Shepherd (1982) reported that in timed tests of arithmetic facts, LD children performed at a slower rate than nondisabled students. However, when the ratios of number correct to number attempted were examined for both groups, little difference was found between groups. Strategies for arriving at correct answers existed in the LD students, but these strategies were not as efficient as those of their nondisabled peers.

The provision of efficient strategies can be translated into lessons on how to memorize. No definite recipe exists. Nonetheless, some guidelines to facilitate memorization can be gathered from the literature. The types of memorization called for in mathematics and, in particular, arithmetic deserve a brief examination.

Consider the multiplication statement $8 \times 4 = 32$. Initially the child learns the combination in written form and orally. Examine and compute the answers to each of the examples in Figure 10-8.

The answer in each case required the use of the basic relationship $8 \times 4 = 32$. Nonetheless, in each example after the first two, the combination was actually no longer $8 \times 4 = 32$, but $8 \times 4 \times 10 = 320, 8 \times 10 \times 4 \times 10 = 3200$, and so on. In other words, when a child "memorizes" the relationship $8 \times 4 = 32$, and the relationships $10 \times 1 = 10, 10 \times 10 = 100$, and the rest, he or she is expected to be able to combine these relationships if the knowledge is to serve any practical use. The relationship $8 \times 4 = 32$ is the underpinning for a class of relationships.

A second observation is in order. Initial memorization usually takes the form of oral or written response to the stimulus $8 \times 4 = $ _____ or the same relationship written vertically. Yet in no example after the first one in Figure 10-8 was the combination presented in either fashion. The various configurations in which a student must see the combination are illustrated in Figure 10-9.

Many, if not most of us, make the adjustments easily. Some children do not; LD youngsters often fall into the latter group. The learning of the

---

Figure 10-8 Examples Using the Basic Combination $8 \times 4 = 32$

$$
\begin{array}{cccc}
4 & 14 & 43 & 14 \\
\times 8 & \times 8 & \times 18 & \times 81 \\
\hline
\end{array}
$$

$$
\begin{array}{cccc}
43 & 432 & 432 & 432 \\
\times 81 & \times 81 & \times 18 & \times 810 \\
\hline
\end{array}
$$

$$
\begin{array}{ccc}
8 & 8 & 68 \\
4\overline{)328} & 4\ 3\overline{)3698} & 43\overline{)2924}
\end{array}
$$

Figure 10-9 8 × 4 = 32 Seen Again

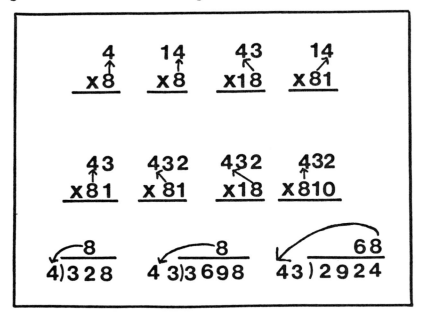

addition and multiplication combinations and their inverses cannot be regarded simply as a paired-associate task, although such association may be an initial step.

With these cautions in mind, let us consider some of the ways in which learning facts and algorithms, with a view to their speedy and accurate use, can be facilitated.

Less Can Be More

When learning the sequence of number names, the very young child determines for himself or herself the number of names to be learned at one time. The number of names is usually relatively small. Some children choose to count to four, others to six, others to five. Not only young children but also investigators into memory recommend that memorization is facilitated when the number of items to be learned is small. Yet one can walk into a primary grade classroom and observe children working on sheets containing as many as 25 facts at a time. Such practices do not recommend themselves for any child. The LD child may become even more overwhelmed than most other children. Decide with the LD child the number of combinations to be learned at one time, and work on those combinations until they are mastered to a level of skill determined in advance.

Oral Drill Can Be Helpful

Oral repetition of the relationships can aid rehearsal and transfer of the relationship to the formats indicated in Figures 10-8 and 10-9. For this reason flashcards to which both oral and written responses can be provided are valuable aids for rehearsal. The timing of the completion of such drills can also be helpful. For suggestions for the use of such material, see Fitzmaurice Hayes (1984), Myers and Thornton (1977), and Lessen and Cumblad (1984). The latter two articles represent the many to be found in the *Arithmetic Teacher,* a publication of the National Council of Teachers of Mathematics.

Frequent Rehearsal Is a Must

Daily or even twice-a-day rehearsal is a must if the child is to experience success. Since the number of facts to be learned in one group is small, these rehearsal activities need not take much time. Since the child is observing his or her progress in learning, the activities need not be boring. Frequent opportunities for rehearsal offer greater chances of success.

Properly used, microcomputers help provide sources for practice. The programs used, however, must allow for the repetition of the same facts over and over again. Most software programs provide the student with a score at the end of a sequence of examples. If the time needed for completion is a variable for the student, some structure for monitoring time should be designed.

Mastered Combinations Must Be Reviewed Frequently

Once a group of facts has been mastered, they must be reviewed frequently by the inclusion of one or two in the daily rehearsal of a new set of combinations and through the use of games.

Unknown Combinations Must Be Available

If instruction in the arithmetic algorithms for whole numbers is to be ongoing while the LD child gradually acquires facility in recalling accurately the basic combinations, the unknown combinations must be readily available. Charts or calculators probably offer the best resource for these answers.

Instruction in Algorithms Should Follow the Same Guidelines

If the LD child's instructional goals include the mastery of one or more of the arithmetic algorithms (and the expenditure of a great deal of instructional time on such goals may not be justified for some children), the principle "less is more" must be kept in mind. As was the case with the basic facts, specific objectives—for example, adding two two-digit numbers with regrouping—and specific levels of mastery should be agreed upon by teacher and learner. Steps toward the goal should be delineated, and the child's progress along the path should be well marked. As is the case with the memorization of facts, daily rehearsal is a must.

One reason frequently advanced for the difficulty in memorization experienced by LD youngsters is a failure to organize the material to be learned. The tasks of organization involve an awareness of patterns and relationships. The need for such a capacity brings us to the fourth guideline of Greenwood and Anderson: a focus on students' abilities to observe patterns and relationships.

PATTERNS AND RELATIONSHIPS: HELPING STUDENTS TO SEE THEM

The structure of mathematics affords endless opportunities for the observation of patterns and relationships. The examples in Exhibit 10-1 provide but a very small sample of these. The exercises require relatively few arithmetic skills. The essential components of the tasks are noting of patterns and relationships and using them to formulate conclusions and/ or to make predictions. Such exercises provide for the formulation and testing of hypotheses.

The skills developed by exercises such as those illustrated can be invaluable to the LD student. Through the recognition of patterns and relationships, concepts and rules are initially formed. Patterns and relationships form the structure for the logical organization of subject matter. The recognition of patterns leads to prediction and the formulation of hypotheses. Such behaviors are necessary not only to the mathematician but to students in all areas.

Needless to say, experiences with patterns would not start with the types of exercises illustrated here. The young LD child can receive help in recognizing patterns and relationships through the kinds of activities

Exhibit 10-1 Finding Patterns and Drawing Conclusions

Exercise 1: Examine each list of multiples. Find the sum of the digit(s) in each product in each list. If the sum is a two-digit number, find the sum of those two digits. The first set is done for you. What patterns do you find?

Multiples of 2	Sum of digits	3	4	5	6	7	8	9	10
2	2	3	4	5	6	7	8	9	10
4	4	6	8	10	12	14	16	18	20
6	6	9	12	15	18	21	24	27	30
8	8	12	16	20	24	28	32	36	40
10	1	15	20	25	30	35	40	45	50
12	3	18	24	30	36	42	48	54	60
14	5	21	28	35	42	49	56	63	70
16	7	24	32	40	48	56	64	72	80
18	9	27	36	45	54	63	72	81	90
20	2	30	40	50	60	70	80	90	100
22	4	33	44	55	66	77	88	99	110
24	6	36	48	60	72	84	96	108	120

Exercise 2: Find the sum of the angles in each shape. Divide the sum by 180. Compare your answer to the number of sides the figure has. What do you conclude?

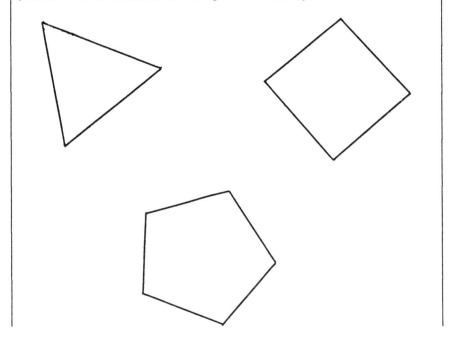

Exhibit 10-1 continued

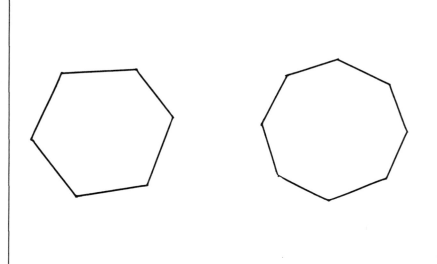

Exercise 3: In the table below, the multiples of the numbers 2 through 9 are listed vertically. In the last column are written the sums of the numbers in the first five rows. Can you predict what the next sum should be, without adding all the numbers? Without doing any of the rows in between, can you tell what the sum of the numbers in the last row should be, without adding them? Check your predictions.

		Multiples						*Sums*
2	3	4	5	6	7	8	9	44
4	6	8	10	12	14	16	18	88
6	9	12	15	18	21	24	27	132
8	12	16	20	24	28	32	36	176
10	15	20	25	30	35	40	45	220
12	18	24	30	36	42	48	54	
14	21	28	35	42	49	56	63	
16	24	32	40	48	56	64	72	
18	27	36	45	54	63	72	81	
20	30	40	50	60	70	80	90	
22	33	44	55	66	77	88	99	
24	36	48	60	72	84	96	108	

described in *Project MATH, Levels I and II* (Cawley, Goodstein, Fitzmaurice, Lepore, Sedlak, & Althaus, 1976). The interested reader can also pursue Fitzmaurice Hayes (1984). Through the careful sequencing of patterning activities throughout elementary school, mathematics instructors can help LD students .to develop and monitor their own organizational skills.

The thinking required for the exercises suggested in Table 10-1 and the expected outcomes represent a form of Guilford's convergent production, the "generation of information from given information, where the emphasis is upon achieving unique or conventionally accepted best outcomes (Meeker, 1969)." Of equal importance to the cognitive development of the LD child is divergent production: "the generation of information from given information, where the emphasis is upon variety and quality of output from the same source [Meeker, 1969, p. 20]." Related to the encouragement of divergent production is Greenwood and Anderson's fifth guideline: the explicit appreciation of novel ways of approaching problems and skills.

ENCOURAGING CREATIVE APPROACHES TO PROBLEMS

A group of first grade teachers had devised a questionnaire to be completed by first grade children being considered for participation in a program for bright and talented children. One item was written thus: "Do you like to share your ideas and ways of doing things with your teachers and the other children in your class?" To the teachers' chagrin, one youngster replied, "You'd better not try to."

Bright and talented children are not the only ones who often have novel ways of approaching problems, nor are they the only ones who learn quickly to keep such ideas to themselves. For the LD child, however, who must often develop compensatory strategies, disapproval of divergence can be very harmful. On the other hand, an atmosphere that encourages creative approaches to problem-solving tasks can be most beneficial.

Such an environment must be replete with two types of problems, those for which no one answer is the only solution, and those that have a solution that can be arrived at in a variety of ways. Examples of such types of situations can be found in all subject areas, but mathematics is a particularly fruitful source of such problems.

A set of attribute pieces, such as the one pictured in Figure 10-10, can serve as the starting point for many problems of the first type.

The following list contains but a few of the many possibilities:
- Sort the pieces into two groups so that all the pieces in each group go together in some way (obvious solutions—large vs. small, curved vs.

Figure 10-10 Models for Attribute Pieces*

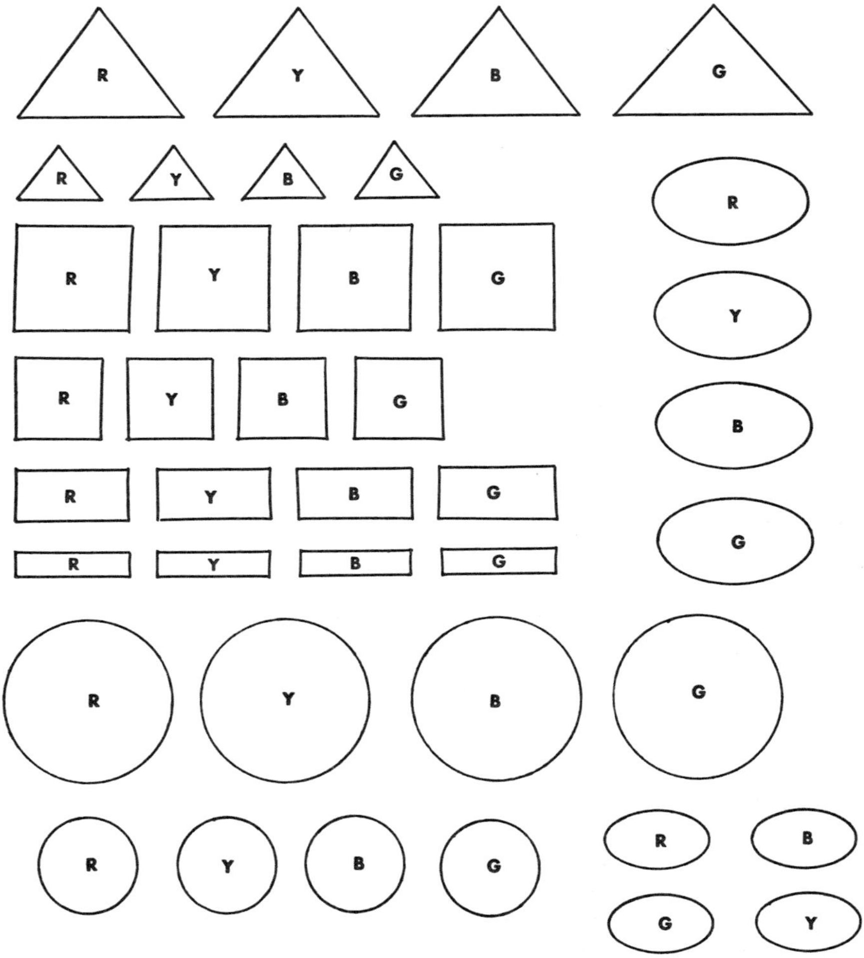

*Note: R = red, B = blue, Y = yellow, G = green.

---

noncurved; less obvious but to be encouraged—circle vs. noncircle, four-sided vs. not four-sided, blue vs. nonblue, and so on).

- Start with the large red circle. Make a necklace so that each succeeding piece differs from the one before it in only one way.
- Use any four of the pieces to make a square region.
- Combine two or more pieces to make a four-sided figure.

In each case, more than one solution is possible. Students should be encouraged to work together to come up with different solutions and to share their results. Most issues of the *Arithmetic Teacher,* in that section called "Ideas," contain suggestions for other types of such experiences. For an example of a different sort, see Slesnick (1984).

Problems abound with only one solution that can be arrived at in many different ways. As a matter of fact, few real problems admit of only one solution path. LD students should be encouraged to seek out different solution strategies, and to share these with other students. Only from such encouragement can students develop respect for their own thinking processes and those of others.

We come now to the last of Greenwood and Anderson's guidelines: the promotion of self-diagnosis, self-evaluation, and self-awareness procedures for all students.

DEVELOPING SELF-APPRAISAL TECHNIQUES

At the secondary school and postsecondary school levels, LD students can often be heard to remark, "I really thought I knew the stuff, but I didn't." In most cases, self-monitoring skills are absent. These skills are essential to good study habits. Many of the suggestions given in this chapter, if pursued, lend themselves to the development of self-appraisal techniques in LD youngsters.

Students who have been encouraged to communicate their understanding of mathematics content orally have a means through which they can check up on their level of understanding and remedy misunderstandings. Students who have been taught to monitor their progress in memorizing content through time charts and checklists, and who know the value of frequent and paced rehearsal, can both plan and effectively use study time. Students who have shared their problem-solving processes with those of other students can profit from more efficient strategies, while at the same time building confidence in their own ability to approach problem solving at some level. Students who receive consistent constructive feedback about their efforts in mathematics will develop an accurate awareness of their own capabilities in the different areas.

Not all LD children will progress equally far, obviously, even in the best of instructional environments. Nonetheless, appropriate instruction can minimize the destructive effects of some learning problems on mathematics learning, and can maximize the learner's chances of success. The LD youngster may be a cognitive phenomenon. Surely he or she can also be a cognitive success.

REFERENCES

Ausubel, D. (1968). *Educational psychology—a cognitive view.* New York: Holt, Rinehart & Winston.

Blankenship, C.S., & Baumgartner, M.D. (1982). Programming generalization of computational skills. *Learning Disabilities Quarterly, 5,* 152–162.

Cawley, J.F. (1984). Selection, adaptation, and development of curricula and instructional materials. In J.F. Cawley (Ed.), *Developmental teaching of mathematics for the learning disabled* (pp. 227–252). Rockville, MD: Aspen Systems.

Cawley, J.F., Goodstein, H., Fitzmaurice, A., Lepore, A., Sedlak, R., & Althaus, V. (1976). *Project MATH, levels I and II.* Tulsa, OK: Educational Progress Corporation.

Fitzmaurice Hayes, A. (1984). Curriculum and instructional activities, grade two through grade four. In J.F. Cawley (Ed.) *Developmental teaching of mathematics for the learning disabled.* Rockville, MD: Aspen Systems.

Fleischner, J., Garnett, K., & Shepherd, M. (1982). Proficiency in arithmetic basic fact computation of learning disabled and nondisabled children. *Focus on Learning Problems in Mathematics, 4*(2), 47–55.

Gagne, R. (1970). *The conditions of learning.* (pp. 200–202). New York: Holt, Rinehart & Winston.

Greenwood, J., & Anderson, R. (1983). Some thoughts on teaching and learning mathematics. *Arithmetic Teacher, 31*(3), 42–49.

Klausmeier, H., & Ripple, R. (1971). *Learning and human abilities.* New York: Harper and Row.

Kosc, L. (1981, October). Neuropsychological implications of diagnosis and treatment of mathematical learning disabilities. *Topics in Learning and Learning Disabilities, 2,* 19–30.

Lessen, E.I., & Cumblad, C.L. (1984). Alternatives for teaching multiplication facts. *Arithmetic Teacher, 31*(5), 46–48.

Levy, W. (1979). Dyscalculia: Critical analysis and future directions. *Focus on Learning Problems in Mathematics, 1*(3), 41–51.

Meeker, M. (1969). *The structure of intellect. Its interpretation and uses.* Columbus, OH: Charles E. Merrill.

Myers, A.C., & Thornton, C.A. (1977). The learning disabled child—learning the basic facts. *Arithmetic Teacher, 25*(3), 46–50.

Slesnick, T. (1984). Problem solving: Some thoughts and activities. *Arithmetic Teacher, 31*(7), pp. 41–43.

Sternberg, R.J., & Wagner, R.K. (1982). Automatization failure in learning disabilities. *Topics in Learning and Learning Disabilities, 2,* 1–7.

Van Engen, H. (1953). The formation of concepts. In National Council of Teachers of Mathematics, *The learning of mathematics: Its theory and practice.* (pp. 69–98). Washington, DC: Author.

Whimbey, A. (1977). Teaching sequential thought: The cognitive skills approach. *Phi Delta Kappan, 59*(4), 255–259.

Whimbey, A. (1979). Teaching analytical reasoning in mathematics. In J. Lochhead & J. Clement (Eds.), *Cognitive process instruction* (pp. 309–314). Philadelphia: The Franklin Institute Press.

Index

Note: Pages appearing in italics indicate entries found in artwork.

About the Editor

John F. Cawley is Chairperson, Department of Special Education, University of New Orleans. He is especially concerned with curriculum and instruction for the handicapped.

About the Contributors

Dan G. Bachor is Associate Professor in the Faculty of Education at the University of Victoria, British Columbia. He specializes in mild to moderate learning difficulties in mathematics and language arts.

Colleen S. Blankenship is Associate Professor, Department of Special Education, University of Illinois. Her primary interests are data-based instruction and mathematics for the handicapped.

Miriam Cherkes-Julkowski is Associate Professor, Department of Educational Psychology at the University of Connecticut, specializing in cognitive development of the handicapped.

Jeanette C. Fleischner is Chairperson of Special Education at Teachers College of Columbia University.

Anne M. Fitzmaurice Hayes is a mathematics educator with extensive research in curriculum development of the handicapped. She is presently Assistant Professor at the University of Hartford, where she teaches courses in mathematics and special education.

Michael O'Loughlin earned his B.A. from University College, Dublin, and his M.A. and M.Ph. from Teachers College, Columbia University. Currently he is a doctoral candidate in Developmental Psychology as well as a research assistant and instructor at Teachers College.

Paulette J. Thomas is Associate Professor, Department of Special Education, at the University of New Orleans specializing in pupil appraisal.